Beautiful
Seeds
of
Change

ENDORSEMENTS

The personal stories of trial and triumph in this book take the reader on a journey along with each author. There will be "aha" moments when you recognize some of your own struggles in their words. You will cry and laugh along with them and ultimately find more strength and determination for your own process of transformation. Perhaps most importantly, you will discover ideas and techniques that helped these authors change their lives dramatically, and they will change your life as well if you are willing to practice them.

Patricia J. Crane, Ph.D.
Author, speaker, trainer
www.drpatriciacrane.com

The presence of the archangels is clearly observed with each of the contributing authors in *Beautiful Seeds of Change*. The collaboration of stories will inspire and awaken you to the important message that you are never alone on your journey. Each writer introduces you to their unique ways they connect with divine guidance which assists them with living the life they were created to live.

Sunny Dawn Johnston
Spiritual Teacher, Intuitive Healer, Founder of Sunlight Alliance
Healing Center
www.sunnydawnjohnston.com
www.invokingtheangels.com

Beautiful Seeds of Change is an uplifting book filled with wisdom, hope and love. Readers will enjoy learning about each author through their personal stories of triumph as well as gaining insight through strategic "seeds" of wisdom to catapult them into living their best life.

Kris Voelker
Musician, Artist, Designer
www.krisvoelker.com

The ability to survive, the ability to change, the ability to laugh and cry. These are all portrayed here with a raw honesty that will inspire you to know that you no longer need to simply survive. Instead you can take your greatest challenges and use them to change, grow and live life to the full. Inspirational, breathtaking, highly recommended.

Eileen Clair
Director, Holistic therapist and trainer
www.eileenclair.com

One of the greatest gifts a teacher can give a student is the intimate peek at their own struggles in their path to overcoming. It takes a courageous heart bent on nurturing healing in their life, and the lives of others, to share their most vulnerable moments in hopes of inspiring change. The authors in *Beautiful Seeds of Change* do just that. By sharing their personal stories of trauma and transformation, they allow the reader to find solace and inspiration. These revealing accounts of personal journeys vividly illustrate that seemingly ordinary individuals can survive, thrive, and grow into extraordinary mentors to us all.

Santalena Caudillo
Motivational Wellness Instructor, owner and founder
Healing Artz Wellness Studio
www.HealingArtzStudio.com

With intention our lives change in miraculous ways. Watch these varied life-gardeners cast their seeds, and then behold the glorious blooms. You can find hope and inspiration through reading these stories and gain strength to continue sowing your own garden.

Mary Ellen Psaltis, B.Ph.
Certified Nutrition and Wellness Consultant
Co-author of Spiritual Vitamins – 12 Essential Nutrients for Women

I was very inspired reading *Beautiful Seeds of Change*, which features extraordinary people who share their own experiences of courage to face life's presenting challenges and overcome them with a positive and selfless attitude to achieve self-transformation. The authors gracefully discuss the importance of being thankful for everything in our lives as all is God's will and God's doing, and we should feel blessed to be part of the Divine mission. They encourage everyone to listen to the heart, be honest with the self and stay determined to progress spiritually in life. They also show us the importance of patience and demonstrate that one's feelings can have impact on one's own mental and physical well-being. Most importantly, we have to do our part as only we can make the change within us. My deepest gratitude to all the authors for sharing your optimism, your selflessness and your love for life!

Hari Conjeevaram, M.D.
Associate Professor of Medicine, Program Director,
GI Fellowship Program, Division of Gastroenterology,
The University of Michigan
3912 Taubman Center, Ann Arbor, MI 48109-5362
Tel: 734-615-4628   Fax: 734-936-7392
E-mail: omsairam@umich.edu

This book is an inspiration. It gifts the reader with many ways to recognise the infinite potential that we each have to sow, tend and enjoy the transformational possibilities of new seeds in our life. The stories in this book invite each one of us to recognise our own perfection, yet still seek to become better and be of greater service in the world. I would put this book on the essential reading list for anyone who is in the midst of struggle and adversity as it gives hope, offers practical tools and demonstrates the indomitable nature of the human spirit.

Juliet Vorster
The Metaphysical Motivator
Broadcaster, author and teacher
www.julietvorster.com

A life well-traveled is something to which we all should aspire. The stories included here are magnificent examples of how different paths can lead to the right destination. Turning hurt and anger and loss and disillusionment into joy and happiness and self-improvement is something each of these authors has experienced. Their lives provide inspiring stories for all readers, especially those that are seeking guidance down their own path.

Bill Townsend
Serial Entrepreneur, Author and Speaker
www.AmatiFoundation.org
www.Interminds.com

Beautiful Seeds of Change shares personal stories of individuals who have awakened from the illusion of despair. Through their journey, they found courage to examine their beliefs of insecurity and create breakthroughs by moving through the pain. This book will inspire you to embrace your challenges and find the underlying gift of all experiences. The authors remind you there is always perfection in the moment as you embody the true self within.

Elaine Lemon, En.K.
Founder of Empower Wholeness LLC, Executive Producer of 'Take It With You,' Co-author 'Beyond Beautiful,' Neuro Energetic Kinesiologist, Spiritual & Wellness Coach, Distance Healing, Licensed Heal Your Life® Workshop Leader, Earth Transitions Practitioner, and Karlfeldt Healing Retreat Facilitator.
www.ElaineLemon.com, www.EmpowerWholeness.com,
www.KarlfedltHealingRetreats.com, www.Apocalypsepictures.net

The journeys and insights described by the authors in this exquisite work spread across the whole spectrum of human experience. For as long as I remember, I have seen life as a road paved with seconds in time. Along that road we encounter life's ups and life's downs. As the seconds tick along, we find ourselves speeding, suddenly changing direction and sometimes even crashing.

It might seem to us like we are actually the passenger and not the driver at all. We yearn for control; we yearn for answers. I believe *Beautiful Seeds of Change* to be a wonderful road map for the many who look for a helping hand or a guiding light. It will also be a heartwarming read and confirmation for those who feel their direction is clear.

Andy Pilgrim
*Champion Professional Race Car Driver, Business Owner, Founder of the
Andy Pilgrim Foundation.
www.andypilgrimfoundation.org
www.andypilgrim.com*

Beautiful Seeds of Change is an inspiring portrait of how, through deliberate choice, we can manifest the life we desire with no more need to be a victim of circumstance left to life's ever changing ebbs and flows. NOW we can attract into our lives all that which we desire by first planting the "seeds of change."

Ken Rakowicz, D.C.
quiropraxiademendoza@hotmail.com

Beautiful Seeds of Change is a pure, intimate look into the journey of each author. Compelling stories, raw emotion, profound wisdom … these are the magnificent gifts bestowed upon the reader. Each chapter is laced with life's deep challenges coupled with simple, yet insightful tools for endurance and success … a veritable gold mine of conventional wisdom and spiritual epiphanies!

Dena DeLuco
*NLP Success Coach, Hypnotherapist, Trainer, Reiki Master Teacher
www.streamsofabundance.com*

Beautiful Seeds of Change is titled so perfectly; such a beautiful sharing of very unique and interesting human stories of taking 'seeds' of disharmony and allowing the alchemy for sprouting them into harmony of living. The action of this being the very change that each author allows for her or himself toward living more fully, more authentically. Reading this book, no matter what details are at play in your life, will inspire you toward living your own life more fully and authentically - allowing joy and love or even more joy and love. I highly recommend it!

Canela Michelle Meyers
*Bestselling Author of 'Right Here, Right Now Meditations'
www.canelamichelle.com*

It is the writer

who might catch

the *imagination* of

young people,

and plant a *seed*

that will *flower* and

come to *fruition*.

~ISAAC ASIMOV

Beautiful Seeds of Change

BECKWORTH PUBLICATIONS

3108 E 10th St ~ Trenton, Mo 64683 ~ 660-204-4088

Ordering information: Quantity Sales. Special discounts are available on quantity purchases by corporations, associations, and others. For details, contact the "Special Sales Department at Beckworth Publications."

Beckworth Publications and the Beckworth Publications logo are trademarks of Beckworth Publications.

Printed in the United States of America.
Library of Congress Cataloging-in-Publication Data.
Hardwick, Lisa
Beautiful Seeds of Change-Inspirational, True Stories of Transformation From Men and Women Around the World
Library of Congress Control Number: 2012934469

Compiled by: Lisa A. Hardwick and Nancy Newman
Cover and Interior Graphic Design: Mike Baugher
Senior Editor: Nancy Newman
Photographer Credits: Photo Studio, Gina Myers Photography, Dan Skaramuca, Kim Coffman, Tella Sametz, Deb Hagen Photography, Karen Leonard Photography, Leewon Photo House, Valeria Rae, HalfCity Productions, Derek George, Starbird Photography, Kami Stratton, Cher Rue, Kaitlin Lampley, Kent Henderson, Kimall Christensen

Table of Contents

Beautiful Seeds of Change

Foreword

by Nancy Newman

All of us are cramped for time these days. There just never seems to be enough to do everything that we want to do or need to do, so we have to prioritize. Reading this book is definitely something you need to put on the top of your Priority List!

I believe that we all come to the planet to experience life and to learn pre-determined lessons along the way. How we react to each lesson determines the threads in the tapestry of our unique life story. For some of us, the lesson may be around our choices with substance abuse, for others it may be with relationships, and for still others it may be around loss – of possessions, health, spouses or loved ones, etc. While we may share common lessons, we all choose to react differently thus creating our own experiences.

Leading scientists, physicians and researchers in quantum physics and other areas agree that each human being is composed of energy, and that we energetically attract to us our experience of life and of health. Louise L. Hay, one of the pioneers of the mind-body-spirit connection, was teaching these concepts back in the early 1980's.

As Louise teaches us, your beliefs and thoughts of the past year, the past month, the past week, the past hour, the past minute have created your current reality. But a belief is only a thought, and thoughts can be changed. If your reality is not working for you, you may choose different thoughts. The point of power is right now. This very minute! Your future will be created by your beliefs and thoughts in the next minute, the next hour, the next week, the next month, the next year.

Most people are doing the best they can, given what they know and understand, including you. If they knew more and were aware of more, they would do things differently.

~Louise Hay

The men and women in these chapters will teach you that even in the depths of despair, there is always a choice that can be made to transform your life. I'm confident that you will identify and empathize with something in at least one of the stories in this book, probably many more. I know I did! And, in that shared experience of their story, by telling you about the choices they made, the new beliefs and thoughts they chose to think, they will show you that you, too, can make a choice to experience your life differently – you can plant your own seed of change!

I believe that through the stories of your brothers and sisters in this book, you will become aware that you are not alone in your experiences, thoughts and feelings. Even with our most shameful secrets, we are not alone. We are all beloved children of the Universe, and we are not alone. We are all one. The authors in this book are from around the planet, so you will see that it doesn't matter what our nationality, our race or our gender is, we all have the same hopes, desires, fears, secrets, experiences, thoughts and feelings! These courageous men and women have shown the way for you by sharing their most intimate personal journeys.

Just as a seed planted in our garden needs time to germinate and grow, we must also tend to our personal "seeds of change garden." A sunflower seed doesn't become a beautiful sunflower, reaching up to the heavens, overnight. So, too, will your seed of change need awareness, thought, "fertilizer," and determination to become your desired change. By becoming vulnerable on the pages of this book, these authors will assist you in your journey by showing you their path to awareness and the changes resulting from the seeds they planted.

I did then what I knew how to do.
Now that I know better, I do better.

~Maya Angelou

Make reading this book a priority. After reading the courageous stories in this book, you will finally have a road map for your journey. You will finally be able to know how to "do better."

I wish you courage and perseverance in your personal journey to your authentic self. My hope is that you can all experience the peace and joy which can result from planting your own seeds of change.

Peace and Blessings.

Namasté,
Nancy

nancy@yourmindfulwellness.com
www.yourmindfulwellness.com

Introduction

By Melissa J. White

Every adversity, every failure,
and every heartache, carries with it
the Seed of an equivalent or greater Benefit.

~Napoleon Hill

This is a book about triumph. It is about the strength of the human spirit. All of the people you will meet in these pages are master gardeners who have used their life circumstances as seeds to create beautiful changes in their lives.

While the stories and individuals you will encounter are diverse, they do share one important, universal theme. They have chosen to let go of the limited, false ideas of who they thought they were, to fully embrace their authentic selves with LOVE. Rather than considering themselves victims to their particular life situations, each of these authors chose to use their circumstances as tools for transformation. Each person was a responsible participant in those changes, while at the same time trusting in the flow of life enough to surrender the ultimate unfolding to the Universe.

In the pages that follow, you will share in experiences of heartbreak, job loss, cancer, obesity, bipolar disorder, paralysis, alcohol abuse, abortion, severe psychological and physical trauma, home transitions, feelings of unworthiness, and responses to calls to spiritual growth and change. You will witness how these individuals used their darkest nights for healing, truly seeing these occurrences as "blessings in disguise." You will see, as they did, that we are not alone – that God never abandons us.

Like the Phoenix, you too, can rise from the ashes of whatever life circumstance you currently find yourself. What within you called you to pick up this book? Was it that voice within, too often ignored? That inner nudging that there HAS to be something better to this thing called life? Or perhaps it was just a desire to share in the celebration of the victories that each writer has bravely chronicled.

Whatever the reason, you should recognize that each of these marvelous, courageous individuals is no different than you. Life is always changing. These stories remind us that we can be active participants in those changes. Each of us can create our own happiness from the inside out.

Life is truly a miracle. There is great love within you and around you. You can step through your fears into that love. Let the stories that follow inspire you as you plant the seeds for your own blooming. Trust that your life, too, can be transformed into the beautiful, vibrant garden it is meant to be.

I wish you courage and vision for planting, inner stillness and faith for cultivation, and many magical surprises in the tapestry of your life!

Namasté,
Melissa

www.mylifeopportunites.com

David Nixon

I dedicate this story to all those who have found themselves in the abyss of hopelessness and despair. I pray that you grab hold of one of these true stories as one would a life preserver the moment after a shipwreck and find a reason to be grateful for this beautiful life we have all been so freely given. Whether you realize it or not, you are wanted and needed here.

Chapter 1

DEATH WAS AN OPTION

Laying there trapped in a prison of self-condemnation and despair, I felt the bed begin to slowly shake, gradually becoming more apparent. I could hear her call, like a wolf in the distance howling at the full moon. As she approached, her call became louder, and her presence undeniable. Her steel wheels gliding along the rails of years gone by. The whole house would shake as she rolled through this town we have come to call home, like a thunder storm moving across the Heavens in the dead of night.

So many nights I would lay awake. That was always the worst for me: After the house had gone completely quiet, and I was left with just me. The booze just wasn't working like it used to and shutting down was increasingly more difficult. I would hear her and her unmistakable call. She was our local freight train that we had nicknamed "Gloria" when we first came to this town, because she came in like "a blaze of Glory."

I would hear that train and think to myself: "I could just stumble out on to those tracks, and it would all be over." I knew I could easily make it look like an accident so my wife would still be able to collect what little life insurance we had. My family and friends would mourn my death; however, in the end, I would still be the hero who always took care of his family, right up to his passing, and no one would ever know the real truth.

What an awful place for a young person in their early 30's to be. From outward appearances, no one would ever have known the pit of despair I was in. To the world, I had the perfect life. I was living the American dream by today's standards with the cute little house, beautiful wife, two cars in the drive way and two beautiful little healthy kids to complete the picture. Everything really was just perfect, and I had become very good at making the world believe that. By all rights I should have been very happy. On the outside I was good at making it appear so, but on the inside I was a train wreck waiting to happen, and I knew that at any moment it all would come crashing down around me. Then everyone would finally see the failure I always knew I was.

I am David Nixon, a 40-something father of four great kids, with a beautiful wife who has seen me at my worst and chooses to love me anyway.

I live in a small town with a population of a little over 2800 people, in a little pale yellow house with a white picket fence to match. Today I have the life that I always wanted when I was younger, and I continue to be amazed on a regular basis how fortunate I am. Even when the world is crashing around me, amidst all its chaos and worry, I continue to feel blessed for this life I have today.

I have never felt more aware of who I am in this part of my journey. I have no fear to speak of and, comparably speaking, my world is free of worry. Even in my darkest hour, I have a knowing about me that everything is going to work out as it should. I recognize that I am just a small fraction of something much greater than me and feel comfortable with who I am as a person. I don't fear death nor welcome it. I simply just accept it for what it is, and if I were to check out tomorrow, I would go with a smile and sincere gratitude for having had the opportunity to experience this life that I was so freely given.

But as you now know, it wasn't always this way, and that is the point of the little story I wish to share with you. I am not sure why it is that you have chosen to read this book; however, I believe there is most certainly a purpose. I have come to a place where so many others have, where I sincerely believe that all things happen for a reason. It is my hope as you read on that you will keep an open mind and try to find the similarities in my story to that of your own unique experience or that of someone you know and care for.

We really have more in common than you may think and just because it has become normal in our society to separate us by politics, race, gender, sexual preference, religion (or the lack thereof) and many, many other characteristics which are too numerous to list, there is one undeniable thing that binds us together which is the one that matters most: The desire to be happy.

Do you believe that? That all of us have that same desire? No matter where we live on this blue planet, how we were raised or what our experience has been, that we all, every last one of us, essentially has that one thing in common? Personally, I have never met one person without this desire behind pretty much every single decision they make or have made. Not one. Have you? Go ahead think about that for a moment. I'll still be here.

Were you able to come up with any? Perhaps you could say a person who seeks power or to be wealthy, that is their desire, and you might be right. But I think in the beginning, their desire was to be happy, and they believed power or wealth was the key to happiness. Many in their quest simply lost their way, and rather than condemn them for the manner in which *they choose* to live, I choose to see them as a person just like me who has the desire to be happy. They are just trying to do their best to find that elusive happiness. I believe that even those who on the outside may appear callus and insensitive to others, have, or at one time had, a deep desire just to be happy.

I try my best not to judge anyone, and believe me, I wasn't always that way. There was a time in my life that I could pick out the faults of a saint, if that meant I didn't have to look at my own character defects! Really, to be honest, it is the reason most people criticize, berate and belittle others. In my experience, by doing so, they do not have to take a look at their own misgivings.

When I am confronted by one of these individuals who, no matter the circumstance, can find fault in it; I try to recognize that this is a very unhappy person, and they have their own road to walk. It is not up to me to try to figure them out, or try to change their point of view. With respect and compassion, I choose to decline their invitation to participate in this counterproductive behavior.

Believe me, I realize that this practice isn't easy. That's why you have to "practice it"! Before you can ever hope to change another's behavior, you have to come to the realization that the only person whose behavior you can change is your own. Most people really dislike hearing me say that, but it is true. When we learn to change our behaviors and reactions to others, they no longer get the reaction they are used to from us. Their behavior toward us will change, but it will be their decision not yours. IT WORKS. When you see it work you will be amazed, but like I said, it takes practice. Be patient, give yourself permission to make mistakes; however, recognize when you do, and just simply give yourself permission to do it differently next time.

If it is your desire to be happy, and you are tired of feeling the way that you do, then you must *become willing* to recognize that nothing on the outside of your life is making you feel this way. Notice I didn't say that "you have to" recognize this. I said "become willing to." Willing, just willing, that is all. If you are truly ready to step into the light, then you will have to consider that maybe you have been looking for your resolve in the wrong places. That just maybe it really has been you all along that has been holding yourself back.

As we move forward, I will be sharing some things with you about me that I hope will make you feel better about where you are in your life today. My desire is that I will share something which rings true with you, and you will have one of those moments in time where the World stops and you realize that it is okay to be right here, right now.

You may or may not know this, but I am going to say it anyway. I don't even know you, but I know that you matter. YOU MATTER TO ME. How can I say that? We've never met! I don't know you! That is a ridiculous statement, how can I say such a thing? Because I truly believe that the decisions you make in your life, in some way eventually will affect me and vice versa. If you have ever tossed a pebble into a pond and watched the ripple go across the water, then you understand what I am saying.

I believe that in some way "We All" affect each other in one way or another. Pretty powerful statement I know, but I believe it's true. That is why I can say: YOU MATTER TO ME. I want you to be happy. I want you to know you deserve to be happy. I want you to know that you have a place in this World. I want you to know that if you are here with us that there is a reason. I want to see your dreams come true. "You have a purpose." And above all, I want you to know YOU matter, because truly, you matter to me.

Equally as important, I would like for you to know that I celebrate your uniqueness. I recognize that you are not unlike an amazing piece of art work with your own special magnificence and that you have your own place in this World where we all come to live and learn.

As I alluded to earlier, I am truly happier today than I ever have been; however, it wasn't always that way. Before, as long as I stayed busy, I didn't have to look at the way I really felt about where I was in my life at that time. That was "my reality." I lived in that way of thinking for a long time, actually for years.

That's why at night it was so bad. Unless I went right to sleep when my head hit the pillow, I would lay awake thinking about where I was, and that place was dark, very dark. There was no denying, at least not to me, that I was in serious trouble, and I saw no way out. I would drink regularly in order to shut my brain down so I wouldn't have to face the reality that I had created for myself. But eventually, the drinking didn't always help. Over the years I had built up a tolerance to alcohol, so unless I drank a lot, it didn't have the effect that it once did. My saving grace was that I had to work, so drinking myself to oblivion wasn't always an option.

Finally after years and years of suffering caused by my own devices, *I had to make a decision.* The fact was: "I just couldn't live the way I was living" any more. Something had to give, something had to change, and that something was me.

I'd like to say there was a huge catalyst, or the gates of Heaven opened up, and I knew it was time for me to make a change. However, the

Beautiful Seeds of Change

truth is – there wasn't, and it didn't. For me, the consequences of where I had come to be in my life had become too much to bear, and I had now reached that stepping off point following years and years of personal persecution and a lack of self-worth – *which I was completely responsible for developing through my attitude and reactions to the things I had experienced in my life.*

I would love to be able to also say that this was something that just came to me overnight, but that wouldn't be the truth. The truth of the matter is: I had to do some real work – work on myself before coming to this realization.

I knew for certain that the first thing I needed to do was take a real look at where I was, and I needed to quit using alcohol to dilute my reality. Believe me, over the years I had tried to go for periods of time without drinking; however, it was not easy. Alcohol had become a staple in my life for so long that the physical and psychological addiction had become too powerful for me to overcome on my own.

The fact of the matter was: *I had no real concept or understanding of what "reality" even was, at least as it applied to me.*

From as far back as I can remember up until this time in my life, I had spent the majority of my time wishing I was something different than I was. I would spend most of my time daydreaming about how I wished my life could really be. My parents were divorced when I was very young, three years of age actually, and because of this, I felt different. When anyone, especially a child, feels this way, it is only natural for them to daydream and fantasize about being something other than what they are. It's a defense mechanism. Not everyone does this, but it is more common than you might think.

As adults, our means of escape become different, and they vary from person to person. I have a friend who reads one romance novel after another, and if she can't find one, or is waiting for the new release, she will actually jones for it (a slang term commonly used to refer to a drug addict who is out of whatever drug they are using to escape their reality). Believe it or not these two people will experience the same reaction when they do not get their fix: for the reader it's a book; for the addict it's a drug. When the reader doesn't have their book they will experience irritability and discontent in the same manner as the addict who doesn't have access to his drug of choice. The same goes for people who use food, video games, television, alcohol or many other things to escape their reality.

I became addicted to fantasy and day dreaming, because it gave me an opportunity to feel better about who I thought I was. But the consequences of this behavior were many. For one, I had a hard time paying attention in school, and actually I never did any homework unless I was forced to do it. To this day, I still cannot figure out why my teachers continued to pass me, because I learned very little. I carried this behavior into adulthood, and when my friends were graduating, getting married, going off to college or entering the military, I was left with no life skills or sense of direction at all.

I spent years feeling desperately alone and worthless. In reality, I had no education and no skills of which I was aware.

When I was old enough to work, I took a job washing dishes. This was great, because not only did it give me an excuse for having poor grades; it also gave me the fuel for the illusion I had begun to create for myself. Whenever anyone would ask what my plan was after graduation, I would tell them that my aspiration was to one day open my own restaurant. Truth was, I had no idea, none whatsoever, what I would do after graduation. After my peers moved on, I took a job at a lumber mill. I made good money, and it gave me some sense of worth, but the reality was I never felt as if I belonged there, and the only time I did feel as if I belonged was when we would go to the bar after work.

You know that saying "Reality Sucks"? It had become my mantra, because I had no idea how to live in it.

By the time I was 26 years of age, I had become consumed by the fact that I had no skills or direction in my life. I had gotten to the point that I was beginning to have difficulty even socializing with anyone unless I had a drink in me. I was so lonely; I had no one to talk to. All my former friends, I had let just fade away, because in my mind they were much more successful than I was and seeing their accomplishments only made me feel that much more like a failure.

I remember during this time in my life, I got down on my knees in this little two-bedroom H.U.D. Section 8 apartment, which I really couldn't afford even at the reduced rate, and prayed to a God I wasn't sure even existed, saying something like this: "God, I don't know if you exist, but I am so lonely, and if you think I am ready to have someone in my life, then I think I am." That was it. I didn't pray often, because my sense of spirituality meant that believing in the God of the Bible only meant that I would have to accept that I was surely going to Hell. So God and I didn't talk all that much, if you know what I am saying.

Beautiful Seeds of Change

Strange thing is, a few short weeks later I met the young lady I now call my wife. Honestly, I would have a better chance of winning the lottery than I did at ever meeting her, but I did. And, I knew when we met, she was THE ONE.

Although I was still consumed by the fact I felt as if I was a huge failure, she did give me a reason to be something better than I was. But even she wasn't enough to rid me of my undeniable truth, although I gave it a gallant effort. I did what I always did: I put on a smile and convinced those around me that I was something that I knew I wasn't.

In a short time we married. I also went back to school, mainly so I could learn how to turn on a computer. After completion, the people there did their best to help me find a job, however the jobs they had in mind didn't pay what I thought I was worth. My ideas had become grandiose and the reality I had grown accustomed to had begun to take hold. I managed to land the big one! To this day I don't know how, only that I was able to convince them that I was something that I wasn't.

This job was overwhelming to say the least; I was a fish out of water in the big boys' pond. Every day, I knew I didn't belong there because I had no idea what I was doing. But I was trapped.   Now I not only had Nicole counting on me, but while I was attending school, she had become pregnant. So, not only was she depending on my promise to take care of her, but we now had a little baby girl as well. The pressure was immense, because even though I knew I wasn't capable of doing the job I was hired for, *the company believed I was*. They had an investment in me; they had flown me across the country for training and were now handing me even more responsibilities.

I was living a lie that had turned into something that I couldn't control, so I did the only thing I knew how to do at the time to cope: I drank. I hid behind a fake smile and a convincing attitude depicting everything as being perfect, trying to persuade people to look at my accomplishments, all the while knowing I was a fraud. I began to believe that I was living the way it should be – the lie had convinced me that it was the truth, and even I, the master of deception, became deceived.

I decided it was time to buy a house and while that process was going on, the company realized their mistake. Although they had invested almost two years on me, it was time to cut their losses. I convinced them I was worthy of staying on long enough to find other work, and they let me hang on for three more months. But I told no one, not even my wife. How could I? If I told anyone, I would have to admit the truth myself; and if I did that, then the lie I now believed would be too much for me to bear.

Two weeks before we were to sign the papers on our home, I landed another job. Of course, I told everyone I had made the decision all on my own, and with a little finagling from my real estate agent, we managed to make it appear as if the two fields were connected in order to show the right amount of work history to the bank. Of course this wasn't true, and I knew it. It worked though. IT WORKED! We got the house and once again I was trapped! *Bound by a lie that I had created and had begun to believe.*

The new job was even worse, and in a short time I knew I didn't belong there either. However, this time I wasn't fooling anyone, at least not my supervisor. I had an ace though. The man who hired me for the job believed in me. I don't necessarily think that he believed the lie, but rather he saw the potential. He managed more than one office, and in a few short months had me transferred to the one he worked out of.

To this day I don't know what he saw in me, but with his help I managed to transition and eventually, became "the guy." You know the one you could count on to get the job done. I actually was capable of doing the job and excelled in it. Although I continued to drink regularly, it was more now because *I felt I had earned the right.* I was the man of the house, my wife was a stay-at-home mom, and although we were barely scraping by, with the help of a second job here and there, I was able to hold it all together. For a while anyway.

Sometimes though, usually at night when the house was quiet and I was just left with me, I would become consumed with the reality that I was not who I had made others think I was and managed to even convince myself I was. I was not even close to being the person I pretended to be. But as long as I stayed busy, didn't give myself too much time with me, I was okay. I managed to keep this façade up for almost three years, staying just one step ahead of the game.

When we found out Nicole was pregnant with our second daughter, although I was very excited, I also knew the reality was that I could barely take care of her and the first baby. Now how could I possibly take care of all THREE of them!

That's when those sleepless nights became more frequent, and I would hear that train and fantasize about stumbling onto those tracks. I knew I had life insurance through my employer. It wasn't much, but I believed that it would get them through for a while.

Thinking back on that time now, it seems very unreal and surreal at the same time. It took some work for me to get over the shame I felt for having those thoughts, but the reality at the time was: *I saw no other way out.*

It's funny how life goes. You see, when I moved to that town, when I was seduced and convinced by the lie, I looked at what was going on around me to confirm that I was doing all the right things.

I remember a few weeks after we moved to this little town, we went over and introduced ourselves to our new neighbors. I remember feeling exhilarated, when I noticed the man of the house holding the same brand of beer I drank. He had a similar jacket on and even worked in the same field I did, by a stretch anyway.

We became best of friends, and although he was older than me, we had a lot in common, even sharing the same first name and naturally curly hair.

The truth is, although neither of us knew it at the time, we had even more in common than either of us imagined. We were living the same lie and had almost become convinced that it was, in fact, the truth. Both of us were very good at reaffirming the fact that we were much greater than anyone really knew.

We rarely talked about the truth, the truth that we only admitted to ourselves. But deep down we sincerely believed that if we could only stop drinking, everything would be just fine. Of course, the only time this conversation ever came up was over a 12-pack. At different times over the years, the two of us would decide to quit forever, and we'd avoid one another until one of us would admit that we couldn't actually do it, at least not on our own, and we would begin the same old cycle all over again.

Eventually that friend made a decision to try A.A. At the time, although I knew I couldn't do it on my own, I wasn't ready to admit that this could work for me. After all, I was young; I still had my house, had never been out of work or even missed work for that matter due to alcohol. *Never mind the fact I had been fantasizing about walking out in front of a freight train*, I wasn't "that bad." A.A. was for people who slept under bridges and pushed around shopping carts carrying all their stuff. Come on! How could I benefit from A.A.?

It seemed to be working for my friend, however, so I decide to give it a try. The ironic thing is: I could have thrown a rock from my back door to the location of my first meeting! Can you believe that? All that time it was there, just waiting. Not to mention the guy I was so excited to see drinking the same brand of beer I did, was the one who brought me in. Just coincidence I am sure. Right! That is a whole other book!

I gave A.A. a shot, and although it was very difficult, eventually by taking things one step at a time, a day at a time, I was able to not drink. After awhile the physical addiction was gone, and all that was left was the mental obsession. I suppose, at least for me, this was the most difficult.

Although as a child I was aware of God or at least the concept anyway, my family wasn't one to attend church regularly. "Believe me, my Mother had enough on her plate." Of course, on occasion I would attend, usually when I stayed the night at a friend's house on a Saturday night and going to church was a part of my friend's normal Sunday morning family routine.

I can remember feeling as if I never quite belonged. I tried a few different churches as a young adult, and I was always left with the feeling I didn't belong. I did believe in God though, or at least that something had to have created all this. To me it was the only explanation.

So when the people of A.A. told me I needed to find a higher power to believe in, I chose God for lack of a better name. The problem was, I knew that if I were really going to believe, which deep down inside of me I always have, I was going to have to accept the fact that this force that I chose to call God of my own "misunderstanding" already knew me – ALL of me. And, if that was the truth, then I had a lot of explaining to do.

That was a real challenge for me; however, I now realize that this is true for many people, not just me. I had a hard time believing that the God I knew as a youth, the punishing God that I was taught about in my brief stints with Sunday school, could ever forgive me for some of the things I had done. What stuck out for me the most as not deserving this forgiveness was the fact that just a few months earlier, I was contemplating my own death. Although I never acted on these thoughts, in my mind having the thought was the same as if I took the action.

I came to the realization that in order for me to begin to establish a relationship with this Power much greater than I, I would first need to forgive myself for my thoughts and behavior I had learned to live by.

Although very difficult, the really neat thing was that once I made the decision to take a look at myself and where I had come to in my life thus far, things just began to start coming together. I began to venture out and offer rides to others who had reached that stepping off place. I would show up to meetings early to help set up and stay late to help shut them down, this gave me an opportunity to get out of "Self" and into service. At night when things grew quiet and my mind began to race, instead of thinking about meeting Gloria face to face, I would practice writing things down. When I noticed

Beautiful Seeds of Change

myself exhibiting a behavior that I didn't like, I would make an effort to take a look at it, rather than just dismiss it.

I began to notice patterns of behavior that began much further back than I had thought, some as far back as before I could even walk. Memories that I didn't even know existed were coming to the surface, and I was awestruck by how much of who I was had started before I could even string full sentences together!

As the days began to pass into weeks then months, and the obsession to drink had lifted, it began to become very apparent to me that alcohol was not my problem at all, but just something I used to mask the truth. *At first it was just to fit in, and then at the end, it was to phase out.* Ironic really when I think about it all now.

Gradually as I began to take a look at where these behaviors began, it became easier for me to accept that in quite a few circumstances I didn't have a lot of control over the situations I was in. How could I? I was a kid! This was an epiphany for me, like a huge weight had been lifted off my shoulders, and I began to find forgiveness for the things I had done and learned to accept that I could use these things now as a learning experience. Every time one of these behaviors that I don't like even today comes up, rather than dismiss it, I will take a look at it to determine where (or who) I learned it from.

One of the really cool things about this whole process is that when I went on this little quest to discover how I ended up to be in this place where death had become an option, almost right away I began to feel better. Weird huh? *The more I worked on who I had become, the further away I moved from that person I became, and the closer I came to the person I am now.*

After awhile other people began to notice as well. They would ask questions like (and this one is funny to me even now): "Why are you so happy?" Oh my goodness! The first time someone asked me that, I actually had to laugh out loud! Then I had to try and explain why I was laughing.

Gosh I tell you, this has been an unbelievable change for me. To be completely honest, at first, as I began to notice that I was actually happy pretty much all the time, I would find myself beginning to worry about it! Because I just knew that the old behavior would come up, and at any moment, everything would come crashing down around me once again.

So what did I do? I did some more work around that behavior and the fear. I asked myself why I felt that way. What caused this fear? Once again, over and over, I was brought back to my childhood. Even now after many years of living completely worry free, I am still amazed at the level of happiness I have achieved. *I like me!* I really do. Because of this whole process I have been able to help countless others as well, and I have been given the gift of watching their lives transform into something much more than they had thought it could ever be.

I believe today that we most certainly bring into our reality that which we wish to. I do, and I am not alone. Many people believe this is true as well. That saying you are what you eat has never had more meaning in my life than it does now. *You become that which you choose to bring into yourself.* You are what you think! You truly are.

If you surround yourself with negative thoughts, then you will attract negative things, such as negative people or illness. If you surround yourself with positive things, then this is what you will attract. This has been my experience and that of many people I know personally as well.

I'd like to share a story with you now that happened not so long ago, which caused me to ask myself how I got to be so happy.

Not so long ago I was coming home from work and began the short drive down the street on which I live. It was obvious someone had recently cut their grass, because I could smell it in the air as I approached my house. It was most likely Mr. Patterson, he has the best looking yard on this street. He should, with the amount of time he spends on it!

I slow down even more as I move closer to my house. There it is. It's the pale yellow one with white trim and a white picket fence to match. I know as I begin to pull into the drive way that at least one of my now four children are likely to come out and greet me. If not, they will be in there waiting for my entry. My wife, Nicole, will be there, too. More than likely she will just be finishing up dinner, she loves to cook.

I remember shortly after we met, a little over 15 years ago when she cooked for me for the first time. Garlic spaghetti she called it, and it was delicious! Looking back now, no wonder! I had been living off of hot dogs, tuna, and those little square packs of noodles that you bring to a boil for a few minutes and then have a meal. Within a day or two after that first dish, I called my mother and proclaimed to her that I had found "The One"! My mother, of course, took this with a grain of salt, as "The One" up until that point had changed for me regularly. I did know though, I knew from the first time we met, this time was somehow very different.

Funny when something like that happens, no matter where you are in your life, it can change in one moment and move in a completely different direction.

No matter what you were doing the day before or had planned to do the next, it all changes.

When we decided to purchase our first home, we had looked at numerous houses over a period of several months. As a matter of fact before our realtor called us on the particular one that would become our home, we had all but given up and had been talking about putting everything on hold until we could get what we had wanted. Our criteria, we thought was pretty simple. We wanted an older home, with a wood burning stove, a front porch, a fenced yard and not a penny over what we had told our realtor we could afford.

This, of course, seemed to be more of a challenge then either of us had thought. Most of the homes we looked at needed more than just a little fixing up, and the neighborhoods were unattractive, which is putting it kindly. Nonetheless, our realtor did call to arrange another viewing.

However, this time we were set on not getting our hopes up and had decided that if this was not the one, then we would put everything on hold.

It was in a small town called Hubbard. Neither my wife nor I had ever heard of it. As a matter of fact, no one we talked to did either. I remember the drive out there with both of us trying our best not to get our hopes up after looking at so many already and walking away disappointed. The directions we were given led us right there, and we actually made it much sooner than we thought and even ahead of our realtor!

As we sat in the driveway, both of us were shocked! We checked the address again and again. The place looked perfect! From the outside it looked exactly like what we had wanted, right down to the front porch. It was a two story, creamy colored house with turquoise trim. It had a tin roof and sticking out from it was a smoke stack. In the front was a huge walnut tree, and on the side next to where we were parked was a beautiful Lilac tree, which just so happens to be Nicole's favorite fragrance and flower. I knew, deep inside; I KNEW: This was "The One."

And, it was. It wasn't long before we were living in this very small two-story house that had been built in 1901. It was our first home, and we loved it! At that time in our lives it was the perfect size for our little family. Alexis, our oldest, was just a little over three years of age, and Nicole was pregnant with Cara, who was due to arrive in just a few short weeks! Back then, we were always entertaining our extended families and friends at our house.

Little did I know that my life was about to change again, in a way I didn't imagine. I can still clearly remember the day that I brought home an addition to the family who was to become an important part of my life. I had been up at the local market picking something up for a gathering my wife and I were having for something or another on that particular day.

I was walking out of the Market, and there sat a little girl. I honestly don't remember too much about what she looked like, but if I had to guess, I would have put her at around nine or ten. She was sitting on the ground with her back against one of the pillars decorating the store front. She had a cardboard box with her and on the outside of it in black marker it read: "FREE PUPPIES."

Of course I was curious! Come on, who doesn't like puppies? Inside the box, I counted five puppies, and one of them stood out like a ketchup stain on a white tee shirt. They were all black or brown with a little tad of white on 'em, except for this one. She was almost pure white, as white as snow with a little pink nose and very fluffy! I immediately reached for this one, and as I was picking her up from the box, I asked the little girl what kind of dogs they were. She told me they were an Australian Shepherd and Collie mix.

Honestly, it wouldn't have mattered to me though, not really. I had already made up my mind when I saw her, kinda like when I met my wife or when we pulled up to our first house. I just knew! It was one of those rare moments in time where you just know that it is right and meant to be.

"I will take this one," I said to the girl, holding the little thing up in front of my face with my hands under her front legs cradling her rib cage so I could get a good look at her. She licked my nose! WHAT A DOLL! Cute as a button, with her little pink nose and white eyelashes. "Alexis will just love her!" I remember thinking to myself.

"That's my favorite, too," the little girl was saying. Then bringing me back into reality, "My folks won't let me have any more animals. We already have three dogs, two cats," she was counting with her little fingers as she's explaining. "I have a rabbit, oh and my brother has a hamster. "Wow! That's a lot!

I thanked her as I pulled five bucks out of my pocket and handed it to her. "My little girl will love her! What are we gonna call this little fur ball?" Right away the little girl says: "I like Gemini! She was actually born in April, but it's the end of May now. Gemini is the astrology sign for this time of year. I know because my birthday is next week, and my mom is into that sort of thing." "Gemini," I say aloud to myself. "I LOVE IT! Gemini

Beautiful Seeds of Change

it is!"

We sure have come a long way since then.

As soon as I start to turn the door knob on that little yellow house, Gemini will begin to bark with anticipation. Like my wife and children, she adores me! Nicole says that Gemini is in love with me, and I think she is right.

When I am at home, it doesn't matter what part of the house I am in, she is there. Sometimes just for fun I will walk down the stairs knowing she will follow, and then immediately turn and go right back up, then turn and do it once again. She is such a silly dog, but isn't it that way, when we are so strongly connected with another, we seem to have that desire to be near them all the time. I know it's not nice, teasing her so, but I don't think she minds! Believe me, she gets plenty of hugs from me, and I sincerely consider her a part of my family. It is funny though, I wonder what she is thinking. My wife says she has no sense! She may be right.

Wow! I can't believe how much time has passed since we found our perfect little house and Gemini, and how my family has grown since then. We have added two more children: AJ who is a strong six, and Lili, who is as old as Alexis was when I brought Gemini home for the first time.
How did I get from back there to here? How did I get this life? That house, those kids, that dog and my wife?

Like I said earlier this didn't happen overnight, and because I had been so focused on trying to figure out why I was the way I was, the fact that things were changing in my life weren't as apparent to me as they were to others around me. It was a very gradual thing, this transformation.

So here it is: Another little story, however not so much a story as an explanation, bringing everything around full circle. It began when I was sitting in my driveway and had one of those moments that blew me away.

You know that child I have been referring to? Me? Well, I was the youngest of four children, and the only boy. I don't remember too much about my father, only a little here and there. What I do remember of him aren't things that were nice. My mother divorced him when I was three, so as you can imagine this wasn't easy for a boy in a house full of women.

I remember from a very early age wanting to have a dad, although the only examples of a dad I had were those of the few friends I had, and those I would see on television like Andy Griffin, Happy Days, Good Times and The Brady Bunch. That was the kind of Dad I wanted. One that worked, loved his wife and children and was there. A dad that wasn't mean when his children made mistakes and helped them to make positive decisions in their lives.

I can remember lying in the grass of the apartment complex we lived in, for what seemed like to a kid FOREVER, fantasizing about what it would be like to have a Dad and live in a house. I would imagine a Dad like Andy, who would take me fishing and toss a ball with me. I would pretend we lived in a similar house as the one on that show, with a picket fence and my own room, as at that time I shared one with my sister. I wanted a Dad and to live in a house so bad that it had become my every wish! Every birthday candle, shooting star, dandelion puff and penny in a pond – if it had a wish attached to it, then this is what I wished for.

Now, for the moment which blew me away. What I realized that day as I was sitting in my driveway thinking about my life today is: I got everything I wished for as a kid and more! That Dad I wanted, the one I learned about from television, THAT IS ME! I am that Dad. That house I wanted, the one I wished for on every single birthday, I LIVE IN IT!

What I realized was everything that happened since I was a little kid led me to where I was that day sitting in my driveway! Everything, not just the great things, but the not-so-great things as well, and I was living MY LIFE!

Because of that day I have realized that I have the power within me to manifest anything I wish into my life. More than anything, though, I realized that I am happy. I am truly happy, from the inside out. Quite a contrast between the time where I would lay awake at night fantasizing about walking out in front of a train, to realizing I have everything my heart desired as a youth.

There isn't a day that goes by that I don't find a reason to be grateful for this life that I was so freely given, and there are times I am still amazed at how beautiful and precious life is.

That is what I want for you: To live the life of your heart's desire, the life you wanted as a youth, and not the one you grew to expect.
The really cool thing is: You know that little girl, Alexis? She is now 15 and instead of lying on the grass fantasizing about being something she isn't, she has a huge posse of friends, is an honor student and plans to be an interior designer after college. She loves volley ball and is an excellent artist.

Cara, our second born, is off the charts! She is also an honor student, who hopes to start taking college credit when she is 16 so she can receive her Master's degree early and begin living her dream of becoming a teacher and a part-time writer. She loves soccer and is learning the saxophone. Wait until you see her work! She is an unbelievable author.

AJ, our little tyrant, has become an excellent little reader, is well on his way to being an excellent student and has aspirations of becoming an Astronaut. He loves Lego's and plays tee ball.

Our littlest, Lili, is just simply a jewel, with a smile that never ends. She loves shoes, playing dress up and at this moment in time she is obsessed with going to the moon.

Although we no longer live in that first little house that brought us to this little town, I can still hear that train as she begins to announce her arrival. Now, however, instead of hopelessness and despair, I feel an undeniable gratitude and an excitement for the future when I hear her call of unbound freedom. Funny isn't it? Our perceptions, that is. Although appearances and sounds remain the same, a simple decision can make it all appear so different. That train really was my ticket out in a sense, and when I hear her coming today, I feel victorious and have even in my mind changed her name to VICTORY!

About the Author

David Nixon is a husband and father of four great children; he is an active member of one the largest nonprofit organizations in the world. He enjoys helping others find their passion in life and encouraging them to LIVE THEIR DREAMS!

David resides in Hubbard, Oregon where he enjoys spending time with his family and friends. He has a real passion for dramatic storms and sitting on the beach listening to all the powerful sounds of the sea. He sincerely believes that the key to one's happiness lies within them and that they truly have a purpose in this life.

dnixon@mail.com

Acknowledgments

I have so many people in my life to thank for allowing me to be who I am without judgment. There are a few that stick out more than others like: My mother, Marie Friend, who always encouraged me to be who I am and not limit myself by the things of this World; My sisters, Barbara Rea, Kathryn and Dawn, who taught me the true meaning of family, and I will be forever grateful for having had the experience of being their little brother; My beautiful wife and true confidante, Nicole, who, even when I thought it was too late and had all but given up, gave me a reason to be something much more than I was, allowed me to struggle and stuck by me through my darkest hour without hesitation.

Nancy Newman, who helped bring my story to life!

Lisa Hardwick, who encouraged me to pursue and ultimately realize my dream of becoming a published author. She is truly a remarkable gift to us all, and I am grateful for having had the opportunity to have met such a beautiful soul. You **rock,** my friend! THANK YOU!

Deb Wright

My story is dedicated to all the courageous people who wore "the face" before me and to all the empowered souls of the future who can now spread their wings and fly free as their authentic selves!

Chapter 2

THE FACE

AND THE OSCAR GOES TO...

Have you ever seen the movie Runaway Bride with Julia Roberts and Richard Gere? It's a cute chick-flick movie about a big city columnist, Ike Graham, who gets wind of this small town girl, Maggie Carpenter, who apparently has major issues (and when I say "major," I mean MAJOR issues) with following through marrying her fiancés.

The opening scene of the movie has Maggie dressed in this beautiful, white flowing wedding gown riding a big brown horse like a bat out of hell through the woods with the most horrified look of fear and desperation on her face. That terrified expression appeared as though she only had one thing on her mind: ESCAPE! The funny thing about that entire scene was U2's song, "Only To Be With You," is playing in the background. I thought to myself how fitting, considering the line that is repeated several times in the song was: "...but I still haven't found what I'm looking for!"

To make a two-hour movie short, Ike heads out to Maggie's little town to dig deeper into her story and to prove she is nothing other than a man-eater. After weeks of following her around, pestering her, pressing all her buttons and driving her just insanely mad, he uncovers the root of her problem. His frustration gets him to the point that he can't hold back any longer and unleashes on her in a huge fight at the luau which was her *fourth* rehearsal dinner.

He points out that she is a lost woman – so lost, she doesn't even know who she really is and doesn't have a mind of her own. Completely stunned, Maggie's only come back was that in her mind she was "being supportive of her men." DING DING DING, give the man a prize because he just hit the nail right on the head: THAT'S ME!

Her soon-to-be groom, Bob, ends up walking in on their tension-filled spat and causing them to silently end things through dagger-filled looks at each other. Ike manages to get the last word in by asking her a weird question, "How do you like your eggs?" A simple question: How do you like your eggs? But she couldn't answer it. See, Ike found out that with her first fiancé, Gill, she liked her eggs fried *just like him*; with #2 Brian, it was scrambled *just like him*; and with #3 George, it was poached *just like him*. Maggie was so livid with his ridiculous question, she stormed off! But Bob turns to Ike and says, "egg whites only *just like me*," before he walked away, too. At that moment in the movie I lost it, bawling my eyes out: I realized Maggie was me!

Her "supportiveness" went so far as following The Grateful Dead and faking a tattoo for Gill, the hippy guitar player and fiancé #1; playing with bugs with Entomologist George, fiancé #3; and becoming a walking cheerleader for her mountain climbing, sports nut, football coach, man-of-the-hour Bob, fiancé #4! Not sure why they didn't get into #2 Brian that much, I guess it's because he became a priest. She spent more time and energy encouraging them and bragging about all their great accomplishments than sharing one thing about herself with anyone ... *EXACTLY THE SAME AS ME!* To me she wasn't a man-eater, she was a man-pleaser!

Like Maggie, I, too, came to realize not one of the men I was ever involved with were allowed to let get close enough to me to even know who I was, because I was too busy convincing them that I was everything they wanted and needed me to be. As Maggie proclaimed to Ike at the end of the movie, it was a good thing that she didn't go through with all four of her marriages because it would have been a lie, because SHE didn't know the real her ... and from what I can see about myself, neither do I!

DADDY'S LITTLE BOY?

When did I first turn into Maggie? When did I convince myself that the only way I would be happy in love if I sacrificed all that I am in support of being all that they needed me to be? That as long as I was making them happy then I would be happy, too ... wouldn't I?

As far back as I can remember I have always been that girl. As every psychiatrist's cliché goes, "I blame my parents!" For a while, I DID blame them! I pointed the finger at my Mom for the longest time thinking if she tried harder, then maybe my Dad would finally show her love. And at the same time, I was so angry with my Dad for not being sweet and romantic with her. I thought maybe if he was more like Prince Charming then my Mom would be happy, too, and we could all live happily ever after.

But in reality, the more I learned about myself, the more I didn't blame them at all. It wasn't their fault I am the way I am. Somehow, in some way, I made the choice all by myself to become a self-sacrificing "pleaser" in the name of love. Believe it or not, I remember as a little kid making the conscious effort of becoming everything my Dad wanted me to be in hopes of gaining his love. Sound familiar, Maggie?

My Dad wasn't really the lovey-dovey, cuddly daddy's little girl type growing up. He was, and still is, a hard blue collar worker. That's just what he does! Every morning he would get up and do the same routine: have his coffee before the sun even knew what day it was, go off to work before we were up for school, come home and work around the house before dinner, stop for a bit and eat, then work a little more on whatever project he had going on and finally end his day sitting down in his recliner and watching TV until he passed out. That was my Dad.

He would work even if he wasn't at work! Growing up, he would work on the house or the cars on his days off. I never saw him just take the day off and relax, play with us or do "family-like" things such as go to the park or the zoo. There always seemed to be something that had to be done or fixed. It seemed like family time was whatever home renovation was going on or working on whoever's car was broken down. So, as a little kid, dying to be a part of her Daddy's world, I learned to like what he liked. I figured if I came into his world and loved all the things that he loved, then maybe I had a chance at him loving me, too?

I learned to work on cars, rebuild engines, swing a hammer, build additions, use power tools, paint rooms – you name it, I learned it! I believed that was the only way I could get my Dad to spend time with me. It made him happy, which made me happy. I thought if he needed me and wanted me there working alongside of him, then he loved me. Starving to feel that praise of a proud parent, I became the best son my Dad could have ever wanted!

The older I got, the more I thought I had this great relationship with my Dad. Every weekend my Dad and his dad, my Pop-Pop, would get together and go to the junk yard, get parts and work on their cars. As far back as I can remember, it was just a normal part of my life. My little sister, Re, and I would be all excited on the weekends because Pop-Pop would bring us donuts before they would head out! Woooo Hoooo DONUTS!

After they would get back, Re and I would spend the rest of our day fighting over who got to run out to them the sandwiches my Mom made, who was getting the next Schaffer beer for them, and what tool we could grab for the two pairs of legs popping out from underneath the car! I thought my Dad and my Pop-Pop were so close, just like two peas in a pod. That father/child example was what I wanted, and from where I was sitting it was pretty freaking awesome!

I wanted that with my Dad! And March 19, 1989, that opportunity sadly presented itself. After my Pop-Pop suddenly passed away, my Dad changed. I never saw my Dad cry before that day. It broke my heart into a thousand pieces. I wanted to fix his pain and fill the void left in his heart. So, I devoted myself to becoming my Dad's new working buddy. I loved what he and my Pop-Pop had, and to keep the tradition of them alive, I volunteered to fill those shoes.

We spent the weekends working on the house or working on my Mustang (that had belonged to my Pop-Pop). I grew into a regular motor head tom-boy, and my Dad loved it. Always eager to please my Dad, I devotedly became everything he wanted. I gave it my all to be the perfect side-kick for him. My cartoon doodling and oil painting in my spare time became architectural plans on graph paper for expanding rooms in our house and designing dream homes. In my mind, it was all about coming into his world, and I couldn't help but change and adapt my passions to suit that desire. He was my Dad, why wouldn't I want to make him proud of me?

My Dad was not a real emotional man, and it wasn't until I was much older that I heard him tell me he loved me. He wasn't the type to get all mushy over my art exhibit at school or do cartwheels over an A on my paper. My Mom was always the cheerleader and making big deals over our stuff. So, I just figured that dads don't do that, only moms do!

I don't know what kind of people-pleasing seed I planted all those years ago, but what I do know was there wasn't anything that was going to stop me from feeding it. I was set on doing whatever was in my power to make it thrive! I even went to the extreme of letting my Dad and my boyfriend at the time decide what my college major would be and what career path I was going to take, even if it wasn't what I wanted.

My Mom said that even before I could walk and talk I had something in my hand to draw with. I was a natural artist and wanted to be a cartoonist who would one day work for Walt Disney. How many kids do you know whose heroes were Charles Schultz and Walt Disney? I would doodle the *Peanuts* gang on my school books and had Mickey Mouse items everywhere in my room. I knew I was good at it, and it made me happy! Ummmm HELLO... what kid doesn't want to go to Disney World, it's the happiest place on earth! And, all I wanted to do was make that magic! But I guess that wasn't a realistic dream because my Dad seemed to have other ideas I should pursue. And, of course, I was a good girl who always did what I was told. Silly me for thinking otherwise.

DIRT DIGGING CARTOONIST

When I was in my senior year of high school, my Mom, Dad, boyfriend and I all went over to my boyfriend's college for an open house. Because I didn't have the money to go away to school, this college was an option for me since it was a satellite campus near my house. My Mom, Dad and I all got in line to sign up for the Fine Arts program, while my boyfriend went off to do something else. I wanted to continue my passion for art, and it was a state university that I could commute to, so I could afford to swing the costs. Sounds like a win-win situation, how could I beat that?

If my memory serves me well, my Dad wasn't really buying into the whole artsy-fartsy career move and really wanted me to get into something that had a possible future in it. He had a point, and I believe his heart was in the right place trying to combine my art skills with the construction background that I grew up with. Honestly, at the time I was all for it, why wouldn't I be? My Dad was a God in my eyes, and I hung on every word he said.

While my Mom ducked out of line to go to the bathroom, my boyfriend came over to my Dad and I and asked us to check something out. Next thing I know, I'm signing up for the Landscape Architecture program instead of the Fine Arts major I was there for. Loving them both, I became enthusiastic about it and was bragging to all my friends about going to Temple University for Landscape Architecture. None of my classmates had heard of that major before, so I thought I was special because I was one-of-a-kind!

This attention and curiosity made it so much easier to be happy on the surface even though deep down inside I was heartbroken over giving up my Walt Disney dream. So, I did what I did best … put on *"the face"* and was ecstatic over the choice. I believed my Dad and my boyfriend wanted what was best for me because they loved me, so I dove in head first without hesitation, convinced this was what I wanted. Little did I know I was doing what they wanted at the price of what I wanted.

THE FACE

"The face," as my sister, Re, and I call it, was a June Cleaver seed planted a long, long time ago by my Mom. Yes folks, this incredible hidden ability of acting like everything is perfectly fine even if it isn't, is a true art form. It is not to be sold short or underestimated in the slightest bit because it takes some serious talent and skill to pull it off to those closest to you.

Yeah, you can put on the happy face and act as if everything is peachy-keen to co-workers and random people you run into at the store, but to be able to paint the ideal picture to your close friends and family ... well honey, that's a completely different ball game! To be able to look someone you love point-blank in the eye and depict that everything is great when knowing in your heart it is all a big fat, fake lie is a hard thing to do! Oh, and my Mom was good – very, very good! I learned from the best.

I do believe, though, over the years I have surpassed her to become the master of *"the face"* myself. Even though my Mom can see right through me, 99% of everyone else in my life has no clue of what goes on behind MY closed doors. I present myself as the perfect ray of sunshine wherever I go to whomever I am with. It truly IS a gift and a curse all rolled into one.

It wasn't until I was much older that I realized that my parents were the classic teenage tragedy that TV shows and movies were made about. They were a young high school couple whose untamed love meets the unexpected fate of an unplanned pregnancy, causing these former senior sweethearts to head down the road of marriage because it was the right thing to do. With their crazy teenage days behind them, these once full-of-life kids end up spending the rest of their youth struggling through hard times trying to survive the hand that life dealt them. Yep, that was them, and that was how my story began.

My Mom must have started *"the face"* then. There cannot be any possible way my Mom was tickled pink over having to drop out of high school and raise a baby at 18 years old. Yeah, yeah, yeah, she will claim over and over again that she loves me, and if she could do it all over again she would NEVER give me up ... but still, 18? She was a kid herself, are you kidding me! What about her dreams, her future, her journey... all pancaked for me? Do you know that to this day I still don't even know what my Mom wanted to grow up and be? That is sad; so, so very sad to me! Sacrifice after sacrifice, as long as my Dad, my sister and I were happy, she was happy. WOW, I guess my Mom was a Maggie well before I was!

From the get-go, she put on *"the face"* of loving to be a mom, of getting to marry her high school sweetheart, and building a life with my Dad. Painting the perfect June Cleaver life without having two nickels to rub together was something she did well... a little too well, I must say. Trust me, when you look back at the photos or hear the stories, it looked as though this was really what she wanted, what they wanted. Sometimes, I couldn't really tell the difference of what was an act and what was real.

Matching "Mr. and Mrs. Wright" shirts, BBQ's every year with their friends for my Dad's birthday and their anniversary, holiday dinners, working on the house together, making my Dad eggs and bacon for breakfast on Sundays, packing his lunches in his igloo cooler before he went off to work, she did it all with a smile on her face!

On the surface she looked like the supportive wife and everything seemed fine, but behind that closed door you could tell she was empty and lonely. They both were! I can't remember ever seeing them hold hands, cuddle on the couch watching a movie, kissing under the mistletoe, or going out for Valentine's Day. I just thought people really didn't do that kind of stuff. I guess what else can you really expect from two kids who were forced by a higher power to grow up very fast and were pushed down a path in life that they never really were ready for. It was hard, unbearable at times – and why wouldn't it be?

They may have loved and cared about each other, but I don't believe they married for love. How could two high school kids, with their whole lives ahead of them, really know what love is? To me, they married because it was the right thing to do considering their situation. Kudos to them for taking the chance!

Sadly, the charade only went so far. Our tension-filled home was very stressful at times, filled with fighting, crying, and this uncomfortable silence between my parents that you could cut with a knife. I grew up thinking this kind of environment was normal, and that's just how couples are.

By the example I saw my Mom set, I believed with my whole heart that if you want to have someone love you, you must give up what you want for that to happen; say goodbye to all your dreams and devote yourself to making their dreams come true. By willingly becoming exactly what they want and need you to be, you will be happy spending the rest of your life convincing them that you are all that and more. That's marriage! Hmmmmm, live a lie with *"the face"* on and they will love you … I guess somewhere along the way I thought if my Mom can do it and she looked happy, I could do it, too. *"The face"* seed was planted. The older I got the more hungry to be loved I became. I am ready, coach, put me in!

MUSIC & MAKING-OUT

Middle school – ahhhhh, the ugly, awkward years of bad hair, raging hormones and young preteen boy crushes. Yep, you guessed it: A deadly combo for a girl who so desperately wanted to be loved. Chasing that feeling of love had me so desperate and so willing to do whatever I needed to in order to get it, that I was heading down a road that was destined for failure. By 12 years old, I was starting to grasp the concept of *"the face"* and being able to work that smiling, charming, "everything is great" persona to win someone's heart.

My 7th grade year began by joining what I would soon learn is the butt of most school jokes … I became a *bona fide* clarinet-playing Band Geek! Only a couple of practices into it, I learned that there is some unsaid law of nature that has the woodwinds always messing around with the drum line. Man, did I love the attention, it was awesome! Every day, I watched that clock tick by waiting for practice time to come! Innocent flirting led to my first boyfriend, if you can call a 7th grader and an 8th grader figuring out the birds and the bees a real relationship.

Sitting together on the band bus, hanging out over at each other's houses once in awhile, and showing me how to ride his skateboard with his buddies was all we ever really did. He was passionate about fire fighting, loved it more than life itself I would say. I can remember buying him a model to build for Christmas that year. I was into him, his drumming, his fire trucks – it didn't matter as long as he wanted to be with me. Whatever he wanted to do, talk about or mention, I was in 100% because I just wanted to be with him.

I was so caught up in this new puppy-love feeling that I didn't realize what lengths I was willing to go to hold onto it. That was until one afternoon when it all became crystal clear. We were all alone in his room. The door was shut, music was playing, the mood was set, and he quietly asked me the simple question on every young boy's mind. Terrified, I didn't know how to answer him. I didn't want to make him mad, and I sure as hell didn't want him to dump me because I was afraid. This was the first boy who had ever looked my way, who had picked me out of all the other girls in band – scaredy-cat me couldn't blow it now!

Sick to my stomach with fear, my shaking, flat-chested, tiny little body got down on both knees like the good little girl I was. Looking up at him through my badly permed hair preparing myself to slide into 3rd base, I could see that I WAS doing the right thing because he looked so happy. Did it make him love me? No, no it didn't. As an adult I would say you can chalk it up to a teenage kid who wanted to see how far he could get with a girl. But the 12 year old me won't believe that for one darn minute! And, after all that, he still broke up with me later.

After our break up, I took some time off from boys, but apparently the sabbatical didn't faze my Maggie-like obsession. Towards the end of my freshman year I met this slim, dark haired, dark-eyed upper-classman guy who lived around the corner from me. He had this bad-boy personality that

Beautiful Seeds of Change

just lit me up like a Christmas tree. He pursued me, chased me, and made me feel wanted. The attraction was insane, I felt like this desirable prize he had to have. For a teenage girl, it didn't get any better than that! That feeling was like a drug, a drug I could not live without. I started changing once again, this time to morph into *his* perfect girl.

SCORPIO PASSION

Initially, the transformation began with the small things like listening to his kind of music. Feeling like a badass, we would thrash down the road with his arm around me in his Chevy pick-up to the sounds of Metallica, Testament and Slayer blaring from the speakers. He made me feel special, he made me feel untouchable – like a woman who could be anything and do anything. I was confident with him, and the more I felt alive, the more I worshiped the ground he walked on. The passion between us grew to levels that people couldn't touch, we were invincible together.

That passion had us inseparable: Kissing every chance we had, making out in parking lots after dark, and in the back of movie theaters – he couldn't keep his hands off me, nor did I want him to. He showed me what he liked, and this time around, I wanted to do those things with open eyes and a willing heart. I wanted to master my new skills because I knew it would make him happy. I was good at loving him, catering to his every need, and bringing him the happiness he sought after. The highs were high and the lows were even lower; we loved with passion, and we fought with passion. That's what you get with two Scorpios in one relationship. I craved the rush, the wanted excitement, and the sexual infatuation we had with each other. What we had was amazing. The more he wanted me, the more I was willing to do whatever it took to hold onto him.

I was changing rapidly, more and more every day becoming less of me and more of his girl. I wore his letterman jacket to school with pride even though our schools were arch-rivals. He loved blondes, so I bleached my hair with peroxide. He loved fishing, so I learned how to fish. He watched Beavis and Butthead and the Simpsons faithfully, and so did I. I became a HUGE sports fan. Football Sundays and hockey season were like air to him, they now were to me, as well. I never thought twice about it because I loved him!

With that love, I followed him to college at Temple University. He treated me well and made me happy. I felt like a queen with him, so why wouldn't I want that to go on? We spent two years there together. When we were together and a couple, it was good; and when we broke up for the summers, it hurt… I mean, it hurt BAD! I felt like a revolving door as he would come and go out of my heart.

It was his idea to take the summers off so we could explore other people. Today, looking back, I can completely understand why he suggested that. He thought this was what was best for us because I was 14 and he was 16 when we first got together. We were just kids! In his mind there was a whole big world out there waiting to be discovered. In my mind, I loved him and only wanted to be with him. So the devoted me silently suffered through what he wanted.

Summer after summer we did this, and I would just wait for him to come to his senses and come back to me. And in a way he did… sort of? Even though we were seeing other people, we were still hooking up and sleeping with each other. To me, I believed it was because he was deeply in love with me and could not resist me. In reality, I was just torturing myself by hanging on to someone who clearly wanted to let me go.

The torture continued each fall when we would get back together, celebrate our birthdays, the holidays, ring in the New Year and cap it off with a romantic Valentine's sexfest before the next summer breakup. Who wouldn't think the man was in love with me? We were together for all the important stuff. He was with me and not them. I thought that I must be doing something right because he kept coming back to me… right? WRONG!

My metal music loving man graduated and left me to finish off my last couple of years of college on my own. He was 21 years old and out in the real world, hitting clubs, meeting people and living life, while I was just sitting around waiting for him like a lost puppy sitting at the door eagerly anticipating her master to come home. Hopeless me was still hanging on to my high school sweetheart, the boy I started dating six years ago in 9th grade! I, too, should have been out there living and loving what were supposed to be the best years of my life.

Eventually, I could finally see that he was running back to me after the summers off less and less and wanted to be with the other girls more and more. Even so, it was hard to let him go because we had spent six incredible years together, and we had learned a lot about life and love from one another. But, somehow I found the strength to start loosening the grip he had on my heart and stopped trying to win him back by being his perfect girl.

FLOURISHING PHEROMONES

As his door started to close, I met a guy who was the total opposite. He was the big, strong, rough and rugged mountain-man type. Our relationship didn't last very long, not even a year actually, but the pheromones between us sparked a fire inside of me that I hadn't felt in a long, long time. He was several years older than me, and I found that completely fascinating and intriguing. He had a past that made him mysterious. Every time I was with him, he was leaving me wanting to come back for more.

Unlike my experiences with my high school boyfriend and the few casual guys I dated in between, this was a completely different and foreign experience to me. He lived on his own, was mature, older, and had some notches on his belt that I wasn't sure I could compete with. I had only been with one person before him and needed to come up with a better plan if I wanted to hold onto this amazing guy. I felt like a kid with a grown-up not knowing what to do and too afraid to ask. So, I did what I do best ... I watched and learned so I could become exactly what he wanted!

He opened my eyes to a whole new world. Being invited to his apartment made me so nervous, he was the first person I had ever met *with an apartment*. I felt like such a child still living at home with my parents. He was gentle with me and treated me like something he treasured. He held me in his arms as we fell asleep – I thought that was just something you saw in the movies. Sleeping over at someone else's place and waking up with someone was something I never did before. I liked what I was experiencing. I liked it a lot, and there was no freaking way I wanted to give that up!

He was way into the outdoors and landscaping, so I became little "Debbie do-gooder" and strived to be the perfect little student in school. We joined clubs together and organized events on campus together. We spoke at local schools together encouraging art students to explore landscape architecture as an option. We went on camping trips with fellow classmates and instructors. I was an all around star joiner, and it made him happy as can be! I even started dressing like him with my flannels, jeans and work boots.

Things seemed great, and I felt like I was doing everything right. We were having a blast and everything seemed fine between us. To be honest, I am not really sure how or why our relationship unraveled, but it eventually did. He believed that there was someone better out there for him. That kinda stung a little. Why did every guy who dumped me say that there is always someone better for them than me? Wasn't I everything they wanted? I don't get it?

Like Maggie, I was in denial about failed relationships. After all, I *WAS* supportive and the perfect girlfriend – wasn't I? In all three of my relationships, I had done nothing less than love them, support their interests, and encourage their dreams. But did any of them really know me? I doubt it. Did any of them really try to learn who I was? No, not really. Did I ever give them a chance to know and love me… NOPE! I was always too busy being what they wanted to let them in.

It saddens me though to think I once lowered myself to the point of performing sexual encounters to win a man's heart, or physically change my appearance to win another's. What kind of person am I to allow a man, or anybody for that matter, to make me feel less than who I am? I was EXACTLY like Maggie, hiding the real me, protecting my heart with a huge brick wall so no one could hurt me!

OUT OF THE BLUE

My senior year of college was right around the corner, and I was having a blast. Three more semesters to go and I would be a college grad! I was focused on making my parents proud of me for all that I accomplished. I felt empowered and confident about my work. I had my entire future ahead of me, and I escaped the family curse … I HAD IT ALL! Everything seemed to be going my way.

Out of the blue, this shy, soft spoken guy, who was in the same major as me, somehow ended up in my criminal justice class. I had never seen him around campus EVER! I was always there, and pretty much knew everyone around school especially in the landscaping department. Little did we both know that everything we knew as our life was about to take a most unexpected turn.

I don't know if it was because my wounds from striking out in love time after time were raw, or the hunger to be in love again was just bursting to come out, but from the first date I threw myself into him hook, line and sinker. We dated for a while, which eventually led to him always sleeping over at my house and us spending the weekend at his. Don't judge – we were two kids paying for college on our own and couldn't afford apartments. Our parents understood. They may not have liked it, but they understood.

Being in the same major, we got along great together. I helped him through his design studios and the more artistic classes, and he helped me with the classes that I was struggling in, too. We made a good team. We complemented each other: where he lacked, I was great; and where I fell short, he made up for it. Working together, we were unstoppable.

As time went on, I started doing the same Maggie-like things. I got into his music, started hanging with his friends and backing off of mine; I even went as far as hanging out with his sister over my very own. I don't

48   *Beautiful Seeds of Change*

know why, but I was determined to make this one work. I really can't give you a reason why I consciously made the choice to consume myself with this particular relationship more than the others, but I did.

To this day, I live with a regret that this obsession compelled me to do. I had a beautiful friend, who I had met on our very first day of kindergarten. Every memory of my 13 years in school was with her. She was my best friend; we rode the bus everyday together, played on the play ground together, had every birthday together, dated best friends together, went on school trips together, were in marching band together, went to the prom in the same limo and went to Europe together. We did EVERYTHING together! And, on her big day, the day every little girl dreams of, I bailed out after the ceremony so I could go to my boyfriend's college graduation party. I hadn't even known him two months, while I had known this girl my whole entire life. What in God's name is wrong with me to do something like that?

Is there any length I would not go for love? I walked out of my best friend's reception without an ounce of remorse at the time. I was having too much fun drowning myself in his world to even think straight. We went to Dave Matthews concerts and college parties with his friends. We went to Penn State games, and hit all the clubs in the city. We were having a good time; we were great friends and got along really well, maybe it's because I was playing in his world and not mine... who knows?

HISTORY DOES REPEAT ITSELF

A year into our relationship, we tossed around the "M" word. I was graduating from college at the end of the year, and we figured it was the next step. We picked out a ring, and he popped the question at a TGIFriday's one night. The stress of a future wedding after I completed school started to bring some of our differences to the surface. But I think it was mostly because I started opening up a little about what I wanted. I should have just kept my mouth shut and went with it. More differences created more problems, and the more problems created a big break-up... an ugly break-up! After a couple of weeks, we tried working things out and with that came the fun make-up sex.

Well, as we would soon realize, as we chipped away at putting our relationship back together, the heavens had bigger plans for us. It was my last week of college forever, and I was in the deepest trenches of my finals. And, let me tell you having three history classes in one semester is a tough challenge! I was under a lot of pressure and a ton of stress, so it would be only natural for your body to be a little messed up... right? But something told me that maybe I should take a pregnancy test, so we bought a couple of boxes of them. After peeing on stick after stick, seeing the plus sign over and over again, I was convinced they were ALL broken. I couldn't be pregnant, there is NO FREAKING WAY!

That was impossible! Absolutely, physically impossible! I have endometriosis; I have had it since my teens. After several different procedures, my doctor sat me down with my Mom at 18, and told me that I was infertile and would not be able to have children. I learned to accept my fate and thought in some twisted way this was the Heaven's gift to breaking the family curse. As far as I knew, the curse started with my Mum-Mum, who got pregnant with my Mom when she was 16, my Mom pregnant with me her senior year of high school at 18 and now me pregnant at 22 during my last year of college... this can't be happening to me... NOT NOW! I had accepted my fate of being kid-less. I had planned out my future based on that fate. I thought I had endless possibilities in my grasp... why God, why?

After a long, long... long talk in the bathroom we decided to make a pact. We were in this together, sink or swim, no matter what. We proceeded to tell our family and friends; there were many mixed emotions all around, some good and some bad. For the first time in my life, I decided to take my destiny into my own hands. There was no way I was going to raise my daughter while still living with my parents, who at this point were still married only for us kids. I needed to take the initiative and make a plan. I can do this, I had to do this, I didn't have a choice. This baby was coming either way. It's go time!

During the course of one year I had my degree, I had a single family home, and I had a precious daughter to love. All that was left to do was to get married. So that's what we did. Was I like my Mom and Dad who got hitched because that was the right thing to do? Maybe? Or, maybe it's because we did everything else already, and this was what we were supposed to do next.

I remember my Mom asking all my bridesmaids to give us a moment alone while she put her veil on my head. She said to me, "Debra, you don't have to do this. We can figure something out." I looked at her, trying to hold back the tears filling my eyes, and I said to her, "Ma, I am not you. I can make this work, I can do this!"

I didn't realize that my stubbornness and determination to not become my Mom was EXACTLY what I was doing! With every step I took down that aisle I was doing nothing but walking in her footsteps. I do believe wholeheartedly that the man I was about to marry and I did have a close bond and a deep sense of caring for each other. We knowingly took on this tough road together. He never quit on me, and he never gave up on us no matter how hard things got.

In the beginning I saw him as a good man and a very hard worker. In a lot of ways he reminded me of my Dad who I loved and worshipped. His zest for sports brought out this enthusiasm and excitement of his inner child hidden away in his everyday life. Sports were his passion, his pleasure and his escape. His gentle demeanor diminishes when it comes to sports. He comes alive, full of energy and really allows his emotions to fly free. It really is the only thing I have seen that spikes this fire in his soul and puts a genuine smile on his face.

When he is watching ESPN, he appears so comfortable in his own skin that happiness illuminates from him and his authentic self comes out. His soft spoken voice would become exuberant with loud and crazy cheering. His excitement would fill the air like the smell of coffee in the morning. He was having fun, and I wanted to be a part of that world. So, I put on my Maggie hat once again and became the supportive sports wife, in hopes that he would shower me with an ounce of that passion he displays for his favorite sports teams.

"The face" didn't just stop at being sports nut wife. I put on the apron and became the June Cleaver wife planning all the BBQs, birthday parties, holiday events and everything I could to make us appear like the perfect little family. With every year and every event I would consciously bury more and more of myself, committing all my energy to living up to the standard of the perfect Stepford wife swirling in my head.

This driven obsession to be the perfect wife to him and everything he wanted pushed me into this insane depression. You could see the physical toll it was taking on me: stress causing acne on my face that made pizza look pretty, losing weight because I was starving myself to the point I looked as though I was a chemo patient, and bags so black under my eyes from tossing and turning on the couch at night that I looked like a was a Goth follower.

Depression consumed me, and I didn't know what to do. I did not want to be my parents living in misery (which I obviously was), and I did not want my marriage to fail like theirs did either. I was determined to prove them wrong. I was convinced I could make it work, no matter what the cost!

CRYSTALS, STARS AND GUIDES ... OH MY!

A few years into my marriage, we were driving back from a family function one evening, and the stress of everything finally took me down. I LOST IT! Within the 45-minute drive home, I went from pulling off the perfect *"face"* to a full-fledged nervous breakdown. I was hysterical, overwhelmed, not making sense whatsoever and just a downright, out-of-control mess. We decided that it was time I got some help ... professional help!

I can't remember how I came across Jim in the beginning. I am not sure if it was the yellow pages, a referral, or what, but Jim entered my life and introduced me to so much more than a therapy couch could ever offer. For years, he helped me through a lot of my past demons, my current issues, and my problems with relationships. I told him my secrets and my fears. He made me feel safe, so safe that I finally cried somewhere other than alone in my shower. I cried thousands of tears in his office without judgment, without regret and without fear. This was so new to me, to finally have someone care about me. I was the one always caring about them, not the other way around. This was so hard for me to understand, and it was even harder for me to accept.

I would meet with Jim professionally on and off for ten years while he helped me though a lot of stuff. The more we uncovered and the more he showed me about my life of lies, the less I wanted to be there. I didn't want to see the reality of my life, I did not want to look at who I really was in the mirror, and I did not want to admit that I was the self-sacrificing martyr he believed I was. So, I would stop showing up to appointments and would disappear for months sometimes years on end until I would hit rock bottom again and come crawling back.

Just like Maggie, I didn't believe I was doing anything other than supporting those who I loved. Jim said I spent so much energy caring for everyone around me that I did not have anything left for myself. And since I was such a giver, I wasn't receiving anything back to fill my soul. There was no balance, and my soul was starving.

He told me that he thought a different kind of therapy could help me. He said if I was open to it, he would like to introduce me to some work with crystals. This was something I had no idea had ever existed ... all I knew was it was something to do with really pretty rocks. He showed me a room with a table draped with a white sheet in the center, beautiful crystals everywhere and intoxicating, therapeutic smells in the air.

From the very first session I felt rejuvenated, awakened, relaxed and free. He opened my eyes to things I never thought I could see or feel. I was connecting my chakras little by little with each session. I began seeing things in my mind's eye more clearly and discovering more about myself that had been buried deep for decades. He was no longer my therapist, he was now my spiritual guru, my teacher and my guide to a world I wanted to be a part of.

Crystals were just the start for me. My interest in them helped me expand my curiosity in the direction of astrology, tarot, chakras and more. The most amazing things began to happen to me, information was just pouring into my dreams, and I finally started to feel whole and see the real ME!

People who were like me were being drawn into my world. One time I was wearing this unique azurite and malachite necklace which someone special gave me to my daughter's dentist, and this woman who worked there noticed it. Little did I know that she would not only become my friend but this porthole to an array of people in the metaphysical world. She introduced me to this enchanting woman who became not only my spirit guide but another close friend. Christi and I had an instant connection. She helped me listen to my elders and all the messages I had been ignoring all my life. Our chats would last for hours, but the information she helped me see would last a lifetime.

She shared with me this vision she had of me: an angel with big, beautiful white wings – so big and so magnificent, glowing and waiting to fly. Sadly, this incredible creature, who was me, was shackled with heavy chains around her wrists, just wanting and waiting to be set free. Oddly enough, she told me, the angel holds the key to her own freedom right in her very hand. All that I needed to do was unlock myself, and I would finally be free. Her messages from my elders and guides have completely reshaped who I truly am.

A FIGHTING CHANCE

The more I got in touch with my authentic self, the less I felt like I fit into my life. I started to see the differences in my relationships with people. The flaws in my marriage became evident, and all the problems floated up to the surface one after the next but I wasn't ready to face it. The more I saw me, the more I saw the life I was living was nothing short of a masqueraded lie. I was an actress staring in the leading role of a big, fat phony, and I did NOT want to admit that to myself nor anyone else for that matter!

Honestly, did my marriage ever have a chance from the get-go? The poor man was married to a fake – a stranger, a liar. I never gave him a chance to know *me*. From the moment I put that white dress on, *"the face"* came with it. It was my "something borrowed" from my Mom, hahaha! Every day of our marriage was one challenge after another, but no one ever knew it.

We spent more time surviving than we did enjoying our time together. Excuses after excuses, we pushed on instead of figuring things out between us earlier on with our relationship and marriage. For one reason or another, we hit rock bottom more times than I would like to say, but we never quit on each other. Because of his devotion to our survival and our situation, I wholeheartedly committed myself day after day, year after year to his needs and his world. The problem with that was, I finally caught a glimpse of the real me, and I liked it.

I needed to make a huge choice… the man who never gave up on me or my authentic self?

MY ANGEL, MY SAVIOR

Struggling with the choice, I started suppressing what I learned about myself. I didn't want to admit how different my husband and I were. I was realizing we were strangers under the same roof, and I was a prisoner in my own life. I stopped seeing Jim, because I didn't want to keep looking in that mirror of reality. It was just easier if I started ignoring myself again and started loving and supporting my husband.

Depression was my new best friend, sadness filled my days and tears kissed me good night. Gluing *"the face"* on tight, I reverted back into that desperate soul who would do anything to hang onto her man, her marriage and her family.

Just when I thought things couldn't possibly get worse, one night around 3:30 in the morning my worst nightmare came true. I saw the dim glow illuminating the bottom of my 12 year old daughter's bedroom door. As I cracked the door open, I caught her texting someone from her bed. Angry she was breaking the rules, I grabbed the phone and told her we would discuss this tomorrow, and I stormed out of the room.

By the time I got to the kitchen, my hands were trembling, my head was spinning, and I thought I was going to puke my guts out. My sweet, beautiful daughter was texting with a boy who wanted her come over in the middle of the night to lay naked with him. She was agreeing to it, even though he had been calling her degrading names earlier in their conversation because she was resisting his advances.

The more he was trashing her and throwing her away, the more desperate her texts sounded to hold on to him. She kept saying, "I will, because I love you." It made me so sick to my stomach. I was crying, I was scared and confused and then it hit me: Oh my God … SHE'S *ME!*

What do I do? How could I break this chain? She is becoming the next Maggie. I don't want her to be me; she has a chance at true love without wearing *"the face"* to get it. Yeah, negative attention is still attention, but is that really how I want her to be … NO! Since the day she was born, I have always worried about how I would look in her eyes. Would I be the strong role model she wanted to grow up inspired by, would I be someone she admired, would I make her proud? Instead I have done the opposite, I let her down, I showed her the way to repeat history. I needed to change this and change this NOW!

IT'S TIME TO CHANGE

My daughter's actions saved me. She woke me up from the life of lies I was leading and gave me the courage to change my ways. This rude awakening planted a new seed in my heart giving me the desire and drive to not only change for her, but for myself as well. I don't *EVER* want her to be afraid to be herself, and I don't want her to *EVER* hide who she really is for anyone! She doesn't need to convince anyone to love her. If she believes in all the beauty that she holds, then the right person or persons will love HER for all that she truly is! The funny thing about all this was that I was not listening to myself at all.

How can my daughter believe one word I am saying if I am not living what I preach? How can she allow someone to love her for herself if she is seeing me hiding who I am everyday from everyone? She will never be proud of me if I am completely ashamed of myself. In the movie, Maggie leaves Ike at the altar, not because she didn't love him and not because she was trying to be what he wanted. She left him because he broke through that huge wall she built around her heart and saw the real her, but she didn't. She didn't know who she really was; she didn't even know what kind of eggs she liked.

I didn't know myself either. But the more time I spent in crystal therapy with Jim, the more time I spent with Christi, the more astrology research I explored and the more I uncovered about myself, the more I got scared. I was terrified to let people see who I really was – what if they don't like me? What if I won't be loved for who I am? Isn't it just easier to hide than to take the chance and let someone in? YEAH, it's easier to hide, and the example I am setting for my daughter was to do just that… HIDE! She deserves nothing less than to shine as bright as the stars and be surrounded by amazing people who love and adore her for all that she is, and SO DO I.

Looking back at all four of the men I have been seriously involved with, I have noticed one common thread that stands above all the other similarities they share. Every single one of them has been nothing short of their authentic self. Every single one of them never gave up their passions, their hobbies or their interests. Every single one of them followed their dreams in some way or another. Every one of them stayed true to themselves.

I was great at loving them, I was great at supporting them, and I was great at giving up myself in order to do that. I obviously had been blind to see that I was living through them and not with them. I was continually devoting myself to people who were true to themselves, not realizing what was right in front of me. I wanted to be the free spirit that I saw in all of them. I wanted to be comfortable in my own skin without fear of judgment or what people thought. I want that now more than ever.

Can I change overnight the way I have been thinking since I was a little girl? No, I can't. But every day I make the conscious effort to allow a little piece of me to shine through this very large brick wall I built around my soul. I try every day to take *"the face"* off and without regret let people know how I feel about things. It is a struggle, I have to admit. I get scared a lot and want to run and hide. It would be so much easier at times to put *"the face"* back on and smile my way through things, but I know I wouldn't be being true to myself. Every time I want to just cave and not stand my ground on how I feel, I think of how I cannot be a doormat any longer.

I have gone back to what Jim has taught me about the difference between an acquaintance and someone who truly loves you. After playing that story over and over in my head, I took the time to see the difference in those who have only loved me when I was loving them and not for me being me. I need to believe that people will love the real me if I give them the chance to. I believe I am on the path to loving myself, seeing all the wonderful gifts I possess and how special I really am. I am getting there, slowly but surely I am.

And when I do, I believe I will find the life full of love I have chased after since I was a kid. And I will find someone to share MY life *with* instead of *through*. And that someone WILL see me as the amazing person they love like I do them. I know none of this will ever be possible if I don't love and adore myself first.

I need to want those things for myself as well as for my daughter or anyone else I devote my heart to. I need to believe that I, too, deserve those things as much as anyone else. I know that I need to find the courage to believe in myself, to find the desire to want to love myself and most of all USE the key that I hold in my very own hand to unlock all the magic of the real authentic me. NOW, is my time and the change is up to me!

By the way... I like my eggs over hard with broken centers!

About the Author

Deb Wright is a Landscape Designer by trade, and artist, photographer, and dreamer by heart. She owns and operates a residential and commercial landscape design company that serves many of the contractors in her area outside of Philadelphia, Pennsylvania. To her, lush gardens, courtyards and award winning projects are only a small reflection of where her true passion lies. Through the expression of her charcoal drawings, oil paintings, creative photography and now in her writing, the real her truly comes alive. Deb's zest for life comes from the people she meets, the stories they share and the fascinating world that surrounds her.

justdebb@comcast.net
www.justdebb.net

Acknowledgments

I would love to thank my daughter, Mickayla, whose love opened my eyes and saved my soul; my Ma for always looking past my "face" and seeing me for who I really am; my sister, Re, who will always be the yin to my yang; Dan for always standing by me and never giving up; my Dad because without him this would not be my story; my munchkin, Shawnnie, for always loving her mommy; my dear friend, Robyn, who helped make my dream possible, and a special thanks to all the amazing people who have blessed my journey so far!

Diane S. Christie

My words are dedicated to the always present and Universally available power of choice.

Chapter 3

CHOICES: CLOSER TO THE BONE

I been high and I been low, I been people that I don't know...
~Bruton, Burnett, Goodwin, Neuwirth, Hold on You

It was a Friday night in June, the last night my husband and I were together. We were going our separate ways: one north, the other south. Different directions were a knowing statement and apt summary of the state of affairs of our marriage. Since our move from Alaska back home to Washington State, we had argued frequently. No matter the topic, we picked at each other. We could not agree on anything. Under much stress of being without direction, we each behaved poorly and lashed out at each other.

Following our move from Alaska, I had a new job, and he changed careers. His new career, with a partner, was as a general building contractor. Our most recent explosive argument was when he discovered that his new business partner had lost all the money from my cashed-out retirement plan, which had been invested in the business. The missing money had gone to gambling. Following our new knowledge of the missing money, and now of the covertly hidden clamor of unpaid contractors, the business partner committed suicide. This was absolutely the last straw. There was no way the situation could be any worse.

In a piercing experience of shock, pain, rage, and disgust all rolled together, we cried, screamed, and cast blame on each other about the myriad of symptoms and choices made. He wanted to talk to me. I would not talk. There were no words left to say. I knew separation was the best action. There is no memory of tears, hugs, sadness, or elation on that Friday evening. The only thought I had was that we were acting out the logical conclusion to an accumulation of grievances, arguments, and despair. The only way to resolve the layers of conflict was to separate and then to divorce, as quickly as possible.

The next morning, Zorro, our loving and joyful black Lab, and I drove away. My husband stayed, packed up, probably swore, perhaps even cried a tear or two for himself, and then moved out. I returned on Sunday evening to a strangely silent, half-empty rented house. The rooms echoed, the floors and toilets needed scrubbing, and Zorro moped. The overall feeling was numb.

On Monday, all my work processes were on automatic pilot. For many days, driving anywhere on the Interstate and in the city was a blur. The blur was from incessant tears, sobs, and gasps for air. Drastic change had occurred. The marriage was gone, and all the illusions of a stable relationship were gone, too. Lots of long walks, cleaning cupboards, vacuuming the house, and other physical movement helped to calm my heart. Direction was not necessary, just action.

Separation and divorce statistics were in the newspapers and magazines. The rate of divorce was 50%. Our outcome was normal and along with half the married population, divorce was bound to happen. I had no control over this outcome … it was just the way life turned out.

All the people around me certainly heard that life had changed. Most everyone, especially immediate family, agreed with me, of course. The most common phrases were 'he was wrong, ''he shouldn't have….,' 'he's awful, ''he took *WHAT* from the house?!' and so on. When said, these comments felt loving and supportive of my indignation and helped ease the sting of being by myself again. I had also now lost relationships with two step-kids. What remained was the sick-in-the-gut feeling of being a complete failure.

The days came and went. I put one foot in front of the other, and did what was necessary for mental and physical equilibrium. Besides taking long walks and scrubbing the house, it was important to figure out the money situation. Financially, life would be okay. I had a good job, could pay the rent, and put food on my and Zorro's plates. My workplace, coworkers, and client group were pleasant, familiar and comfortable. I understood the environment and knew what to do, how to think to get the job done right. Work was a place of stability when everything else had turned upside down and was so unknown.

For many weeks, one friend in particular, Susan, listened. She heard my anger and woe. She lovingly suggested that I might be interested in attending a personal growth program that she herself had attended. She said that she thought some of the ideas could help me sort through issues. I remembered being shocked and offended at the suggestion of attending a self-help program. I offered comments like: 'He's the one with the problem!' and 'He did this, he did that, and my needs are … ' The most memorable comment of that conversation was that I said 'You are full of shit!' There likely was more said, but better now that other comments are forgotten.

Time moved on. There was work each day. When at home, I cried and usually watched TV and then sat out on my patio and endlessly smoked cigarettes. I spent a lot of time alone thinking about the state of affairs called

Beautiful Seeds of Change

'my life.' I reached out to various people from all aspects of life that spoke right up, were supportive, and affirmed my thoughts that separation was the right decision. There were amazing, agreeable conversations with Zorro.

In September, the first of the legal papers appeared in the mailbox. Oh my. Not only was there a petition for divorce, but the petition included a provision to change my name. My heart raced, and my face flushed. His effort to change my name provoked anger that surprised even me with the depth. This was the final insult. My name, professional and personal identity, was under assault also. All right then, no part of life was sacred anymore. Of course, other people were shocked and angered also. There was a lot of support from others as they all agreed that this last action was too much. I hired a lawyer.

One day in February, I was at home with a packed suitcase waiting for a ride to the airport, ready for a much needed trip to visit friends in Alaska. The TV was on and Oprah Winfrey was interviewing John Bradshaw. His name, as an author and speaker, was only vaguely familiar. He talked about family dysfunctions and family patterns. He described the wounded inner child present in all of us. He said he would lead a guided meditation, on national TV no less, to help access and contact one's inner child.

Curiosity prevailed, I focused, and then decided why not? No one will see or hear me. So, I let myself be in the moment right then with John Bradshaw and Oprah. The next thing that happened was a spontaneous and tearful conversation with me, as a child. Her nickname was Dinnie. She was that blond, naturally curly haired, blue eyed, sweet and smiling six year old girl in that beautiful, red and white cowgirl outfit that my Mom had sewed for Christmas day. She was right there. She was looking at and talking to me! And, I talked to her. We cried together... tears of joy, sadness, and recognition. She jumped straight into my heart. We found each other, were intensely together, and I felt a missing part of me was back where it belonged.

While on vacation, I told my friend, Pat, about 'meeting' John Bradshaw, the meditation experience, and being with Dinnie. Pat was then in her Master's program in psychology. Pat 'happened' to have the entire series of Bradshaw tapes at her house. Those tapes came home in my suitcase. I listened and listened, and listened more. What was there to know? Something in my brain was shifting as new information and ideas were presented. The Bradshaw information made sense to me. Then the thought and question came to mind: 'Was it possible that the earlier idea of self-help may have merit and that I could look deeper at life?'

Back home, I looked around at the rental house. It made sense to move closer to work. A few miles from the office, I found a cute little house that was just right for Zorro and me. The house was so cozy, and all the furniture would fit nicely. There was room for the two of us and extra space for visitors and maybe even a friend or two for dinner. Packing used energy doing something productive. I asserted an independence that was difficult to define, yet felt liberating. This was a new start and moving to a new place was right. A new place would be the perfect space for dimming old memories and creating new ones.

Mom and Dad helped pack furniture and household belongings. While they were at the house boxing items, a legal process server showed up at the front door. Mom called at work to tell me about the delivery of the legal papers. Immediately, I left work and went home. To this day, there must be imprints on the steering wheel from that drive. The papers were from an attorney who advised that the Internal Revenue Service was looking for me. After reading the papers, the shock and anger were overwhelming. The letter documented that the IRS had been sending notices to my husband. The staggering amount owed was $45,000. I had no knowledge of this debt and no knowledge why I did not know about it.

The story unfolded, one nauseating detail of omission and governmental threat after another. Most of the time I did not think there was room in my head for another piece of awful information. Surely brain matter was going to explode all over the dining room table. Yet details kept coming. Screaming, guttural questions pierced the air about how this information was unknown and not seen. Then the underlying question came about what I did not want to see: It was being done to me again.

Zorro and I moved and settled in quickly. It was a new place to sleep, a new neighborhood to explore, and it was closer to work and social activities. Zorro loved his big back yard. He loved to chase after his blue rubber chew toy. We both would run and play, and run and play some more. He loved being able to sniff out the corners, and he could poop wherever he wanted. It was his yard. I cleaned up after him. I even learned how to mow the grass as part of being the renter and took pride in a nicely mowed yard and most certainly having a yard that was dog poop-free.

Soon, a second attorney, one who specialized in tax matters, was part of the legal mix. This attorney had also once worked at the IRS and knew the ins and outs. He became part of the 'Diane team' working with the family law attorney who was navigating local divorce law. Always, I went to my job every day focusing as I could on work and doing the best job possible. What an effort, and often struggle, to plan for upcoming projects. All I wanted to think and talk about was how to get out of the mess I'd been put in. I was suffocating in stagnant air. Life was an ongoing tumultuous clump of questions about what was happening, going to happen, and why 'it' was happening. None of this emotional upheaval made sense. Please, just stop.

As the year progressed, however, the thoughts were changing, but I still did not specifically understand why or know how. I now took more time to think things through and did not react as quickly. Change was happening, yet in an unknown direction, and the 'why' of too many events was still unclear. Like a Fourth of July firework, a spark of survival kept me waking up each day. I was proud and conditioned to be Scandinavian stoic.

Deep down there must be another side to this story, somewhere, sometime soon. The path was out there. What I knew about myself was that when there was an idea in mind or a goal to accomplish, I was single-minded and made things happen quickly and efficiently. As a matter of fact, some have described the approach as being 'like a dog with a bone.' I would not let go, usually ever. This behavior worked for me.

Over the year, Susan and I socialized in a variety of ways including movies, meals, and family gatherings. We talked about many aspects of life. She seemed to empathize with me. She introduced me to some different thoughts than I had ever had before. Mostly though, our time was time to laugh. It was a respite from pain and confusion.

Also, throughout the year, I noticed how Susan was moving forward in her life. She kept getting such interesting results in her endeavors. She enjoyed both her jobs and was happy with her relationships. Sometimes we would talk about the idea of results, and she would suggest that there was another way or perhaps many other ways to look at situations. Rejection of her ideas was still the basic response. After all, I was the victim here and deserved the attention and sympathy.

One sunny Saturday morning, in the front yard of the sweet little house, the neighborhood suddenly looked different. This was a convenient location, and it was fun to be in this place, but it was not fun being with the neighbors' dogs that pooped in my front yard. I had asked around the neighborhood for help in keeping others dogs to their own yards, put up little fences, and used repellents.

On this particular day, in the front yard, I was again cleaning up other dogs' poop –and boy was there a lot of it and BIG piles! This continual scoop parade effort was frustrating, and certainly not a fulfilling experience. It was difficult to understand life. Life was like a never ending circle of poop everywhere. At the moment of that thought, tears started to flow down my face.

Then I had a new thought: Might there possibly be something to the idea that I could use some help and thus help myself as had been suggested? What I was doing in my front yard at that moment was a metaphor for life. It was not a pretty sight. Lots of other questions and thoughts were right there in front of me, like on a billboard in the brain. Such as, possibly I did not have to do everything by myself; that life did not have to be smelly; that I might actually learn something from 'self-help' ideas or some similar program; that my results could be different.

A shift occurred. The idea that had been planted a year ago had resulted in the questions appearing right now! My body was shivering, yet it was warm outside. Breath came faster. I did not know why or what was happening. It was like a bright white light beam lit up all my surroundings. Even the dog poop glistened at that moment! For sure, my thinking was changing.

I called Susan and made a date. When we met, we discussed thoughts and the effect of thoughts on actions. With as much humility as could be mustered at the moment, I asked her about the program she had attended, what she had learned that had been important to her, and asked when I could learn more. Changes in my view of the world took place in that conversation. She told me when the next meeting was going to happen, and we made plans to attend together.

Not long after, as her guest at the introductory meeting, there was a description of the Pursuit of Excellence program by Context International. I listened, and now was intrigued by the idea about learning more about oneself. Mostly I was interested in the idea of how to change the results in life so that I could be happier, and maybe, just maybe, I might experience joy in my life.

There was such an interesting mix of people at the meeting that evening. In talking with other people who had already attended the program, the same general theme was expressed. The theme was that of optimism … that change really could occur, that there were answers to whatever issues existed for any of us, and yes, it did require personal work. Not only was personal work required, but that a safe learning environment was present, and they promised fun. I thought that was a contradictory mix, and that I had not experienced those three dimensions together, ever.

For the first time, I was conscious of breathing more deeply, of opening up, not closing down. After all, given that life seemed to be all about cleaning up poop, mine and others, here there was discussion of possibilities for different information, perspectives, views. This opportunity offered specks of light in what were some very dark days. My choices to attend were 'yes' or 'no.' 'Maybe' was not an option because that really was a 'no.' I said 'yes.' After all, I am all about results.

Two weeks later, in July, and thirteen months after the marital separation and one month of being newly divorced, I showed up in the meeting room at the Seattle Center near the base of the Space Needle. In the program room, there we were, over 100 of us. For whatever the reasons, each of us had said 'yes' to the idea of learning something new, to reflect, to participate and discover.

There were young and old, men and women, from all walks of life, all of us with what seemed like one thing in common … our lives were at an intersection point and we each were seeking a skill set or ideas that could help create personal change. At first, it was overwhelming with so many people, and I felt lost. But this atmosphere was different. It was electric and energizing. I actually smiled. This environment offered hope and energy. I was off to 'find' Dinnie and me.

As each program exercise unfolded, I judged it, sometimes even verbally, to be fun, boring, stupid, exciting, and all the other descriptors I could conjure. There was an acute awareness of how my body temperature changed in response to each new experience, of when there was fear of being judged by others, of when there was excitement to explore an idea, of when I was tired or angry, and when I was laughing and connecting with other people. Somewhere, mixed into all the new information, there was the question: 'Would you rather be right or happy?' Now, there was a thought. I had never examined my thought patterns before and instead reacted to situations around me. Now was the time to look within, as within is where thoughts were. Like a dog with a bone, I went for it.

Curiosity prevailed. Who in this universe is the most important person to know and really understand? Self-learning was happening and information became self-knowledge. What fun! What work! Each day, life felt a bit brighter. That is, until Saturday when there was some group activity that evening.

What I remember was that we were asked to just freely let our energy out through dancing, jumping jacks, or something physically expressive. In my view of the world right then, it felt foolish to dance around and let out my energy. What would others think? Whatever the reason, this form of expression did not feel safe. The music was fabulous, people were laughing out loud, and dancing was everywhere. Only one thought was present in my mind: 'I am out of here!'

I stood, looked around at all these fun-having people and grabbed my jacket and purse. Bumping into many people and chairs along the way, I made a rapid and determined beeline for the back door. With a racing heartbeat, little beads of perspiration on various body parts, and a white knuckled hand, I turned the door knob and opened the door muttering, 'Time to leave this place. This was not in the plan.'

In the noise of the room and in my brain, another thought popped in which was: 'This is what always happens when life feels rough, when the answers are not right there, when an image of life gets in the way. You leave.' For what seemed like ten minutes, yet was probably only about 30 seconds, I stood there paralyzed. At that moment, another decision point presented itself, and I turned around and walked back into the program room, to the music, to the people, to the expressions of joy and excitement, to life.

The next evening was graduation. I was mentally at least a thousand pounds lighter. I had discovered so much about me and about others. Nobody told me what to think or how to think. It was true what the leader had said … they presented an idea; I explored the idea and decided how it worked for me. I knew that now I had found a way to grow and to help change my life results.

What happened next? During the training and leading up to graduation, the next program, *The Wall*, was mentioned. This was an opportunity to decide if this was the right next step for me. Yes, *The Wall*, is exactly as it sounds: Explore and uncover stopping points – walls. I learned strategies to recognize and address the walls, understand behaviors, take different actions, and get different results. For sure, there were tears. There were shocks, often followed by shame. There were smiles and laughter. No matter the length of a lifetime, it was hard to let go of deeply embedded and cherished beliefs.

The most important insight right then was that living as a victim was painful, exhausting, and unrewarding. As a victim, more circumstances always presented themselves so that being picked on was normal. My place in the world was rapidly moving out of poop-covered darkness and into a clean light of self-discovery and of taking different, productive actions. On a piece of butcher paper, I drew a new picture for my life, for Zorro and me.

While attending *The Wall*, another decision point occurred. The next program was called the *Advancement of Excellence*, which would start a few weeks later. This program was about advancement in life and consisted of several weeks of putting into practice what had been learned up to this point. Personal advancement consisted of setting goals and taking steps to achieve those goals. Then there was another amazing concept – teamwork for support. Support had always meant that others agreed with me. Not now. I learned quickly to hear the ideas of others, take in suggestions for strategies, to discover when I was fooling myself, and to gracefully accept a gift. I had some great ideas, too. This team thing was enjoyable, and fun was everywhere. Perhaps, I was even experiencing JOY.

One difficult and wonderful day, a teammate, after patiently listening to all the talk about stages of divorce, stages of grief, and IRS experiences, looked straight at me. She pointed and wagged her index finger at me and said, 'There is a book you need to read. It is called *You Can Heal Your Life* by Louise Hay.' I said 'Okay.' Thus began another dramatic turn on the path and of the journey.

Here was information about the thoughts people think and how important those thoughts are in creating what happens in people's lives. I learned about mind, body, spirit connection. The book contained scores of examples of how to uncover limiting thoughts and turn the thoughts around into a life affirmation. I learned to state and believe that 'I am precious and cherish the miracle that I am,' and 'I am a powerful person, and I can create miracles!'

As I learned more about myself and my values became clear, I accepted responsibility for my actions and made decisions. Here is how everything unfolded:

- The tax attorney helped reduce the tax liability to $15,000. I negotiated a payment plan with the IRS. It was clearly understood that in US law, my ex-husband and I were each jointly and individually liable for the debt. His declaration of bankruptcy did not alleviate the IRS obligation. Despite us each having a payment plan with the IRS, my goal was to have mental and financial freedom soon. For freedom, I made the decision to pay the debt.

  At Mom and Dad's house, on a sunny, Sunday afternoon, while choking back sobs, I screamed out loud: 'I don't know how I will do this, but I will pay off this debt!' Zorro heard me. Life shifted, and the earth moved. On the following Wednesday, Dad received a call from the Swedish consulate who stated that he had inherited $15,000 from his aunt. He gave me that money. We went to the IRS office together. This was especially sweet as he was a CPA. There is more. I clicked my heels and danced in the IRS office. I shouted whoops of excitement. Dad and

I enjoyed the looks of others and embraced their smiles. The debt notice said 'PAID IN FULL.'

• After his bankruptcy, my ex-husband was cleared of most debt. Those items we had jointly signed for and that were still owed were now mine. I negotiated settlements with credit card companies. I sold most of my jewelry. I cleaned out closets and sold as much as possible. The debts were paid, and my name was clear. On a PBS special, Dr. Wayne Dyer stated 'Pay attention to the details of your life.' I understood.

• I chose my own name. I learned the value of a signature. I learned the value of me, and how I showed up in this world.

• Another level of training presented itself. It was called *Mastery*. I had new friends who helped me in this deeper discovery. Sometimes I had to let others go from my life. That decision was usually sad, yet freeing for all. I was here to live and to be alive.

Of course, to every story there is so much more. There were those days of such sadness, maybe what could be called depression, at the state of my life. There were moments and prolonged periods of sheer terror. There was self-doubt about ability to do what needed to be done. It was frightening to keep unearthing buried attitudes and remnants of actions. All this drama and confusion needed to end peacefully, for all … let us just move on.

Yet each time there was a new decision, a new resolution to fully step into life and be responsible for my thoughts and actions, each and every cell of my body responded with a resounding 'thank you.' It was all a process, asking why thoughts were what they were, examining life and decision processes, moving out of the fog and into light. Many wonderful layers upon layers were peeled back and revealed themselves.

It is important to mention another decision and discovery: I volunteered. I gave back to those programs that helped me so much. This was the notion of paying it forward. Then I learned the law of circulation – giving and receiving; what one gives out comes back. These are laws of the Universe.

The opportunity to assist a *Mastery* program was presented. I accepted. What a memorable decision. Being away, helping out, and seeing life through others' eyes would be a soul satisfying way to spend my December birthday.

Off to a beautiful place called Orcas Island, in the San Juan Islands of Washington State ... to a Boy Scout camp called Camp Orkila, to five-plus days in a rustic, green, wooded, and beachy environment. There were four of us who travelled together from the Seattle area to the camp. It was dusk, and it rained hard. There was lots of bumper-to-bumper freeway traffic, and we were cramped in a small, smelly car. We made it to the ferry in time, crossed to Orcas, and soon arrived at Camp Orkila. We were all happy to arrive safely and more than a bit grumpy after the drive. It was good to stretch and breathe fresh air again!

The assisting team had now all arrived. We met in the program room, settled in to meet the program leader, Peggy, from Vancouver, BC. It was a time to look around, appreciate the beautiful surroundings, say 'hi' to each other, and to take in the fact that we were all there together. Tomorrow the participants would arrive. Then all of us would begin sharing next steps on a journey, from very different perspectives.

I was happy and felt fluttering throughout my body. There was movement in the air. Surely there were butterflies everywhere, just not visible. It was a relief to be here. It was such a great combination to be assisting and to celebrate a birthday. It was another chance to deeply reflect on the last 2-1/2 years since 'that' Friday night, and in completely different surroundings.

The assisting team introduced themselves. In addition to the four of us from the Seattle area, there was a fellow from the province of Alberta. Then there was Bill, who said when he introduced himself, that he was from a small farming community in western Saskatchewan. He said that he had been en route for 23 hours to be on time, and that he, too, was happy to be here safely. It was embarrassing that I had been grumpy after only six hours on the road!

I took another look at Bill and thought 'something is different here.' It was unclear what that was, but when this man spoke, my vision was clearer, and I listened intently. Suddenly, my personal radar was loudly beeping, and there was a high alert in the room and around my being!

The team settled into our work for the next five days. Our goals were to support the needs of the program and the participants as quietly and unobtrusively as possible. Throughout the program, Bill and I, along with the rest of the team, worked together, laughed and talked together, and ate together. We all did our part for a wonderful and fulfilling program to occur, and we were in service.

On Sunday, we all left for our homes. We drove to the ferry, in our separate cars, soon to be dispersed to Alberta, Saskatchewan, British Columbia and parts of Washington State. Bill and I sat together on the ferry. Yep, something was different, AND we both knew it. He was rural, I was urban. He had always been self-employed. I had always worked in a corporate or government setting. He worked with the earth, machines, and the air. I worked with people. He was more liberal, and I was more conservative in our social views. We celebrated some of the same holidays, but our two countries had many different holidays. We lived in different time zones and in different area codes.

Over the next almost three years, Bill and I dated. Our efforts to be together were extraordinary. We travelled and met all over three western Canadian provinces and four western US states for dates of usually five days or more. We contributed substantially to the profit statements of our respective phone companies. The details make quite a yarn that we tell. Yes, something was different for sure.

He was the person whose presence helped open my heart to yet another layer of possibilities for my life. The question that surfaced was, 'Is it safe to openly express who I really am?' There had been so much learning through the ideas of self-help and personal exploration, I was no longer reacting to circumstances based on old thoughts or other people's ideas. The ideas and thoughts were mine.

In January, 1995, during a 2 hour and 35 minute telephone call, I said to Bill: 'It is time to shit or get off the pot!' Oh my, there was that idea of poop again! Except … now we each understood that poop is what we make it. This time, the word was a verb, not a noun. We each had 'let go' of many old beliefs and were ready to move on. We each learned that we can change our thoughts, we can be honest with ourselves and each other, change our behaviors, and heal the wounds of our pasts.

Bill immigrated to the US. We were married in November, 1995, on the beach at Camp Orkila, on Orcas Island. Our intimate group of six friends listened to individually written vows and then joined us in loudly singing Elvis Presley and Rita McNeil songs while drinking champagne. We did it our way. On the day we married, the rain stopped for a few hours. We looked over the water and there was a brilliant rainbow. We believed the rainbow was symbolic of the joining of our lives, and the linking of families, sets of friendships, and of our countries.

Over the years, we've had many challenges. We have had lots of 'discussions,' shed many tears, and shared many a laugh. We each deeply felt the loss of sweet Zorro. We comforted and cared for each other during the experiences of the losses of all four of our parents. We each have lived through car crashes, thrived through cancer and other health experiences, grown through job changes, and reinvented ourselves through career changes. We regrouped.

Together and separately, we reached out for spiritual support and attended both Unity Church and the Center for Spiritual Living, and participated in many opportunities in each place for classroom and experiential learning. We shifted thinking, and thus changed our experiences. We each learned the importance of forgiveness, especially of self. We are 'in it' for the long haul. Each of us is always self-helping. Each of us is always helping the other. We choose to be a witness for each other. We both always have people in our lives who love each of us enough to tell their truth of a circumstance and provide insights and encouragement.

I now have family from the Northwest Territories to Newfoundland. He now has family from Washington State to Florida!

As this part of the story closes, here are poignant words from a favorite songwriter and the album, Closer to the Bone:

> *Let the walls come down*
> *Let it all come true*
> *When it all comes down*
> *It's up to me and you.*
>
> *~Kris Kristofferson*

My experience is that all of us are seeking peace in our lives, connection with others, and certainly a safe place to truly unearth and express who each of us is, at a heart level. Not who others expect us to be, but who we really are. Whatever you want to learn, however you want to grow, help yourself. Life is all about getting 'closer to the bone.'

Will you join me?

About the Author

Diane S. Christie, SPHR, is a licensed *Heal Your Life®* Coach and Workshop Leader in Olympia, Washington. Diane partners with people to get to the heart of a matter and (re)discover their unique skills and abilities. Her passion is helping others learn how to move beyond limiting beliefs and take the next steps in their lives to create meaningful results.

In 2011, Diane was a recipient of the Governor's award for Leadership in Management as a Human Resource Manager.

Diane and her husband experience joy in constant learning through worldwide travel and spiritual adventure.

info@dianeschristie.com
www.dianeschristie.com

Acknowledgments

Thank you to….

Bill … our journeys continue.

The Spirits of my beloved mom and dad, Norma and Chet, for your ever-present love and belief in my abilities.

Diane, Linda, Mary Ellen, and Terry for gently delivered insights, laughter, and intense support, on many levels, over many years.

Susan for listening, hearing, inviting.

Zorro, who wagged his tail no matter what happened.

Families, both biological and of choice; and teachers in and out of the classroom, past, present, and future. I appreciate your presence and many gifts.

Sandra Filer

First and foremost, this story is dedicated to the love of my life: Mr. Kim Coffman. He is the pea to my carrot. Without him this love story would be incomplete. To all the women who have been hurt, betrayed, or abandoned, may this story give you hope. There is great love for you.

Chapter 4

FROM HEARTACHE TO HAPPINESS:
A GODDESS-INSPIRED LOVE STORY

It was December 31, 1999, just before midnight. The venue was a deserted office building that had been transformed into a multi-level dance party. There was music blasting, lights flashing, people dancing, couples kissing, and drinks pouring. People were everywhere, wearing everything. It was a high-energy, not-to-be-missed celebration, welcoming in a new year filled with such anticipation and promise.

As the time drew closer and closer and closer to the midnight hour, one could just feel the excitement build. The music got louder. The dance floor grew fuller. People got more and more drunk. The countdown started .. 60, 59, 58 … Oh no! This meant that the unavoidable New Year's Eve kiss was just around the corner. Yikes! Something inside of me felt sick. Dressed in my full silver spandex body suit, an ivy headdress, glitter platform sandals, and completely covered in silver glitter, "Miss Millennium Girl" darted to the porta potty. Safely seated and gazing up at the vent on the ceiling, the countdown finished: 3, 2, 1 … HAPPY NEW YEAR! The crowd went wild outside. Inside the porta potty, crumpled in a sad slumped over position, Millennium Girl cried buckets of tears and kissed no one. You see, my life was in the dumps.

How did this happen? What went wrong? Allow me to take you on a short journey into the story of my life. By sharing it with you, perhaps it will help us both heal.

It is always best to start at the beginning.
~ Glinda the Good Witch of the North

On a beautiful fall day, in a Catholic church located along the shores of Lake Michigan, friends and family gathered as I exchanged sacred vows of marriage. It was September 13, 1997, and the seventh anniversary of our relationship. It was the perfect day to be married. Trees were slightly dusted with color. Lake Michigan was sparkling a stunning shade of blue. Everything had been woven together to make this magical day come true. To ensure that this union was blessed, I had my first marriage annulled … not a fun or uplifting process. I became a Catholic. And, we met weekly with the priest for "Goddess" knows how long. It seemed like forever.

In keeping with tradition, I spent the night at a boutique hotel and upon awakening, I will always remember stepping out of bed, taking in a big breath, and throwing back the curtains to bask in the scenery and experience of the moment. Dropping to my knees, with tears of happiness, I took the time to thank God for my life. Little did I know that this dream would be dashed almost faster than I said, "I do." You see, he had other ideas about whom he wanted to spend the rest of his life with.

Fast forward to a bittersweet day in the fall of 1998. It was another BIG day. We had decided it was time for a change in our lives. We sold our home in the Midwest, packed our bags, said good-bye to our friends, grabbed our dog and headed west. The only thing we left behind was happy memories. Prior to arrival, we had selected a wonderful home in Pearland, Texas. It was an amazing property that came with lavish landscaping, incredible window treatments, a two-level back deck and a hot tub. Bliss! We had arrived.

Shortly after, the moving van pulled up. All our accumulated things were being delivered. It was exciting; and yet, there was something brewing underneath of the surface. As the men began to unload, "Bill" decided he needed to run to the office. Hmm? This seemed quite odd given what was transpiring. However, he left. The truck was being emptied. The moving team came in and out of the house, depositing each box, each table, each lamp, one after the other. All the decisions of what to place where were left to me. This just didn't feel quite right. Suddenly, that sick feeling started to bubble inside of my stomach. Intuition guided me to investigate. I listened. Glancing across the kitchen, I noticed Bill's Franklin Planner. A force greater than myself took over. With a rapidly beating heart and shaking hands, I flipped through the pages, going backwards. What was I looking for? As someone very wise once said to me, "Be careful what you look for."

I wanted to vomit. I wanted to run. There, on the pages of his planner was the proof: a hotel reservation number from a day in the not so distant past. Out of my mouth came a scream that shook the movers. With big eyes, they came running into the kitchen to find me crying hysterically. One of the kind and caring men asked me very delicately, "What is wrong?" Wracked with sobs, I choked out, "I just found out my husband is having an affair."

Their eyes grew like saucers. As their pace of unpacking picked up exponentially, I could see the fear they felt. To put them at some amount of ease, I let them know that I would not freak out and would wait to confront Bill until their departure. Like any distraught person, I ran to the telephone. I needed to talk to someone. After all, I was in Texas for God's sake, 1500 miles away from any friends or family. Thanks, Bill.

Beautiful Seeds of Change

As I waited, I started to recall the days leading up to this day. I distinctly remembered "the day" in his planner. For validation, I dialed the phone number. Very brilliantly, I asked the hotel employee to assist me. The words just came out. I explained that we were traveling on business, and I was in the process of filling out my expense report. The only missing piece was the dollar amount of our stay at their hotel. She placed me on hold to retrieve the information. I waited. Returning to the line she said, "Yes ma'am, I have it right here. It was $79 paid in cash." I could feel the blood drain from my face as I whispered, "thank you" before ending the call.

What is hidden in the dark
will always come out into the light.
~ Zenobia Carter

After what seemed like weeks, Bill arrived home to find one very upset, yet strangely calm new wife. (Yes, new as in we had only been married eight months at this time.) Sensing something bad was about to happen, he began to fidget. With a level of courage that I never knew I had, I asked him to sit down. He refused. I demanded he sit down. He complied. We sat face-to-face, eyeball-to-eyeball, and the inquisition began.

The opening statement went something like this, "Now Bill, clearly there is something that I need to talk to you about. As I begin, please remember that I am not a fool." He began fidgeting more. "While you were away, I looked in your Franklin Planner." (Silence.) "Can you please tell me why you made a hotel reservation on the very same day that you were supposedly having lunch with your work associate, Beatrice?" The blood drained from his face. (More silence.)

Next, out of his mouth came the most ridiculous statement. Apparently, he had not heard me when I told him that I was not a fool. Bill said that he had rented a hotel room to have lunch with Beatrice so that no one would see them in a restaurant together and think they were having an affair. Seriously?? If it weren't so tragic, I would have laughed. Because now, in sharing this, it seems completely ridiculous. Here was an educated and seemingly intelligent man telling me such a crazy story. Really? Try again.

A bit of time passed. Decisions needed to be made. Each of us contacted therapists. Mine suggested that I secure an attorney. I explained that I wanted to save the marriage. Her advice surprised and shook me: "You've paid me for my services. Please do as I say. You need to hire an attorney." The very next day, I dug out the piece of paper where she had scribbled the phone number of "the barracuda in the court room disguised as a blue-eyed, blonde Southern belle," and I made my appointment. Her advice would prove to be "spot on." She told me on this day all of the behaviors to anticipate. It was as if she had peered into the crystal ball of my life because they each played perfectly out. And, I was well prepared for what happened next. Or, was I?

THE WRATH OF A WOMAN SCORNED

During this awkward time, an envelope arrived in the mail from Southwest Airlines. Intrigued, I carefully opened the piece of mail to see what was inside. Lo and behold, it was a ticket to Chicago. Interesting. Note to self: Some of that advice was about to be put into action. Get ready! Lying in bed one evening, Bill shared that he was going to be going to Austin. My ears perked up like a cat taking a nap and hearing a food can open. He further explained that his friend had a dental appointment, and he wanted to support him as he was terrified of the dentist. Here we go with one of those ridiculous stories again.

In complete disbelief, I told him (once again) that I was no fool, and he should be smart about his choices. He seemed perplexed. I further went on to remind him that he was, after all, married. He got angry. This resulted in him spouting out: "You think you are so damn smart, and yet you are stupid." Wow. Very calmly, I cooed, "You have no idea just how smart I am." He would soon learn, and it wouldn't be pretty. It would, however, be brilliantly planned and expertly executed.

The plan got complicated. What I had discovered was that I could not get a divorce in Texas for six months. I needed to have domicile. I could have a divorce in Michigan or Illinois; however, each of those states were no fault states. Ugh! Texas on the other hand is an at fault state. Meaning, if I could prove fault in the marriage, it would be a disproportionate split. Game on. I hired a second attorney based in Illinois. The two attorneys would conspire together to support my plan. Keep the divorce "in process" for six months, and then have it overturned to Texas, where the judge was a nice Baptist man who did not agree with adultery. Well played.

DON'T MESS WITH TEXAS

Bill left for "Austin." All the players were ready. At the request of my attorney, I faxed over a current photograph of Bill. The Illinois team made a poster with his face and last name on it. A process server was hired. Documents were drawn up stating that I was filing for divorce on the grounds of adultery and the adulteress was named in the document. This was something that would prove to be a party pooper as she, too, was married.

Beautiful Seeds of Change

Meanwhile, a locksmith was called. All the locks on the house were changed. He had decided to leave. I decided to claim what was rightfully mine. Once again, I was guided to the next step to drive to the airport and find his car. This was necessary because the garage remote was in his car and that was the last way he could enter the property after the locks were changed. With determination, I drove to the airport and combed the parking lots until I spotted his vehicle. Using the spare set of keys that were still mine, I quickly got in and secured the remote. Success!

Now, onto the next step in the plan: Call her husband. Yes, I know this was horrible. It felt horrible. I knew, however, that it had to be done because I felt it was only fair that all the players know what was happening. Before I made the call, I checked with the Illinois team to see what progress had been made.

With horror, I listened as the attorney's assistant shared what I knew would be true. Yet, I still did not want to believe. Once again, I wanted to throw up. The plane had an on-time landing at Chicago's Midway airport on a crisp fall day. Bill joyfully departed the plane anticipating a weekend away with his paramour, Beatrice.

At the gate, she waited for him to deplane. She was not the only one waiting for him. Just as they embraced, one of them spotted the big sign displaying his photo and name. Intrigued, of course, they approached the man. The next part, I must admit, is quite "movie worthy." As Bill approached the sign-wielding man, he said, "Hey that's me!" To which the man replied, "Really? You are Bill? Great!" A camera snapped all of this as the man handed him an envelope and said, "You have been served." Ouch! I'm quite certain that this put a slight damper on the "dental" appointment.

Back in Texas, I swigged a bottle of courage. I leafed through the White Pages and found the phone number for Beatrice's soon-to-be ex-husband. After a few rings, he answered. The situation was shared. This time, it was he who felt like vomiting. It was a feeling I knew quite well.

Bill returned home to discover that his "stupid" wife was actually quite smart. He walked up to the locked front door. Rifling through his pockets, he dug out his keys unsuccessfully making another effort to open the lock. With a heart beating completely out of control, I carefully watched through the curtains. He was angry! Next, as I knew he would, he got into his car to search for the remote. Darn! It was gone. Now, he was really angry. After lots of yelling, I decided to give in just a little. I opened the door and tossed out his hockey equipment and told him to be on his way. He never looked back.

As you would probably imagine, the drama did not end there. In Illinois, Beatrice managed to obtain her divorce within a matter of two weeks. Bill was not so lucky. Six months had now passed. Attempts had been made to settle out of court. Nope, that was not going to happen. This future goddess had her feet firmly planted. I was going to get what I deserved! Next, mediation was attempted resulting in a full day of negotiations with no resolution. We would now move onto a full out court battle in the bible belt of Texas. Maybe there was a reason I moved to Texas? Yes, there was, and this would only be the first gift to be discovered.

As promised, my attorney proved to be a soft-talking barracuda with a sweet Southern accent. She pointed out all of the indiscretions to the court. There were scads of evidence found in his subpoenaed planner, check book register, and credit card statements. Plus, his admission in court to this one question that will forever linger in my devastated ears: "Is it not true, Mr. P, that you had sex in the back seat of your wife's car while she was at work?" In one of those "feeling like I am going to vomit moments," he replied, "Yes. It is true." A stirring happened in the courtroom, and the rest is a blur. The end result was what I had wanted: a disproportionate split. Indeed, I walked away with the 70 percent and he with 30 percent. While it seemed like a victory, in my heart, I felt agony.

How could I be so unlovable? What could I have done to make him cheat on me? I felt ugly, fat, stupid, distrusting, gullible, dejected, scared, alone, devastated, distraught and certain that I would NEVER trust a man or fall in love again.

A GODDESS IS A GIRL'S BEST FRIEND

Life truly does support us. My story certainly will prove that to be true. As they say, there is a silver lining in every cloud. Mine happens to be laced with silver linings, as well as a pink one.

During this dreadful time, I found myself in a dreadful job. I was miserable at home, and I was miserable at work. What in the world was happening? Something had to change. Soon, it did. On one of these miserable days while traipsing down the hallways at work, I spotted a burst of color swishing by. It was a colorful pink skirt being worn by a temporary employee. It was like a breath of fresh air in what would ordinarily be a very stuffy office. Immediately, I was drawn to this person. She was young, beautiful, and happy. Just like her skirt. Her name was Ellie. We became fast friends. I wanted to be just like Ellie. She took me under her wing and helped nurture the ugly duckling back to swan-like life.

One of the greatest gifts that Ellie gave to me, besides her friendship, was a book. Actually, I will call it the "magical manual." Now, being a very good student, and trusting her completely, I began to read the book from cover to cover. The magical manual was designed to teach me the way of the Goddess. This was absolutely intriguing. I had never heard of such a thing. In addition to teaching me the way of the Goddess, it was also supposed to enlighten me as to how to attract the "right" love into my life. Wow! Clearly I could use a bit of assistance in this area as I had two "was bands" on record.

In the evenings, after work, I would get my magical manual and go out on to my little balcony patio of my new apartment. The book suggested that I light a candle and wear loosely fitted clothing, preferably something in white. Another tip was to use a pen with purple colored ink. Finally, to make this especially effective, I was to use a nice sheet of paper. I improvised just a bit and settled upon a piece of red construction paper. The night sky was growing darker, and the moon was becoming brighter. The timing was just perfect. The instructions were to relax, dream, imagine and begin to write on the piece of paper all the qualities that I desired in my perfect soul mate. It is interesting to reflect back upon this experience because, at the time, I thought I was done with men. Silly little Goddess.

With focus and attention, I drafted the list. Some of the things I wrote were:

He cries at sad movies.

He lets my dog sit on his lap.

He holds my hand when I feel sad.

He is strong and sticks up for me.

He is trustworthy.

He is kind.

He puts me first.

He laughs at my stories.

The exercise said to be as specific as possible when making your wish. I was serious. At the end of the evening, I folded the paper up, as instructed, and anointed it with cinnamon oil. Next, to power it up, it was left under the light of the moon and the sun of the day for 24 hours. From that point on, I slept with it under my pillow. What could it hurt?

The magic manual was a powerful tool for me. I became so infatuated with the ideas presented that I decided to begin calling myself a Goddess. Diosa actually, which is Goddess in Spanish. Even more specifically, I declared myself: The Happy Goddess. So be it and so it is. I was having fun with all of this newly discovered information. It was real to me, and I treated it as such. I secured the email address of happy goddess in Spanish.

Then, the next step is really exciting. During this same time, I decided that I deserved a sexy new car. Yes! Why not? I purchased a jet black 2000 Pontiac Trans Am with ram air. Varoooom. It felt so liberating to drive such a powerful muscle car. The icing on the cake was when I treated myself to a personalized license plate. I gleefully secured: DIOSA.

Meanwhile, the awful job continued. The drama heightened. I was working long hours and in a very stressful, unhealthy environment. However, the pay was really good. And, I really needed the job. One night, about nine hours into the day, while my dog was at home locked in his crate, the boss just kept at it. She was concerned about my travels the next day and felt compelled to keep me late to go over the details.

Her main concern really had nothing to do with work. It was a matter of her distrusting the relationship that I had with a woman from another office, and she was fearful that I was going to "air her dirty laundry." Goodness! Too much was too much. I was up to my eyeballs already. Finally, something inside me just snapped. Before I knew what was happening, the words came out of my mouth. "I quit, "I shouted. "I am done. I don't know what I am going to do, but I will clean toilets before I work another day for you!" I cleaned out my desk that night, packed up my car, and cried all the way home. What in the world was I going to do now? I was without a husband, and now I was without a job.

THERE IS A SILVER LINING IN EVERY CLOUD

Volunteering was something that I had always loved to do. For some reason, I felt particularly drawn to working with teenagers. The church that I was attending had a need for volunteers to work with their youth. Since I had nothing else better to do while I found a new job, I decided to sign up to help out. The job search was not going so well because quite honestly, I was so depressed, I just knew that I could not operate as a Vice President in a bank; which was my profession prior to the big D.

I just kept praying. Then, like a miracle, in sharing during a Thanksgiving youth gathering on how we can't always judge a book by its cover, I broke down and shared with the kids that while I drove a fancy car, lived in a nice space, had decent clothes and wore jewelry, I did not

Beautiful Seeds of Change

know where my next dollar was going to come from, and I did not have any money to buy a turkey for Thanksgiving. Nor, did I have anyone to spend the holiday with. The whole room got very quiet. I held back the tears and the fears that were welling up in my throat. The feelings were almost overwhelming. After the meeting, a woman came up to me and said, "This may or may not be what you are looking for, but we could sure use a receptionist in our office. It only pays $10 an hour."

I decided to take the position. What the heck? I knew I could at least answer a phone. The job was in a plastic surgeon's office. It turned out to be exactly what I needed. This Goddess in training found herself working with women that created laughter in the workplace every single day. These women were like angels to me. They listened. They provided counsel. They invited me into their homes and treated me like family. We played pranks on each other and the temporary job, along with the magic manual, was beginning to effectively re-build my very bruised self-esteem.

It was during this time that I knew, in my heart, I was not going to be leaving Texas. For a while, I thought I would return home to Michigan. But, deep within me, I sensed that there was no going backwards - only forward. There had to be a reason I was relocated to Texas. Soon it would be revealed. Apparently, the exercise from the magic manual was working, unbeknownst to me.

At the office, preparations were being made for the annual charity ball raising money for cleft palette surgery in third world countries. How exciting! I'd never even known that balls really happened. The only ball I was aware of involved a pumpkin and a prince. It was going to be a black tie event. The dress code for women was a ball gown. Since I was going to be working the event, this meant that I was to come in a ball gown. Uh oh. There was no room in my budget for a ball gown. Suddenly, I remembered that my Grandmother had lovingly gifted me a ball gown that she had worn in her early 30's. I vaguely remembered that it was on a hanger jammed in my closet somewhere. All I remembered at the time was that it had a lot of sequins on it and it was really, really heavy.

When the opportunity presented itself, I found the dress all scrunched up on the hanger. Holding my breath, I pulled it off. In amazement, it looked like it could work. It was a sleeveless, iridescent ivory sequined dress with a dab of orange sequined details. It was designed to be a skin-tight dress. Thankfully, having been on the divorce diet (barely any food being able to be eaten), I was as thin as I had ever been. Trying the dress on, I found it was a perfect fit. Of course, it was.

As the night approached, I grew nervous. I'd never been to such an elegant affair. The good news was that I would be working the event and that would keep me busy. One of the nurses and I were put on the task of collecting tickets at the entrance. It was a busy night. In addition to collecting tickets, we were able to take some breaks, enjoy a meal, and indulge in a cocktail or two. My mood lifted. I was having fun. The only distracting thing was that the event photographer kept taking our photo. How annoying!

While I found the photographer's behavior to be annoying, others did not share in my opinion. In fact, it seems my angels, disguised in ball gowns, were busy playing, laughing, and consorting with the photographer. The next thing I knew, one of my co-workers was winded and giggling. She came up to me and very excitedly announced, in her Southern accent, "He is so cute. He is single, and I think he wants to ask you out." What? I was shocked. How could she have had such a conversation with him! I said, "Look at him, he is brown. He is wearing a brown suit, brown shoes, brown glasses and has brown hair." She just kept giggling with that big twinkle in her blue eyes. "Come on," she coaxed, "He's nice. Let's dance!" Before I knew it WE were on the dance floor, all of us, including the photographer.

The night finally drew to a close. It had been a long one, and my emotions were all over the place. I quietly went out to the parking garage all by myself. It was dark, and it was quiet. In backing my car out of the really tight space, I rubbed the door of the car parked beside me. Shifting my car into park, I carefully got out of my car to assess the damage. As I am bent over examining the car beside me I hear a voice say, "Is everything okay?" Naturally, it was the photographer. I feared it was his car. It was not. After we established that the car was fine, and I was fine, he launched into his "let's go get a drink" campaign. After several attempts at saying no, there was just something in his determination that stimulated me to say "yes."

In separate vehicles, we drove to a piano bar. It was all so surreal. There were scads of people all over the place. It seemed dreary and dingy. As we made our way through the crowd, I felt random strangers touching me. We settled upon a spot along the wall. Lighting up cigarettes and washing them down with a drink, we began to share. After quite a long time, he finally said to me, "Now you know, I am not looking for a relationship!" What was wrong with this guy? Having carefully studied my magic manual, I knew it was time for me to speak my truth. Tossing any fears aside of being rejected, I confidently stated, "You are the one that asked me out. I don't even like men." It felt good to stand in my power. This was something quite new to me. Especially, when dealing with men.

At the end, he asked me to breakfast. I graciously declined. He asked for my number. I gave it to him. He then took a deep breath and said, "I am going away for two weeks. I will call you when I return." Sure, that's what they all say, I thought to myself as my stomach growled loudly. My breakfast would be a bag of Fritos purchased from a vending machine still wearing my Grandmother's vintage ball gown at 3:00 in the morning.

Time went by - - two weeks to be exact. I continued reading the book Ellie gave to me. It guided me to putting myself first. One of the most important rules shared was to let male suitors know that Goddesses are busy. Therefore, when/if they call, the instructions were to refrain from jumping at the chance to go out, or to change previously made plans. Remember, you are busy. The manual also explained that, in nature, the male species is the one that is more colorful and has to win the love of the female. I found this all to be so incredibly fascinating. Somewhere along the line, humans messed that all up. I was taking notes. Further into my reading, the book shared that a way to a man's heart was through his stomach. It also revealed that a magical ingredient or, a sort of elixir was the spice cinnamon. This stuff is so cool!

As promised, my phone rang in two weeks. I was shocked. Being a very good student, I allowed the call to go to voicemail. It was bittersweet. There was one part of me that felt giddy that I actually followed through, and there was the old part of me that was fearful that I would lose him. The new me stayed strong. I wanted to do things differently. I believed in the magic manual, and I was convinced to play full out. I listened to the message over and over. Finally, the next day I returned the call. He asked me to have lunch with him. After careful consideration, a day was decided, and we met for lunch on a quiet street under a canvas canopy.

The year was beginning to draw to a close. It was soon to be the end of 1999. It was a year I was ready to put far behind me. It was a year riddled with pain. My friend Ellie and her friends were throwing a big New Year's Eve bash called the Y2Groove. In preparing for the event, I dressed up in my Millennium Girl costume, dreaming about how the evening would unfold. With every stroke of mascara and dusting of glitter, I was romanticizing the evening's events.

Going outside of the Goddess teachings, I momentarily lost my mind and mentioned to Kim, the photographer, that the party was happening, and if he wanted to, he could stop by. He never did. No wonder I found myself slumped over a porta potty toilet sobbing buckets of tears. After being completely shaken by an unfaithful husband, I had allowed myself to almost fall in love again. But was I ready? Later, I would realize he wasn't ready for a big New Year's date, and neither was I. We both needed to take it slow. A Goddess takes it one step at a time.

SOMETIMES I THANK GOD FOR UNANSWERED PRAYERS

The dating dance began. Or, more realistically stated, the romance blossomed. This time, I committed to moving forward as instructed in the magic manual. We dated when it worked in my calendar. We met half way. I paid for some of the dates. He paid for some of the dates. It was amazing! There were so many things that felt so incredibly dreamy.

Of all things, he was a photographer at polo. This meant that I would be invited to go to a polo match as his guest. Now, like the ball, I didn't know that this actually existed. The only experience I have ever had with polo was watching Julia Roberts in Pretty Woman. And, it actually felt a little like that.

Aside from polo, something that we really enjoyed together was cooking. This was something entirely new to me as, in my previous lives, it was always I alone in the kitchen. It was fun to co-create dishes together. Of course, I found a cookbook designed for Goddesses. Each time we got together we would cook, laugh, play and enjoy some delectable dish that was always sprinkled with a hint of cinnamon. Kim was very open to the idea and seemed to get a kick out of me. In almost complete disbelief, I found myself in a relationship with a man that actually listened to what I had to say, opened the car door for me, served me dinner first, and poured my glass of wine first. We talked for hours and hours. We sat on opposite ends of the couch so we could look into each other's eyes as we spoke. At night, we would sit on my patio balcony and look at the stars. I found him to be kind. Once, when we were watching a sad movie together, I spotted tears. And, after several visits to my apartment, before I knew it, my cocker spaniel was sitting on his lap. Could the exercise be working?

I am happy to report that after 12 years, Kim and I remain blissfully together. About six years ago, we moved in together. It was time for us to cohabitate. We were ready. In packing up my things, I discovered a faded and folded red piece of construction paper tucked deeply in a box. Curiously, I unraveled the folded paper. To my surprise, it was the special red paper that held all of the things I had wanted in a relationship and the traits I wished my future husband to have. With astonishment, I went down the list and realized that Kim had all of those qualities and more. He is an amazingly loving soul that treats me like a Goddess. The love we share is one of those gifts that I was to discover.

Beautiful Seeds of Change

I'm glad I stayed in Texas. I'm grateful to Bill for dumping me here. And, I am eternally grateful to Kim for sweeping me up and loving me. I believe in the magic manual, and I hope you do too. I believe that everyone deserves a love like ours.

Here are my ideas on how to create the love of your life in your life:

- Love yourself first.

- Follow your bliss.

- Play and thrive in love.

- Be clear in what you are asking for and never settle for less.

- Believe you deserve it.

- Trust your intuition.

- Forgive and let go with grace.

- Be open to receiving.

- Live full out.

- Love fully.

- Use cinnamon in every dish.

I wish for you great love. It really exists. I know. If it can happen to me it can happen to you.

Wishes can and do come true.

About the Author

Sandra J. Filer, MBA, is a gifted artist, speaker, author, beauty consultant, and licensed *Heal Your Life*® Coach & Workshop Leader. Sandra is also actively involved with the Woman Within Organization and the Empowered Girls Alliance. She is passionate about empowering people to live happy, healthy, and love-filled lives through coaching and workshops.

Sandra lives on a quiet, lantern-lit street with her love, Mr. Kim Coffman, and six fabulous felines. She enjoys her family, friends, having fun, creating art, being in nature, and escaping to her favorite island in Florida.

diosafeliz@hotmail.com
www.thehappygoddess.com

Acknowledgments

A special thanks to all the amazing women who have loved and supported me, especially my sister, Mary. For this particular story, thank you to Ellie Windsor, the Goddess of Light, and Charlsie Kendrick for talking to the "photographer."

Beryl Huang

To my mother and father who, through their love and courage, gave me the strength to find my life's calling, thank you. To my dear friends, Andy, Amy, and Bill, who believe in me and challenge me, thank you for your friendship and love. And to all the readers who upon finishing this book will set forth on a new and better life's journey, pursuing and finding your own significance, thank you for doing your part to make our world a better, more joyful place.

Beautiful Seeds of Change

Chapter 5

FIND YOUR SIGNIFICANCE

"What an unattractive little girl," the woman said aloud, jabbing her finger toward my face like a thief waving a gun at a bank teller.

"You're so big and ugly. You're the abominable snowman," said my fifth grade classmate, the words ripping my heart, like a dagger slowly being turned in circles.

"Ugly duckling! Ugly duckling!" sang the teenage girls as they taunted me, tearing away my pride and self-esteem.

How is any young person supposed to cope with bullying, harassment, and demolition of their confidence when so many, perhaps unwittingly, constantly degrade the person? How do you overcome name calling and the destruction of one's self-esteem, and still expect to be able to become the person you're capable of becoming?

How do you find your significance when it seems everyone and everything is fighting against you?

This is the story of how the ugly duckling, the troubled teen, the rebellious daughter, found her significance through a journey that would take her from Taiwan to Germany to the United States.

I was born in Taiwan in a family with my parents and two brothers, one older and one younger. As a little girl, my eyes were small, my nose was flat, I didn't grow much hair, and I cried a lot. Compared to my two brothers who both won the Gerber baby competition, I certainly was considered the ugly one. And everyone made sure I knew that.

When I was four years old – and to this day I remember it vividly – something happened that was hurtful and left me in tears. Little did I know at the time that it was just the start of what became years of pain.

Our neighbor had just gotten married. I was so excited to go next door to see the new bride. While I was there, the bride looked at me and asked the people standing around us, "Who is that ugly girl?" They all turned to me, gave me sorrowful looks, and then one lady told her that I was the neighbor, Amy's, daughter. The bride was shocked and exclaimed,

"Wow, how sad, her mom is so pretty. How come the daughter looks like that?" Yes, you heard it right, that was exactly how she said it, and she said it in my face. I remember I ran home and cried in my room the rest of the day. It was my first great disappointment in people, but not nearly my last.

As I grew up, I was always the tallest kid in my class. By the time I graduated from elementary school, I was the tallest person in school, which included all the students, and even the teachers and staff. I never felt pretty or had feelings of self-worth, because I felt so different from the other kids.

As the school years passed, I seemed to feel even worse. I got bullied a lot and was constantly called names. The other kids even had a song to make fun of me just because I was taller and bigger than them. While they thought they were being funny, they didn't realize their cruelty was harming me and would set a pattern that I'd fight for years.

By the time I was a teenager I hated myself very much and disliked who I had become. I pushed some of my anger onto my parents for I felt it was their fault I was so tall and different than other girls. I just didn't fit in and worst of all as a teenager, boys didn't like me. In fact, a boy I had a crush on asked me to deliver a love letter to one of my girlfriends. I pretended I didn't care but I cried so many nights after that incident. I wondered if I would ever be loved and wondered if I could ever love myself. I now knew I was different, and nobody would ever understand what I was going through.

Despite my incredibly low self-esteem, I was doing very well in school. The teachers called me "super student." Any exam, any competition, any task I was asked to do, I won them all. I tried my very best to be perfect as I thought being perfect would mean people would like me. I thought if I was a winner in title, I'd be a winner in life. I thought if I was always number one, my relatives would accept me, a girl, as an equal like a boy. I thought wrong.

No matter how good I was, how hard I tried; it seemed it was never enough. I brought home countless awards, but never felt they were appreciated. One day I was competing against students from across the nation, and I returned home earning second place missing the first place trophy by only one point. Expecting words of congratulations and praise, I was dumbfounded when my teacher blamed me in front of the whole class, berating me and yelling, "How could you not get first place? Why didn't you win?" I was crushed. I felt devastated. I had beaten hundreds of other students and only failed to win by one point, yet here was a person of authority saying I was a failure.

It was at that moment that I turned my back on everyone and began a rebel's journey.

Within weeks I went from being a good kid to a kid that would be every parent's nightmare. I rebelled against everything. My aunts and uncles wouldn't allow their kids to speak or play with me. My parents threw up their arms in frustration. My brothers tried to ignore me.

I did everything I could to make everyone else angry, upset, and uncomfortable. When they'd say "don't do it," I'd do it anyway. When they said "do it," I didn't. My father turned to physical punishment, beating me countless times because I wouldn't listen to him or my mother. I was rebellious and was out to prove I didn't need anybody, and that I was right. When he broke a 2x4 board across my back in an attempt to teach me a lesson, I stood defiantly, never shedding a tear.

No one liked to talk or play with me. I was alone. I was an outcast. My uncle told me I was not welcome at his house because I was a bad influence on his child. I was barely 17, yet my rebellion cost me my family, my friends, and even worse, my pride.

I wanted to be anywhere but home. I was dying to get away, and when I found a chance to run away I did. It would be more than three years before I would speak with my father again.

I went to a school far away from my hometown and struggled to stay in school while working in a restaurant. I rented a small room from an 88-year old man who had rented rooms to three other students as well. My room was meager, about 10 feet by 12 feet, with one wooden bed and a desk and chair. That was it. No dresser. No mirror. No nightstand. No closets. Nothing else. It was sparse, depressing, and lonely.

I could never see this room as a home. It ultimately became my prison: a hole that I resigned myself to living in even though I hated it. I couldn't afford to buy a warm blanket, and I often ate only once a day because I didn't have enough money to buy food. My prison kept me down and alone. At some point I even started to feel sorry for myself. Even though I had put myself here; I started wondering what I had done to deserve this, what I had done to end up like this?

Looking back, I realize that I wasn't rebelling to be bad; I was rebelling because I wanted attention. The more I yearned for attention, the lonelier I became. Ironically, I grew up in an upper class household with housekeepers and drivers and each child had our own nanny. What a fall I had taken.

Reality was setting in. Life on my own was not easy at all, and certainly not what I was accustomed to. My stubbornness and rebellious spirit—and perhaps what little pride I had left, kept me from calling out to my family for help and forgiveness.

I was beginning to learn and understand some life lessons. I learned that being a troubled teen most often means living with a lonely heart. I learned that youthful ignorance is no match for the wisdom of our elders. I learned that pride can help you reach your goals, but can also blind you to reality.

For every upbeat moment, I started to feel I was having five moments I'd rather forget. I struggled to get by. I was seriously and dangerously questioning why I was alive. I learned that life was hard and unfair. And then, out of the blue, a simple act of compassion seemed to shatter the darkness and give me a spark of light to find my way.

It was a bitterly cold winter evening. It was so cold in my room I thought for sure I'd freeze to death. I didn't own a heater nor did I have a warm blanket, so I put on every piece of clothing I had, yet still felt the damp winter chill scraping at my bones. As I lay in bed, teeth chattering, I heard someone knock on my door. I opened it to find the owner of the house holding a big, puffy, warm blanket. He pushed the blanket to me and said four words, "Tomorrow, go home kid." Then he turned and walked back down the hallway without as much as a smile.

I wrapped that big blanket around me and tried to sleep, but his words had shocked me into realizing it was okay to admit I may have been wrong. It was okay to ask my parents for forgiveness. It was okay to let people know I needed their help and attention. For the first time in a long time, not only was my body warm, but my heart, too. The next morning I called my parents and asked them to let me come home. Of course, as parents often do for the love of their children, they opened the door and their arms to me. It was then that I learned the concept of unequivocal love.

Many say we cannot go back in life and I am sure this is true. Even though I was so happy to be home in many ways, living with my parents again proved difficult. I had always had conflicts with my father. I now know that my father and I were so similar in personalities, but at that time, I would have laughed at anyone who even suggested such a thing. I was behaving very badly, and the relationship with my parents became more and more tense. I considered leaving again when I got another wakeup call.

My beloved grandma had a heart attack and was hospitalized with the grim prognosis that she likely would not survive much longer. I visited her as much as I could, and the very last time she was still coherent, she held my hands and told me, "You are a good kid, so stop acting like you are not. I want to see you be good." Her words hit me like a sledgehammer to the head.

I realized I was about to lose the only person who was always consistently with me, giving me her love no matter what I did. When everyone else didn't want to talk to me, she was the one who always opened her arms to me. As she lay there, I promised her I would change. I swore I'd make her proud. That was the last time I spoke with her, as she soon fell into a coma and passed. I realized I would never did get the chance to show her how I could change and make her proud.

Her death made me realize that life was too short to live it negatively. I had to turn my life around, and there was only one person who could do it ... ME! I could not help being tall. I had to learn to forget the unkind comments about my appearance from long ago. I finally silenced the voices of my cruel, heckling of classmates. I knew I could find my way back to being the "good kid" my grandmother believed I was.

I now found myself with a new focus. I wanted to see if there were others out there like me. I determined that if there were, then maybe I could use my experiences to help them find their way.

I became fascinated with the field of psychology and how the human mind works from an intelligence and emotional standpoint. I sought out answers to what causes rebellion, what drives self-doubt, what makes one lose their self-awareness, and what causes people to fall into a downward spiral from which many can never break free.

I dedicated myself to my studies and earned my undergraduate degree in Taiwan, and then my Psy.D. from one of the most prestigious universities in Germany. After graduate school, I moved to America where I worked in Hollywood, completed additional coursework in the field of psychology, and then opened my practice. I know I will always be searching for answers to my own problems, yet along the way, I learned how to help others with theirs.

As of 2012, I have been counseling patients for over 13 years. I have clients who are actors, sports stars, business executives, housewives and lots of ordinary people seeking extraordinary lives. I have done this through private practice, seminars, workshops, and even television and radio shows. The field of psychology has certainly illuminated my own life path.

The paths and roads I travelled were a mystery to me for so many years. It has been through my dealings with clients' problems that I have unlocked the answers to many of my own frequently asked lifelong questions. My clients' often real and sometimes perceived life troubles very often provided me the wonderful by-product of answers and solutions to my own experiences and decisions.

We frequently worry so much about what we will become tomorrow that we forget that we are someone today. That troubled teenager that used to be me was lost in what I might not become, instead of focusing on who I was. I was listening to others instead of listening to myself. I lost sight of who I was because I let others define me. This is often the start of a downward journey for so many.

When I launched my practice, I was scared at first and wondered whether I could survive financially. A service business like psychology takes clients, and getting clients isn't easy, especially in a field where the clients must first admit to themselves that they need help. I wondered if clients would find me. I even questioned whether I could help them once they did.

It is human nature for most of us to doubt ourselves. We find our minds reeling with "what if" scenarios. What if they don't like me? What if I fail? What if they say "no"? What if my spouse gets mad? What if I lose my job? What if I can't pay the mortgage? What if I am not pretty? What if I am never loved? What we don't realize is the self-fulfilling nature of our worrying. We ignore the common sense that says if you tell yourself something enough times it will come true.

So we fill our mind with negative thoughts, and then we're not surprised when these negative thoughts come to fruition. I've heard clients exclaim, "Oh, I just knew I would lose my job," or "I knew my business would fail before I started it," or my favorite, when I asked a client how long she'd been suffering from a cough said, "in three weeks it will have been a whole month!"

We have to turn these negative thoughts around. Instead of asking, "What if I fail?" you should say, "What will I do when I succeed?" As I've coached clients in this positive, predictive thinking technique, I've witnessed dramatic changes in behavior and outlook with people being able to overcome years of self-doubt to lead stronger, more fulfilling lives. It is wonderful to witness.

Most of our issues are created by ourselves. If a challenge presents itself, and there is nothing that can be done about it, you can either choose to worry or put it aside until it can be addressed. The former will increase stress, and guess what, the latter will decrease stress. The latter will also empower you to focus on much more important things because you are not filled up with worry.

It should not be your concern to make a difference in those things that we cannot change. Instead, focus on what you can change, and do so with the goal of leading a better, more rewarding life. Learn from your mistakes and certainly, don't make the same mistake over and over again.

The last several points I made are of course common sense to any reader who is not in a difficult place in their lives. I must tell you that I have used these common sense points with countless numbers of clients over the years. I have blended simple thoughts into their particular stress scenario with remarkable results. Even the most intelligent and successful person can be positively affected by something so simple. Very often, a seemingly simple and obvious statement can be the key to unlocking different thinking or shining light on a particular problem.

We can never have all the answers, but we can all give 100% to figure them out. We will all make mistakes, but we should never be afraid of mistakes that are made honestly. Those mistakes are going to give you the wisdom and strength to make better decisions in the future; to better take on all of the opportunities that line up in front of you.

The journey of life will give us all something. I call these life scars. A life scar is something that we are not born with, but that which we earn. We earn these scars for many reasons: to challenge us; to make us fight; to make us humble; to make us proud, to prove we can overcome. Life scars are badges that we should proudly wear, symbolizing and celebrating our life experiences. Some of these experiences we would rather forget. But once you accept that it is these very scars that make up the unique individual you are, you can proudly wear the collective experiences, rejoicing in what they've created.

There were many lessons I learned while living on my own in that little 10x12 foot room. One of the most important lessons involved the word "choice." This little word has enormous meaning in most of our lives.

Choice is ultimately always ours to make. Learning how to mold reaction to life's challenges is the secret to overcoming most of the obstacles in your path. Learn to stand up for yourself, to take time to answer your own questions, and to focus on continually moving forward and achieving your goals. Try not to let others' opinions stop you or redirect you. Stay strong.

Choose your path, stay on it and go for it.

My early life's path left me with a lot of bad memories. I can tell you that trying to release bad memories is a very difficult thing to do. It takes a lot of tears, work, and introspection to break the chains of the past. Understanding my anger and pain helped me to stop blaming others for causing it. It allowed me to love life again, to see the beauty in every experience, to be non-judgmental and be open to new relationships and a new life.

Jonathan Adler* is a client I first met in early 2010. A successful executive with a large home, a wife and two children, a luxury sports car, and the financial means to vacation twice a year to any location he chose, Jonathan would appear to have had everything he could want. By outside appearances he was a great manager, taking ideas and building them into successful initiatives and having hundreds of employees report to him.

But the more he worked, the less connected Jonathan became to his family. He felt he had lost control of his relationship, not having any common threads with his wife, and eventually the two divorced. Jonathan next fell into an emotional roller coaster of a relationship and moved halfway across the country only to see that end. He began questioning his self-worth, wondering what he was doing wrong, doubting his every ability. He quickly began a downward spiral that led to depression and feelings of inadequacy.

He had worked tirelessly to acquire things that he thought would make him happy, but he didn't have time to enjoy them. In our first session he described how he would buy things to make himself feel better, and months later find an unopened box with something he had ordered. He was at the point where purchasing became the means to his *supposed* happiness. What Jonathan was doing was exactly what thousands of others – perhaps even you – do: they look for happiness not from within, but through others. In this case, the others just happened to be retailers who were all too willing to take Jonathan's money.

He knew there was a hole in his life yet he had no idea what was supposed to be there, or how to go about filling it. Simply put, he had not found his significance. For all his monetary success, he was emotionally bankrupt. He was afraid to fully fall in love again for fear of getting hurt or going through another failed marriage and possibly leaving another child behind. He had no hobbies or means to release his anger so he'd more often than not take it out on people closest to him. He led an unpleasant life with little meaning.

Beautiful Seeds of Change

Over eight sessions we discussed what was holding him back and began identifying ways to help him find his significance. Through attitudinal psychology techniques, he began changing his mindset from feelings of failure and emptiness to genuine emotional control where he would determine what he wanted and how he would react to life's changes.

He learned to accept that which he could not change and began opening himself to new emotional and day-to-day opportunities. At 52 years of age he began taking drum lessons and found the physical and auditory experience a great stress reliever. He created a list of emotional and intellectual goals that he will reach by age 60. He begins each day by looking in the mirror and verbally convincing himself that he is in control; that he is responsible for his thoughts and actions; that nobody can challenge his dreams; and that he is open to falling in love and willing to accept it. Like a light switch, he turned off his negative thoughts and by daily recitation of positive messages that will predict his happiness; he is training his mind to focus on all the good things that are yet to come.

Has it worked? I checked on Jonathan the other day and asked, "How is it going?" In an upbeat and eager voice he replied, "Superb! It's the only way that it can go!"

Jonathan found his significance.

What is your significance? What are you doing with your life that will fulfill you? Whether you believe it or not, your significance is waiting for you to discover it. If you believe you can, you can! Open your mind and heart to discover what you really want out of life. It's not who you are that holds you back, it's who you think you are not. If you don't believe in yourself – if you don't love yourself – how do you expect others to? I know that our beliefs about anything and everything have a direct impact on our lives.

It took me a long time to get to this point; but I remember when I started to believe in a better future. It was a moment of clarity when I quit blaming myself and others and began believing anything was possible. I started being grateful for and appreciating my blessings. I realized life was a process, a continuing dynamic, an ever changing ebb and flow. There was no need for me to be stuck in one mental rut. I got rid of those old negative, defeating mind-sets and attitudes. I started thinking bigger and better! Almost overnight I realized I was happy. Internal and external success soon followed.

Life can be beyond predictable. We all face adversity. We all fall down. We all fail. Sometimes it really is out of our control, with no wrong choices involved. If you do fall or suffer from adversity, be strong and make sure you learn so you can prepare for the future. Stand up when you can and step forward to new success.

Keep learning. Keep growing. Keep pressing your limits, pushing your boundaries. One day you will look back and say, "Wow look what I have accomplished," rather than looking back and saying, "What if I had taken that first step?" The primary reason we fail is that we quit too soon. If things don't work out on the first try, we quit. Bad move. Skills and abilities take time to develop. I have lost a lot in the past but I gained them all back and more. Don't give up if you haven't done your best and tried everything you can. Keep practicing! Life gets better when we get better.

I have always found that a smile can open doors to buildings, life and hearts. Live your life with a smile, a willing spirit, and faith that the pattern you set will not add to the sorrow and pain of the world, but to the mystery and joy of it all. Live your life fully and completely without regret or dread. It can be tough, but no more than we can handle. Be happy for life and look forward to each new tomorrow.

If in the course of your journey you fall, don't try to get up immediately. It's not realistic. Stop, breathe, and look around and see if there is something you can pick up first. Learn from the experiences. Live by choice, not by chance. Make changes, not excuses. Be motivated, not manipulated. Choose self-esteem, not self-pity. Live the life YOU want.

The choice is yours. Learning how to predict your reactions to life's challenges is the secret to overcoming the obstacles in your path. Learn to stand up for yourself, to take time to answer your own questions, and to focus on achieving your goals. Don't let others tell you what you can or cannot do. Decide now how you will react to challenges. Be positive. Choose your path and go for it. Find your significance. The only way to get there is you.

*Name changed to protect client's identity.

About the Author

Beryl Huang, Founder of the American Institute of Attitudinal Dynamics, is a leading attitudinal psychologist helping thousands of people each year through her private and group sessions in motivation, self-improvement, hypnotherapy and past life regression, as well as seminars and workshops in America and Asia. She has been featured in media in North America and Europe and hosts two TV talk shows on Chinese television and a radio live call-in show in Southern California.

www.berylhuang.com

Acknowledgments

I thank my parents who gave me love and support even when I was the rebellious young girl. I thank them for never giving up on me. I also thank my brothers for their patience and love over the years, even though we have been in different countries for many years.

I also thank my clients for entrusting me to help you conquer your fears, surpass your expectations, and find your significance. You have taught me so much and expanded my commitment to helping more and more people overcome life's challenges. Without you, none of this would be possible.

I have received help, love, support and advice from a few very special individuals who entered my life from nowhere. They have provided unconditional strength over many years. Their knowing eyes looked past the anger and the frustration of a young woman; their voices spoke directly to my wounded soul; and their hands pulled a frightened little girl away from danger. Thank you, a million times thank you. Without you, I may have never found my significance.

Kailah Eglington

Dedicated to my beautiful angel babies and my wonderful son. We will all be together again one day.

Chapter 6

SEEDS FROM THE GARDEN OF MY LIFE

*Regardless of what has happened to you in your life,
regardless of how young or how old you think you might
be, the moment you begin to think properly, this something
that is within you, this power within you that's greater
than the world, it will begin to emerge.*

~ Rev. Michael Beckwith

The first time I saw the garden, I knew it would be beautiful again. I saw it as a symbol of me and my disability. Like me, the garden wasn't working in places; there were pockets of the past that needed to go. And yet there were other areas where the brief spark of what it once was shown through; a flower here, a graceful bough there.

The garden, having begun her "proper" life was much older and wiser than me; she had seen more life than I ever would. By the time I was born, she was already into her 40th year. Yet, here she was, on her 87th birthday in very much the same position as me – not blooming as she was meant to bloom, worn out, in need of some TLC and not quite knowing where she was going next. Both of us needed a good overhaul.

I initially viewed the garden as I had done with so many things in my life. I actually imagined I would have her back to her flourishing self within three months!

It was the same for my disability. All along, I had expected that I would wake up one morning and miraculously be as I was two years ago.

One morning I finally did wake up, but it was with the realization that both projects were going to take infinitely longer than I had anticipated because my "disability" had begun long before the accident that took away my ability to walk. In some ways, I think that morning was a turning point for me. My physical, emotional and spiritual rehabilitation was going to take time; and so, too, would the garden's transformation.

A new kind of patience was born within me. I decided that for once, I would do it properly. Perhaps this is what had been intended all along – that I would learn how to actually live life, rather than getting it over and done with as quickly as possible. Perhaps I was also meant to do more than the usual superficial patching up of problems that was my legacy. The same would be true for the garden. I would plan her debut, slowly and meticulously. I would ensure that her very foundations were sound, the soil in perfect condition and the flora that would adorn her would be exactly right.

For me, I would take my steps, one at a time, starting with acceptance, then build on that. I would ensure that I had all the right foundations and equipment to arm me properly for a new existence. I would stop and smell the roses.

The garden bonded to my spirit and together we would heal. Every inch would be cleared, tended and re-born. The lonely path leading down to an abyss of weeds and neglect would become a winding, glorious doorway into a secret, yet exciting future.

I wheeled myself onto the patio, turned back and looked on my destiny. "Tomorrow, we begin."

That was ten years ago, and four years later; I did walk again but that was not the only transformation that happened. For many years before a freak accident had left me facing one of the biggest challenges of my life, the fact that I could no longer walk, I was already disabled. My story goes back much earlier than that because what was holding me back was more than the wheelchair. What had been holding me back was me.

So, here is the story of how the power of forgiveness, gratitude, positive thinking and reconnecting to my spirituality helped me on my journey to healing and wholeness.

With this story, I hope to show you that courage, never giving up, giving to others when you think you have nothing left to give and believing absolutely in that extraordinary and untapped power and strength you have within you, can help you overcome physical, emotional and spiritual adversity.

I hope you will learn that there are no limits because you have within you the power to achieve whatever it is you want to achieve, and the power to embrace whatever it is you desire and become the person you want to be.

Although it was difficult at times to retrace the seeds of my life, I sincerely hope with all my heart that my story will show you that even when you are at your lowest ebb and even if your life is broken and shattered, it is possible to pick yourself up and start again by simply changing the way you think about things.

THE EARLY SEEDS

As a seed buried in the earth cannot imagine itself as an orchid or hyacinth, neither can a heart packed with hurt imagine itself loved or at peace. The courage of the seed is that once cracking, it cracks all the way.

~ Mark Nepo

One of our deepest needs is to be loved and to feel as if we belong. This was denied to me from a very early age, and in its place I was punished, though I never quite knew what I had done wrong. I grew up with my life full of guilt for simply being alive. In my mother's eyes, whatever I did was wrong and when she was in a bad mood, which was frequent, I would be shouted at, berated, hit, punished or locked in the cellar for whatever my transgressions might have been.

Although I remember crying out, "I'm not a bad person," on more than one occasion, I was convinced that I must be bad. This was backed up regularly at church where we were constantly reminded of our sinfulness, and how we would burn in Hell if we did not confess our sins and repent. Fifty-seven years on, and I can still see a vivid picture from my first catechism showing sinners reaching up to Heaven pleading for release as the fires of Hell burned them.

The seeds of unworthiness were planted early and continued to grow stronger. Even though I was a top student at school, bringing home straight A's on my report card, it still wasn't good enough for my mother, and I was told that I should have done better and that my efforts weren't good enough.

I loved music and was told by my grandmother, who played the organ professionally, and my music teacher that I was an exceptional pianist with great potential. I remember music being one of my great loves, and how it moved my soul.

My teacher was so sure of my talent, that she thought I might get a scholarship to The Juilliard School of Music. I would not believe her, thinking she was making it up because the Juilliard School was and remains the reserve of truly gifted musicians, dancers, and actors from around the world. It would surely not want someone who was as clumsy and inept as me!

Although I found it hard to believe that I had such talent, I earned a great deal of praise from my teacher and others for my recitals and performances. My own negative thoughts were given credence, however, when my mother announced one day that "any asshole can play the piano." I was so devastated that I stopped playing and didn't go near a piano again for decades.

One after another, my aspirations were crushed; my flair for foreign languages, my artistic ability, my writing capabilities, my debating skills, my affinity for acting and drama, my mathematical prowess, my natural way with people and animals. Each skill was berated, criticized and tossed aside until every ounce of confidence I had was destroyed, and I was no more than an empty husk going through the motions of life.

It was a heavy burden for such a young girl to have on her shoulders but this was how my early belief system was formed. I was talentless; whatever I did was not good enough; and therefore whatever I tried in the future would not be good enough. If whatever I did was not good enough, I was destined to fail. If I failed, it was further proof that I was useless and merely taking up the valuable space that someone else more worthy than me should have.

THE SEEDS OF DARKNESS

Courage is not the absence of fear or despair; it is the capacity to continue on despite them, no matter how great or overwhelming they become.

~ Robert Fanney

I was 16 and had received my driver's licence. Back then, driving lessons were part of the school's curriculum and didn't cost anything, so I had jumped at the opportunity to learn to drive as this represented freedom to me. I had been given an old, beat up Chevy Nova that my father had bought for $100, and I believed that life was about to change. My father had remained predominantly in the background of my life, unable to stand up to my mother, so I was ecstatic with his gift of the car. I felt he must have loved me after all.

This act of kindness from my father meant that I would no longer be a burden. I had a car and a licence. I would get a job, save my money and go off to school to become a medical research scientist. In one of my more optimistic moments, I truly believed that I was going to find a cure for all birth defects and with my car and licence; there would be no stopping me! Or so I thought.

I had never been accepted as part of the "in" group at school, my family having moved to the town mid-way through seventh grade when friendships had already been formed. I had a few friends, but was considered a bit odd, partly because I was becoming more interested in social causes and partly because I had a spiritual side that many did not understand. I was constantly teased and tormented at school and could not wait to graduate and leave the cow-town mentality behind.

I had grown into a tall, lanky, long-haired young woman with dark, almost black eyes and black hair to match. Some of my relatives said I was a classic beauty with striking features, but it was not something I had particularly thought about. I was more interested in the growing animal liberation movement, protesting the Vietnam War, stopping poverty and preserving nature, rather than my looks. However, that was not to be the case for one boy, whose interest in my looks was to result in the next major turning point in my life.

Rape. The act itself is horrific enough, but how does a naïve and gentle 16-year old girl rationalise losing her virginity against her will, not only being called a whore by the rapist but being forced by the rapist to call herself a whore, or she will be killed and then being treated like a criminal by the police when she is the victim? I rationalized it by reverting back to my belief system that I was no good, that I was unworthy and that I deserved to be treated in this way because I was a bad person.

As if that wasn't difficult enough to cope with, about six months later when I was taken to the doctor after suddenly gaining a lot of weight, it was discovered that I had fallen pregnant from the rape. This time it was my mother who called me a whore.

Several weeks later, without my knowledge or consent, my mother and father drove me to some wretched hospital in New York City where I was given an illegal saline-induction abortion; a technique that I found out later not only poisoned and killed the baby but could kill the mother as well.

I cannot begin to describe the horror of it. My torment and screams meant nothing to my mother, or to the doctor and nurses who held me down as they stuck the needle into my abdomen. I knew the second my baby died, I felt my baby die, and I knew it was very, very wrong. As naïve as I was, I knew I was too far along to have had the procedure done, especially when the doctor said (and I shall never forget his words): "What we are doing now is completely legal," as this perfectly formed baby was finally delivered hours later. The baby was taken away to where, I do not know; but years later, I was told it was probably to an incinerator.

A few hours later, I was packed back into the car, driven home, and no one ever said a word again. This has been my deepest, darkest secret that I have carried throughout my life until now.

Although I had no control over what had happened because I was a minor and my parents "owned" me and could do what they liked with me, I felt like a murderer. I have never harmed any living thing in my life, so I could not even begin to accept that an innocent child had been killed inside of me. A deep-rooted sense of revulsion, disgust and self-hatred, combined with the early years of unworthiness began growing out of control until all I felt was blackness, loathing, despair and utter hopelessness. I was convinced that I carried the smell of death with me everywhere I went, not just because my baby had died but because at the still tender age of 16, I had died emotionally and spiritually.

Less than a year later, I was rushed to the hospital for emergency surgery to remove my gall bladder and the gallstones that had blocked the ducts of some of my organs, causing them to begin to shut down. How I had wished for death to take me then. Although I was sick for a long time, I somehow survived. My belief system was strengthened in that survival, and to me it was a further confirmation that I was a bad person and meant to suffer for my sins.

I graduated from High School shortly after and started a new job as a receptionist. Although I cannot recall any of it, I had become engaged to a boy called Jay. All I remember of this particular day is a shadowy image of someone (Jay, I understand) coming into the office to see me about something. The next thing I remember was waking up in the psychiatric ward of a local hospital. I am told that I had finally snapped, though why or how no one has ever revealed to me. I was told that Jay had come in to visit me in the hospital once, had taken the engagement ring and never came back again. My period of darkness was to grow even darker.

Still a minor, my mother once again saw fit to decide what was best for me, without any discussion and without fully understanding what the consequences of her decision would be. I understand that I was diagnosed with severe depression, which is not surprising given what I had been through. The next day I was taken down to a small room with a nurse and two attendees standing by. I was to discover that my course of "treatment" was to be Electroconvulsive Therapy - a series of electric shock treatments.

During that first treatment, I had no idea what was going to happen.

I was moved onto a table and strapped down. Some gel and two pads, a bit like headphones, were put on my temples and a big rubbery block was shoved into my mouth. All I remember feeling was an excruciating pain and then nothing. I woke up with such an intense and unbearable pain in my head, I could barely move for hours. I thought I had finally reached the depths of hell. My punishment for being such a bad person was to now be tortured through electrocution.

Everything is a blank after that. As a result of the intensity and frequency of the shock treatments I received, I suffered retrograde, long term amnesia. About 85% of my memories were destroyed; what I had learned in school, my music, my past and my identity were all gone. When I finally did wake up with some form of cognizance, I could not even recognise simple things like tables and chairs. I would look at something, recognise it, but I could not put a word to it.

The irony of it all was that the memories they were trying to erase – those of the rape and the abortion - remained firmly rooted in my memory, along with other episodes of abuse I had endured as a child. I was a freak. I did not know who I was, simply that I must have been a very, very bad person for all these things to have happened to me. The feelings of unworthiness, of not belonging, of complete and utter failure cut deeply into my soul; only now, there was a black emptiness where the real "me" had lived.

I was angry. Very, very angry.

My physical and practical recovery took a long time, and I had to learn many things from scratch again. Although a significant part of my memory was never to be recovered, I decided there and then that I had to get away, under my own steam, and take charge of my own life.

Taking charge of my own life essentially meant marrying the first man I ran into who would have me. I thought if someone married me, I could at last feel the love that had so far been denied to me, and that I could start feeling good about myself again.

BREAKING POINT

Even when the universe made it quite clear to me that I was mistaken in my certainties, in my definitions, I did not break. The shattering of my sureties did not shatter me. Stability comes from inside, not outside.

~ Lucille Clifton

I met and married the father of my children when I was 21 and was keen to have a family. I thought I could heal the on-going agony of losing my first child if I could be a good mother to my other children, but in another cruel twist of fate, my beautiful, sweet daughters, Jennifer and Melissa, died although miraculously, my son, Joshua, survived. I was only 25.

I was once again in a state of shock and unable to comprehend their deaths. I could not grieve because I thought if I did, I would lose control completely and end up in a psychiatric hospital again. I had to remain strong for my husband and son. But inside, the pain was unbearable. It felt like I was being cut open from the inside out and the pain, anger and sorrow didn't become any less sharp as the days went by.

When we lose a child, especially if it is sudden and unexpected, it is as if a part of us dies, too. There is a strong connection with our children which starts from the time a single seed is fertilized and becomes a living being. For mothers, there is no relationship more intimate than that of a woman with her unborn child during pregnancy.

Because of this, when they die or when we are separated from them, the loss of this "human" connection can bring on the most terrible kind of grief. Because my husband and I were told that we had to "move on", we kept our grief internally, afraid to admit to each other that it wasn't getting any better.

Without the kind of pastoral care we needed to cope with our grief, my husband and I separated. He simply could not cope with the loss, and my being there was a constant reminder to him. My son and I went to live with friends until I could find a job and a place for us to live.

It was difficult enough trying to deal with the loss of my family, home and husband; but I found out that he had taken up with another woman, who had apparently been in the picture for some time. On top of everything else, I now had to deal with my husband's unfaithfulness, the total loss of his love and support and the ease with which he replaced me. The pressure was intensifying as I tried to maintain a job and give the support that was needed by my son, who was profoundly deaf.

I eventually found a job, but I was having little luck finding a place to live. Back then it was difficult, if almost impossible, for a single mother to rent an accommodation. It was as if I was a second-class citizen or an alien. Even though I had a job and was capable of paying the rent, I was still legally married and therefore "owned" by my husband. As an individual, I had no credit, no history and in the eyes of many, I was a risk. At the same time, the friends I was living with were keen to reclaim their space, particularly as my son had started acting out when I was at work and had caused some damage, albeit minor, to a couple of walls in their home. My whole world was caving in on me again.

With mounting pressure, I reluctantly asked my husband if he would look after our son for a few weeks until I could find a place for my son and I to live, and he agreed. That was a decision I was to regret for many, many years. Without my knowledge, my husband took his lover and my son and fled to Mexico, though I didn't know where they had gone at the time. It would be seven long years before I was to be reunited with my son again. Could things get any worse?

My feelings and my grief all took a back seat to the inevitable everyday tasks that I had to carry out just to survive, yet the smallest reminders would bring them to the fore again, reminding me that I had lost everything in my life. The early seeds of unworthiness were growing, confirming that I didn't deserve to have anything good in my life. Every time a birthday or a holiday came and went, when I heard a certain child's cry, saw baby booties in a shop or I caught a child's eyes looking into mine, I felt a deep, dark pain and yearning in my heart, and I was engulfed by a growing sense of hopelessness and worthlessness.

I kept asking myself what I had done in my life that was so wrong. I used to look in the mirror and shout "I'm not a bad person!" over and over again. I started drinking heavily and ignoring my financial obligations, and eventually the sheriff turned up at my doorstep asking for the keys to my car as I had defaulted on the payments.

With no car, no life and the distinct possibility that I would soon be without a job if I wasn't careful, I knew I had to snap out of it. I knew I could not bring my daughters back. I had no idea where my son was, so I had no control over that. The only thing that I did have control over at this point in time was that I had a choice. I could continue to drown myself in alcohol or I could learn how to manage the pain and grief so that it wouldn't continue to overwhelm my life. Then just at the point when I felt I was ready to move on, I was diagnosed with cervical cancer and told I had a 40% chance of survival.

Well, that's just great, I thought. Anyone else care to throw anything else on my plate while we're at it?

THE SEEDS OF ANGER

There is nothing wrong with anger provided
you use it constructively.

~ Wayne Dyer

I got angry then. All this drama was doing my head in and making me sick, and now I had just been told that I had a cancer with not so spectacular odds on getting through it. So, I had a little hissy fit with myself. Was sitting around stewing in my own self-pity day and night really going to solve anything? Had all the self-wallowing helped me to date? Was I just going to sit there, give in and let the cancer consume me, or was I going to get off my sorry little arse and do something? Yep, I was definitely angry with myself.

I had reached the breaking point. I was fed up with feeling lousy and depressed; I didn't want to be at my pity party anymore. I was sick to death of crying myself to sleep night after night, and I didn't want to hear another word of the "woe-is-me" song because it was getting me absolutely nowhere.

I stomped into my bedroom, threw myself down on the end of the bed, scowled at myself in the mirror, then looked myself straight in the eyes and with a very stern voice that meant business, I said: "Okay, let's have a good look at you then. You are not stupid; in fact you are quite intelligent, even though you don't always act it! You have a good head on your shoulders - you were a straight A student for heaven's sake - that shows you have the ability. You can play music and okay, so the music you memorised isn't there anymore, but you can learn it again. You can dance, and you have artistic ability. You can do most anything you put your mind to. You're an absolute whizz at math and pattern recognition. You have serious strength of character and the ability to carry on in a crisis –I mean, how many people would have survived what you have been through? *So, what is your problem? What are you afraid of?* Okay, so you have a few issues, we can sort those out, but do you *really* need someone to take you by the hand and tell you what to do? Haven't you had *enough* of other people controlling your life? Isn't it about time you took the bull by the horns and just got off your sorry arse and got on with it?"

I jumped up, punched the bed, looked straight into those dark eyes of mine, pointed my finger and said with utter grit and determination: "Yes, dammit, it IS time to get off your backside and sort yourself out, because if you don't nobody else will. Got it?" Oh yes, I got it all right.

THE SEEDS OF TRANSFORMATION

You can start with nothing. And out of nothing,
and out of no way, a way will be found.

~ Rev. Michael Beckwith

I was ready to change but I wasn't even sure about where to begin. I decided I needed to get away from everything for a while to gather my thoughts.

It was one thing having a go at yourself in the mirror and quite another to move forward into an unknown world where you would have to look at things you would rather not look at. The first thing I decided to do was to never touch another drop of alcohol ever again.

I then decided to take a short break from work. I desperately needed time to think. There was a forest near where I was living, so I went there, walked for miles and eventually came upon a secluded glen in the woods. It was beautiful. I had forgotten how beautiful nature could be. I have always had a very spiritual side to me and have always had a great affinity with nature and animals, so I could appreciate the beauty and wonder of life all around me. I was enveloped by the nurturing silence, grateful for it and in those moments, something told me that everything was going to be all right. Knowing this, the floodgates opened, and I cried like I had never cried in my entire life. I cried for what seemed like hours, even when no more tears would come. I begged for relief from the pain. And, then I became still.

The silence gave me a profound sense of peace, and it allowed me to finally reconnect with and listen to my inner voice, not the one that was constantly criticizing, but the one that was gentler, kinder and more spiritual; the deepest part of my being. Some would call this voice their essence, the Soul, the Higher Self or their gut instinct. For me, it felt like my Guardian Angel. This voice told me not to give up, that although I could not change the past, everything was going to be all right, and that there were positive things in my life; all I had to do was look around me and embrace them.

The past is over and done and cannot be changed.
This is the only moment we can experience.

~ Louise Hay

I did look around me, and what I saw filled me with indescribable feelings of awe and love. It was as if I had been given a new pair of eyes. I saw the wonder and abundance of nature, shared the joy of a squirrel finding an acorn, was moved by the beautiful symphonies of birdsong, and was enchanted by the variety of colours and shapes of the flora and fauna that surrounded me. I thought of how nature was at that moment renewing itself, and I accepted that this was the time of renewal for me.

I experienced true gratitude then. I knew that I would not have been brought here to this place nor to this moment in time had I not experienced the things that I had. They had been lessons. Would I have been able to experience the wonder and beauty of this glade had I not experienced the bad? I intuitively knew that I had to begin to find something positive in everything I had experienced, good or bad.

I came to realize that life is a precious gift where every minute is to be savored and enjoyed, where our senses are fully opened to the beauty and possibilities that surround us in abundance. I understood that every day we are given opportunities to learn new things, to feel the most amazing feelings, to open our hearts to others, to be the best that we can be and to give back in a never ending cycle of growth and renewal. I knew that sometimes the lessons had been and would be harsh, and the feelings crippling. But I also knew that in opening my heart, although I might be vulnerable, I was meant to experience these things for a reason and in order to eventually fulfill my life's purpose. Although I had been in a very negative cycle for many years, I had always felt that I was put on this earth to help others. Yet at the same time, I knew that in order to help others, I would have to help myself, and so I began my period of healing.

I felt elated! It was like an enormous wave of adrenalin and relief had swept over me. I had at last begun to break through those heavy barriers that had been holding me down. I had made the decision and taken the first step of accepting responsibility for my actions and for my destiny. I knew my transformation wasn't going to happen overnight, but I knew it would happen.

I also knew that it was time for a change. I needed to start afresh, and I knew that my company was looking for someone to oversee the setting up of offices throughout Europe. I decided that I was going to take that job, applied for and was successful and so began my journey to England, which was to become my home.

THE SEEDS OF BELIEF

Your thoughts and beliefs of the past have created
this moment, and all the moments up to this moment.
What you are now choosing to believe and think and
say will create the next moment and the next day
and the next month and the next year.

~ Louise Hay

One thing I was sure of was that I had to re-evaluate my belief system. Somewhere along the line, I had programmed myself to believe that I was unworthy, unlovable and did not deserve to have good things in my life.

When we are born, we are pure; our heart, our thoughts, our love is pure. We express our feelings freely; we love ourselves, our bodies and others unconditionally. We do not judge, criticise, discriminate or compare. We simply *are*, and we are beautiful.

As we grow, however, our thoughts and beliefs develop, grow and change. These belief systems are largely formed from the people and institutions around us. Although no one is forcing us to believe these things, we are taught to respect and obey our "elders and betters."

As we begin to grow up, our belief systems are challenged, the moulding of our personalities begins, and we start to change. Even if it is not what we want to be or do, we can find ourselves getting stuck in traps. We are taught that we should "do this" or "do that"; we should feel and respond to things in a certain way; we should dress in a certain way, we should even think in a certain way. For many of us, we end up being square pegs pushed into round holes, feeling uncomfortable in our own skin and disassociated from our true selves. We can end up losing that uniqueness and beauty into which we were born.

On top of that, we are subjected to endless pressures from society, religion, education, work, our peer groups and cultures; and if we are "different" or don't fit in with the "norm," we can feel as if we don't belong. If we see ourselves as unable to keep up with "the Joneses," we see ourselves as failures. We can lose the natural love and acceptance we had for ourselves. We can lose our spiritual connection with the natural world around us. We can take countless guilt trips, and we can find ourselves in an endless cycle of the "not good enough" trap. When this happens, we can suffer sometimes debilitating mental, physical or spiritual disease. Worse still, we can lose our hopes and dreams.

Throughout our lives, we learn and absorb thoughts from our parents, relatives, friends, significant others, teachers, religious figures, politicians, shopkeepers and many others. We are subtly manipulated by advertising, books, newspapers, magazines, all of them telling us how we should dress, what we should eat or drink, what medicines we should take, how we should think about things. We are told that our breath will be offensive if we don't use this mouthwash, our bodies will smell if we don't use that deodorant, our options will be limited if we don't go to a particular school or we don't live in a particular part of town. The list goes on and on.

Most of what we are taught, see and hear throughout our lives is meant to prey on our fears or the fears of those around us. We are taught things to "protect" us or to frighten us into not overstepping the perceived boundaries of life.

We then apply these "teachings" to our own thought processes and individual experiences, and thus we form our own internal belief systems. These belief systems form the foundations of how we perceive ourselves, how we live our lives and what we will attract into our lives.

A classic example when I was a young woman was that a woman had to be married by a certain age, or she would be left "on the shelf." The concepts of living alone, having a career or perhaps marrying later in life simply did not exist then. This left me and many other young girls scrabbling around at an early age trying to find "Mr. Right" before most of us even knew who "Mr. Right" was, or if we even wanted one!

But, this formed a belief system for me and many other girls that women had to get married; women had to get married before a certain age; if a woman did not get married before a certain age, she became a spinster; if a woman was a spinster, there was something wrong with her; if there was something wrong with her, she would never get married.

Can you see how easily a belief system can be created and how this could affect the rest of a person's life? Not only could this belief system affect a woman's views on marriage and her ability to marry, but it could begin seeping into other areas of her life. For example, a woman might feel that because she was not good enough to marry, she might not be good enough for other things either.

This could lead to a perception that if anything negative happened to her, it could be attributed to the fact that there was something wrong with her and because of this, only "bad" things would happen to her. Her entire thought-process could become negative, which might result in her creating a cycle of continuous challenges, obstacles, and dead ends, attracting only negative things into her life.

My belief system had been distorted to believe that I was not good enough and not worthy of much of anything. If I tried to get above my station, my beliefs would remind me that I was a bad person, that I was ugly, incapable, unlovable and more.

I could now see that I had become stuck in an on-going cycle of despair because I had formed certain negative belief systems, and that everything in my life was consumed by guilt, feelings of worthlessness, shame and a lack of belief in my own abilities. I was convinced that I was an utter failure, and I was wracked with fears and doubts which subconsciously alienated me from everything and everyone around me.

I came to realize that life is a fragile thing and can change with the snap of a finger. I began to re-think my life and re-arrange my priorities, and it surprised me what I discovered.

THE SEEDS OF CHANGE

I cannot always control what goes on outside.
But I can always control what goes on inside.

~ Wayne Dyer

I didn't really know where to start but being an avid reader, I thought the best place to start was with a book. I began to read but once I started, I could not stop. I virtually devoured every self-help book I could find that was offering wisdom, guidance, hope and a way of moving forward.

One book that was to completely change my life was Wayne Dyer's *Your Erroneous Zones*. It was a huge wake-up call and made me realize that I had the power and ability to take charge of my life, no matter what was thrown at me. One of the questions he asked that has remained with me to this day was: "How long are you going to be dead?" Essentially what he was saying is that we are on this earth for such a short time; it makes sense to live life in the way we want to live it instead of living it the way others want us to.

Of course this would mean learning to love and accept myself as I was, as well as getting rid of my guilt, worry and anger, and putting to rest my damaging belief systems.

Self-approval and self-acceptance in the now are the main keys to positive changes in every area of our lives.

~ Louise Hay

Another writer and teacher who was to have a profound effect on my life was Louise Hay. From a difficult and abusive upbringing, she had turned her life around completely through her positive philosophy. Her in-depth work into the mind-body connection showed that certain patterns of thought could cause certain diseases in the body. Her book, You Can Heal Your Life, showed that by reframing your thoughts and re-evaluating old beliefs you can create inner peace and harmony and bring about amazing transformations and healing for your mind, body and spirit. Intrigued, I decided I would see how they might apply to my own life.

I tested her theories by looking up some of my illnesses to see if there was a connection between them and my thought patterns. I was amazed.

She gave the probable cause of a nervous breakdown as "jamming the channels of communication" as well as "fear, anxiety, struggle and not trusting the process of life." I could see that there was a fit following my early trauma. The rape and abortion were never spoken of, and I was certainly fearful and struggling at the time.

On the probable cause of gallstones, she observed: "bitterness, hard thoughts and condemning." Traditionally gallstones developed in individuals who were overweight, over forty, had a high fat diet or had diabetes. When I developed gallstones, I was only 17, thin as a rake and quite fit, but I had just gone through a very traumatic experience which had left a legacy of bitterness and anger, and I was definitely holding onto the past.

It was all falling into place, so I bit the bullet and looked up cancer. Well, the probable cause was "Deep hurt. Long-standing resentment. Deep secret or grief eating away at the self. Carrying hatreds." The definition could not have been more accurate. It was as if it was written specifically for me and my situation.

Like a bolt out of the blue, I realized that whilst I could not change the past, I could change the present and the future by changing my thoughts. After reading numerous self-help books, I could see that my negative thoughts had been contributing to making me ill, and I knew in that moment that I could do something about it. At last there was a way I could take

Beautiful Seeds of Change

responsibility for my life through changing my thoughts and manifesting what I wanted in life through positive affirmations and belief.

I came to understand that why we end up on a particular path is a combination of attitude and choice, be it conscious or subconscious and both can feed each other, in a negative or positive way. We can choose the path we want to walk just as we can choose the thoughts we want to think. If we surround ourselves with negativity, then that is what we will attract. If we surround ourselves with positive thoughts, then we will attract positive things into our lives.

I also came to understand that there is a positive in everything, whether we can see what it is at the time or not. Finding a positive outcome can give purpose to what has happened, so that even the most difficult of situations can be turned around.

ACCEPTANCE & LETTING GO

> *When you forgive and let go, not only does a huge weight drop off your shoulders, but the doorway to your own self-love opens.*
>
> *~ Louise Hay*

Armed with this new knowledge, I knew that in order for me to move forward, I first had to accept and let go of the past and that in doing so, this would leave me free to move forward, love and accept myself and truly heal.

We tend to cling to the past because it can be a form of protection; we believe that if it is constantly in our mind, we can prevent it from happening again. Unfortunately, this can have a reverse effect in that by clinging to the past, we can draw more of the same into our circle.

It can also be difficult letting go of something that has been part of our life for so long. We can see it as our raison d'etre and without it; we can feel quite naked and vulnerable. It is sometimes hard to accept that something happened and there was no reason for it, it just was. We have to understand and come to accept that we cannot control everything.

We can fear letting go because we are afraid of the future, of what might replace what we are letting go. Fear is natural. In Susan Jeffers' book, *Feel the Fear and Do It Anyway*, she says that "underlying our fears is lack of trust in ourselves." So part of letting go is trusting in ourselves by taking ownership and responsibility for our own lives. We can't change the past; we don't know what the future will bring, so we have to live in the present.

The physical problem we have is that the more we cling to the past, the more it drains us of our energy. I can vouch for this, I was exhausted all the time. I kept trying to find reasons why I had been through all that I had. I kept trying to rationalise it, my mind was constantly looking at the "what ifs." I was forever beating myself up trying to remember what I could not remember. The more I could not rationalise what had happened, the more frustrated I became. The more frustrated I became, the angrier I became, and the angrier I became, the sicker I became.

So I had to let everything go. After I had moved to England, I found a beautiful and peaceful wood, where I continued to do my meditations. I went to this place and let myself become still. I allowed myself to breath in the peace and the silence, and become one with all that surrounded me. I then opened my arms and said:

- I accept that what has come to pass cannot be changed.

- I accept that it is me who is still living, and that I will live.

- I accept that I have lost some of my memories, but that I will make new ones.

- I accept that it is okay to grieve all that I have lost, but I will celebrate what I will find.

- I accept that life can be too short, and I will live each day as if it is my last.

- I let go of that which I cannot change and accept responsibility for that which I can change.

- I accept that I am enough just as I am.

And, I let it all go. I had reached the point where I could no longer carry the burden as it was just too heavy and I simply let it all go. Once I had made the choice, it was as simple as that.

A surge of life pulled me from the dead. I gave up mental contamination and started building a spiritual foundation. Something happened inside of me. I stepped into my true identity.

~ Rev. Michael Beckwith

I felt beautiful warmth envelop me. I felt my whole body lift. It felt like the wings of an angel had wrapped around me. I cried again, but this time it was with tears of relief. I could see the light at the end of the tunnel.

GIVING FORGIVENESS

Forgiveness is a gift you give yourself.

~ Susanne Somers

Forgiveness is one of the most difficult but necessary things to do, and although I had started on my healing journey, it took many years before I was able to do so. How could I possibly forgive the man who raped me, or my ex-fiancé for leaving me, my parents for taking away my identity, my ex-husband for making me miss the most important years of my son's life? How could I forgive my babies for dying? How could I possibly forgive myself?

The thing about forgiveness is that we automatically think that forgiveness is condoning the behavior or the outcome. We think it's telling the person who we believe has wronged us that it's all okay now; that what they did doesn't matter anymore.

Forgiveness is the next step in letting go, but if you can't forgive yourself, you cannot love yourself. When you let go of something, you relinquish control of it; when you forgive, you release and *free yourself* of the need to hold onto bitterness, resentment or hatred.

Imagine you have been carrying around a huge bag on your back with a gigantic boulder in it. Imagine the weight and how hard it is to carry it upstairs, to always have it with you, getting in the way. Imagine trying to take a shower or sleep or ski or swim or simply take a walk with this gigantic boulder on your back. Imagine the constant weight of it bringing you down, slowing you down until you cannot walk on any further.

Now imagine cutting the ropes that bind it to you. Imagine walking away and leaving the boulder on the side of the road. Imagine how light you feel and how much easier your life will be without this boulder on your back.

That is forgiveness.

Forgiveness is freeing *you* from a great burden. It is not saying that the behavior or the action was acceptable. It is not saying that you will allow it to happen again in the future. It is not saying that you are opening the door to the person you are forgiving, nor is it pretending it never happened.

It is freeing you from wasting any more energy on the individual or situation and allowing yourself to focus on the positives and on what is truly important in your life. Forgiveness also helps us become more compassionate and understanding of the frailties of mankind and with that gives us a deeper sense of peace within our own lives.

You don't have to forgive the person face-to-face. You can write a letter that you don't have to send; you can find a quiet place and forgive them in your mind or you can simply shrug your shoulders and decide you have had enough and just shout out loud – "You're all forgiven! I don't want you on my back anymore!" The forgiveness is for you, and how you do it is up to you as well.

Forgiveness was not easy for me but I knew I would never move forward unless I gave it. I tried to forgive from a position of compassion, so I forgave the boy who raped me, and rationalized that he must not have thought very much of himself if he felt that rape was the only way he could have a relationship with a girl. I then forgave myself for not shouting louder, not fighting any harder than I did, and for filling my life with hatred and bitterness as a result.

I forgave my parents for not being the parents I wanted them to be and rationalized that they must have been frightened of what would happen to me if I had a baby so young; they may have feared what the neighbors would think and that they probably thought they were doing the right thing at the time. I then forgave myself for not being the daughter they wanted me to be.

I forgave the doctors and nurses at the hospital for doing what they thought was best for me and for not seeing me as a person in my own right, capable of making my own decisions; and I then forgave myself for not standing up to them and making my needs known.

I forgave myself for not being able to save my children and for not being able to find a place to live for my son and me. With each act of forgiveness, I felt the weight on my shoulders getting lighter and lighter.

I forgave many people, and I forgave myself for many things: for losing my spirituality, for holding onto bitterness, for selfishly locking myself away and hiding from everything and everyone, for being afraid.

Beautiful Seeds of Change

The more I forgave, the more I could find a compassionate understanding as to why these things might have happened. Like me, the people I forgave were doing the best that they could at the time, and I tried to understand the grief, fear and heartaches they were experiencing in their own lives. The forgiveness was cathartic, and I felt a light go on within me. I truly felt that life could go on, and I could now move forward.

LEARNING TO LOVE YOURSELF

Be kind to yourself. Begin to love and approve of yourself.

~ Louise Hay

Learning to love yourself should be easy, shouldn't it? I mean, we live with ourselves twenty four hours a day, seven days a week. We know what we like and don't like, so why is it so hard? The simple fact is that our belief systems get in the way, the awful little critical voice that we have in our heads gets in the way, and self-doubt gets in the way. We are our own worst critics, comparing ourselves to others, finding every flaw, convinced that we would be better "if only."

Well, before we can move one step forward, we have to learn to love, appreciate and approve of ourselves. If we can't love ourselves, we cannot truly love anyone else.

Loving yourself is about accepting who you are, warts and all, because that is what makes you so unique and beautiful, and it is important to embrace your uniqueness.

Just look around you at nature. Everything is different and diverse. No two leaves are the same; no two blades of grass are the same; no two snowflakes are the same. There are so many colours in nature and the diversity of the plants and animals on this earth is spectacular. It is this diversity in nature that inspires such awe and also provides us with such abundance. By the same token, nature can be barren, full of dust, bereft of flora and fauna. But it is these two extremes that create a balance in the natural world.

Now look at us. We are all different and diverse. No two people are exactly the same; even twins have something that differentiates one from the other. We are different colours, different heights, different weights, we speak different languages. This diversity is also awe-inspiring. By the same token, we are not perfect either; we all have imperfections or things about us that we cannot change; we all have strengths and weakness, but we ALL have something special that we bring to this world, and *that* is what makes us each unique and special and beautiful. Rather than finding your faults, find joy in your uniqueness because self-respect, a positive self-image and unconditional self-acceptance will help spark the light within you.

Loving ourselves is not about being arrogant or feeling we are better than anyone else. It is about appreciating ourselves and what we can bring to the world simply by being us! It is realizing and accepting that we are as worthy as anyone else.

After years of self-esteem issues, I found the concept of loving myself a difficult one but I knew if I was to continue my healing journey, I would need to learn to love myself. On top of that, I now knew that illness is created and sustained by a lack of self-worth, and it was apparent that I was suffering in a big way in that department. In spite of what I had accomplished so far, if I continued to nurture self-doubts, I would remain ill and unhappy.

I started with little things, like allowing myself long, hot, pampering bubble baths where I learned to appreciate my body. An important part of Louise's philosophy was highlighting the importance of mirror work. She felt that self-approval and self-acceptance were vital to positive change, so every day, I would look in the mirror and rather than trying to find fault, I started talking to myself about the many positive things about me:

- I have strength of character to have gone through what I have gone through and come out the other end!

- I have lovely eyes.

- I am a beautiful and compassionate person.

- I love and approve of myself.

Although it was hard at first, the more I spoke to myself, the easier it became, and the more I started to believe what I was saying. I started eating, sleeping and feeling better; I was walking taller, and dressing smarter. I smiled more, laughed more, and I came to believe that I could become whatever I wanted to become. People were noticing the difference. I was noticing the difference. I was becoming comfortable in my skin.

THE POWER OF POSITIVE THINKING

It has been scientifically proven that an affirmative thought is hundreds of times more powerful than a negative thought.

~ Rev. Michael Beckwith

Beautiful Seeds of Change

The power of positive thinking changed my life. Rather than dwelling on my negative past and seeing negatives in everything, I made a conscious decision to create only positive thoughts not only for the present but for the future. I also decided to reframe how I thought about my past and for me, it had the most wonderful consequences.

Imagine that your thoughts are magnets. When you have a thought, it sends out a powerful "pull," and whatever you are thinking will come back to you. This means that if you are focusing on the negatives or what you don't want, that is exactly what you will draw into your life; and conversely, if you focus on the positives and what you do want, that is what will be drawn into your life.

In his book *Know How to Be Rich*, Robert Anthony explained that: "What you think equals what you feel, and what you feel equals how you vibrate, and how you vibrate equals what you attract."

This means that, without ever realizing it, we can, with our words, subconsciously decide to take a certain path, *even if it is not the one we want or we intended to take*, and the results can be disastrous to us physically, mentally, emotionally and spiritually. We can end up in a terrible cycle of self-deprivation, destructive behavior and denial of our innermost needs, which can result in feelings of failure, worthlessness, self-hate, bitterness, resentment and hopelessness *simply because we are thinking negative thoughts*. If we continue in this cycle, we can end up walking down an unfulfilling path of continuous unhappiness, depression and despair because our negative thoughts have continued to attract negative happenings.

Physically, when we are negative, our body releases toxins into our bloodstream, which cause more unhappiness, negativity and depression. When we are in a positive state of mind, our "happy hormones" are activated, which brings us into a natural state of relaxation and happiness.

By changing our negative thoughts into positive thoughts or actions, we can bring about change in our lives so easily, but the key is that there has to be a willingness to accept change, and a belief that it is entirely possible to receive what we desire.

Even in its simplest form, changing a negative thought into a positive one can make a huge difference to the way you think about things in your life. One crucial example for me was changing the phrase "I am not a bad person" to "I am a good person."

Focusing on the negative words "bad person" had the effect of continually bringing in bad memories, unhappiness, frustration and anger.

Even though I did not think I was a bad person, I was focusing on the words so much that I was continuously brought back to my old belief systems. It became a negative cycle. By reframing the words to "good person," I began focusing on all the things that were good about me, and the effects not only brought about a change in how I felt about myself, but it was obvious to others as well, and good things began coming into my life.

> Sometimes life's Hell. But hey! Whatever
> gets the marshmallows toasty!
>
> ~ J. Andrew Helt

Positive change is not just about positive thinking; it's also about putting a positive spin on everything you do in your life, and I found that adding in a dash of humour made it a lot more fun and a lot easier!

Take something as simple as washing the dishes or cleaning the oven. They are only chores if we choose to make them so. I began to see chores as positive voyages of re-discovery, a way of remembering special or important times and a way to visualize those things that I wanted to bring into my life. I found that I could find something good in everything, even those mundane chores I couldn't get away from.

Instead of seeing a carbon mountain I would have to chisel off the bottom of the oven, I saw the Cinnamon and Brown Sugar muffins I had baked for a friend who had been feeling sad and needed something to cheer her up. Instead of dirty dishes, I saw a grateful husband who had enjoyed a hot meal after a long day at work. Instead of seeing endless laundry to hang out to dry, I saw it as a time to appreciate a beautiful blue sky, to feel a warm cleansing wind and to embrace a wonderful connection with the natural world around me.

Another technique I developed was using ironing as a means of wakeful meditation. The reality of life is that we are subjected to stress and negatives every day of our lives. These can range from small, insignificant ones like the cat threw up on the carpet again, to major, life altering ones such as a death in the family, divorce or an unexpected disability.

The key is how we react to them. My Nana always said that if you spend your day worrying over something that is out of your control, you have wasted that day. I realized that it was good advice, and one day I realized that ironing could be therapeutic and help me release all those unnecessary negatives and worries.

Beautiful Seeds of Change

Here is how it works: I randomly split the ironing into two piles: one represents things that are out of my control and the other is things that are in my control. With relaxing music playing, I start ironing the "No" pile. As I iron, I visualize that whatever I am ironing is a worry or negative over which I have no control. As each wrinkle is smoothed out, I see that particular worry or negative becoming less and less important. I have no control over it, so as the wrinkles get ironed, I gradually let the worry and negative association go.

When I have finished the "No" pile, I start on the "Yes" pile. These are worries, negatives or stresses that are in my control. As I iron, I breathe deeply, focus on the problem and then let my mind go wandering. I focus on the wrinkles, and how I can best smooth them out.

Your mind is a powerful tool and letting it "free think" is a natural way of finding a solution. How you really feel about a situation will come into your mind quite easily using this technique. Your "gut" instinct will direct you, and you will intuitively know what you must do.

For example, if you are in the wrong job, the thought of a new job will enter your mind. Once the thought comes into your mind, use the rhythm of the ironing and the smoothing of the wrinkles to reinforce your confidence and take the decision to find a new job.

If fear of change or a lack of confidence gets in the way, compare an old wrinkled pair of trousers (your worry) with a newly pressed pair (your solution). Ask yourself how difficult it was to change one to the other, then focus on that. It was easy, wasn't it?

What I found was that once I had taken the decision to iron out the wrinkles in my life and view them in a different, more positive way, the rest followed naturally.

When patterns are broken, new worlds emerge.

~ Tuli Kupferberg

I realized that, as my inner voice had revealed to me, there were indeed many good things in my life; all I had to do was look around.

Part of the healing process also meant finding some positive ways of coping with some of the things I had "lost" in my life. There were many things I could not change, relive or bring back but as Anne Morrow Lindbergh, the famous author and aviator once said: "One must lose one's life in order to find it."

I could not change the fact that my children had died, but I could keep their spirits alive and my emotions balanced in doing so. I had always had a love for needlework, so I decided to set up two scholarships in memory of my daughters which were given to two girls each year to learn the art. On their birthdays, I make or buy something that they would have liked, and I donate it to a children's hospice or charity.

One of the most positive and healing things that I did was to write several articles on losing a child, and I was amazed at the response I received from other parents who had felt the same way, and they all said that the articles had helped them. This stirred within me a long ago silenced calling to help others. I knew in that moment that this was what I would do: help others through my own experiences.

I did not know what had happened to my son, but I could hope he was well and happy. I knew intuitively that he was still alive somewhere, and I continued to believe absolutely that we would one day be reunited.

I could not bring back my memory, but I could create new ones. Losing my memory turned out to be a gift of freedom. I was allowed to forget what was unnecessary to remember and had been given a blank canvas where I could learn and experience new things and plant the new seeds of my life, I could aspire to anything I wanted to, and I could become the person that I was meant to be.

One by one, my losses were replaced with the positive lessons I had learned from them and the new experiences that would come out of them. The seeds of darkness had cracked, and the shoots of new life had broken through the soil and were reaching for the stars.

I had found the light within.

INTO THE GARDEN WITH GRATITUDE

Gratitude helps you to grow and expand; gratitude brings joy and laughter into your life and into the lives of all those around you.

~ Eileen Caddy

In my healing journey, gratitude was to become the "glue" that brought everything together and helped me form firm foundations in my life and enabled me to move from a place of negativity to a place of hope, kindness and light.

Gratitude is being thankful and grateful for everyone and everything in your life, past, present and in the future. It is a profound feeling of appreciation and a connection to our deepest roots, our "true self." It is not only understanding that all our experiences are gifts but that in expressing gratitude for those gifts, we can bring even more wonderful things into our lives.

Gratitude is not just about being thankful for the big things but for all things. Even now, we could express gratitude for the eyes that allow us to read this book, or for the hands that allow us to hold this book. We could be grateful for the cereal we had for breakfast, the packaging that held the cereal, the factory and all within it that produced the cereal, the machines and people that harvested the grain. We could express gratitude for the seeds, the soil, the sun and rain that nurtured the seed, the process of germination, the magnificence of life itself. When we express our gratitude in this way, we can see that there is so much to be grateful for; so much abundance and goodness that surrounds us and so much for which we can be thankful.

Acknowledging all the gifts that I had overlooked in my life filled me with a sense of overwhelming love, and filled my entire being with a light so comforting and healing; it is difficult to put it into words. It was an epiphany, a sudden realization that I had not lost everything, but that I had found myself and my purpose.

I began to keep a journal. Every morning I would write positive affirmations for the day, and every evening I wrote down all the things that I was grateful for that day. I found that more and more good things began coming into my life, and that there were more and more things for which I could express gratitude.

I beat the cancer and have been clear ever since. My son and I were reunited in 1987, and it was as if we had never been separated; our bond had not been broken and remains strong. My career reached heights that I never thought possible. I met and married my soul-mate.

There was to be one more trial, though, only this time I welcomed the challenge and the lessons I learned.

I am only one, but still I am one. I cannot do everything, but still I can do something. And because I cannot do everything I will not refuse to do the something that I can do.

~ Helen Keller

On 28 March 2000, a freak accident left me facing one of the biggest challenges of my life: the fact that I could no longer walk. I had no feeling from the waist down, I could not control my bodily functions, and I could barely lift my arms or move my upper body without excruciating pain. I had lost the ability to take care of myself.

Just over a month after the accident, the company I worked for had to let me go, and the car went with it. Losing a full and generous salary had a serious effect on our finances, and we had to move into a much smaller house.

After months of medical intervention, I was put in a wheelchair, told there was nothing more they could do, and that I had to learn to live life as a disabled person. Well, my exact words were "Bugger that for a laugh!" I did not listen to them because I believed absolutely that I would walk again one day. I was well armed with the tools I needed to get through this, too.

I planned my own rehabilitation, which started with acceptance: "I love myself just the way I am" and "I am sexy in my wheelchair," earning me the nickname Ma Hot Wheels from my friends!

Although my movement was limited, I decided to use my disability to help others and affirmed daily that "the lessons I learn each day help me to help others." I taught myself web design and e-commerce, and started an on-line business that helped crafters and stay-at-home mums start businesses on the Internet, and I became a consultant on disabled access for the local council planning department.

It was also important to affirm the fact that I was going to walk again: "I am perfect, whole and complete. I choose to have healthy energy coursing through every part of my body. I am free" and "I am grateful for every step I take."

Many people asked how I could be grateful being stuck in a wheelchair, but I was. It gave me the opportunity to stop and smell the roses. It's amazing how much life we miss at ground level when we are standing, and I grew to appreciate life in the slow lane.

I was grateful for the opportunity to reassess my life, to reconnect with myself and to give of myself to others. I was grateful to experience the difficulties of disabled access and to contribute to making it better through my work with the council. I was grateful for the opportunity to learn new skills and help others. I was grateful to be alive.

I was grateful for my legs and never gave up believing I would walk again. I visualized myself walking again. I believed in it so absolutely that the day I felt a pinprick of feeling in one leg, I thought: "well, it's about time," and then I wept with gratitude.

That pinprick of feeling spread and in 2004, I learned to walk again. In 2006, I ran a 5km race for charity, and I have run two 10km races since.

Eleven years later, I am still grateful. The worst experiences I have had in my life have also been the greatest gifts in my life for they have taught me love, patience, compassion and understanding. They have taught me that there is no greater gift than the gift of life.

And the garden? The lonely path that led to an abyss of weeds and neglect did indeed become a winding, glorious doorway into a new and exciting future that began when I founded Life Seeds.

I am home. All is well.

About the Author

Kailah Eglington is an inspirational speaker, teacher and writer and the Chairman and Founder of Life Seeds, an organization that helps individuals transform their lives and conquer physical and emotional adversity through the power of positive thinking, gratitude and forgiveness. She is a certified executive coach and mentor, life coach, licensed Heal Your Life® facilitator and stress management, relaxation therapy, Reiki Seichem and Meditation practitioner.

She resides in England where she enjoys nature, animals and is also the Chief Executive Officer of an ethical medical research charity.

ke@lifeseeds.co.uk
www.lifeseeds.co.uk

Acknowledgments

To Mike for his unwavering belief and support. To my dearest friend, Janet, for her encouragement, wisdom, love and unending hugs. To my angel babies whose light from Heaven nurtures me. To my son, Joshua, my miracle and a greater teacher than he knows. To the teachers and mentors who helped me along my journey and gave me the courage to share my experiences. To the Universe for blessing me with my life in order that I might help others. To all who made this book possible - may it bring light, peace and hope to all that read it.

Shellie Couch

Dedicated to the love of my life, my husband, who is my soul mate and has been there for me through it all and has always loved me for me.

Beautiful Seeds of Change

Chapter 7

YOU ARE SMART; YOU WILL FIGURE THIS OUT

How in the world did I end up here?" I thought. "And how will I ever get past this?" These thoughts raced through my head as I sat there, locked in. I looked around me, at the others in their pajamas and robes and slippers. I looked down at myself, wearing ripped shorts and a wrinkled and unkempt brown man's tee with little Warner Brother's Tasmanian Devils twirling about in rows of green. All I wanted to do was cry. I wanted nothing more than for the pain to stop … just stop. All I could envision, though, was it getting worse and worse.

In order for you to understand, I suppose I should tell you a bit more about myself, my history.

I was a happy child with a happy childhood. I have wonderful parents who love me dearly and who raised me in a kind, fair and supportive way. The problems were with me, they were internal. These internal problems began around my eighth grade year.

I remember, back in those days, back in the horrid middle school years, being very happy and very sad, all for no reason, within the same day. That was how a lot of my days were, in retrospect. I could be laughing and smiling and having a great time, and minutes later be crying and sad, not able to find a reason to smile.

I can see that clearly, now, looking back, but in the thick of it all, I just thought it was normal teen age mood swings. I saw other girls my age flip back and forth through a wide range of emotions. I think we all just thought that our lives were just that dramatic and that it was normal to go through a huge range of emotions.

During those dark days of eighth grade, I made a couple of half-hearted attempts to end it all. They weren't well thought out, and they weren't taken seriously. Looking back now, I am glad they weren't, because without the experiences that I have had, I wouldn't be who I am now … but I am getting ahead of myself.

The summer between my eighth grade and freshman years of school, I was fairly reckless. Well, let's be fair, I was fairly reckless from that summer on through my high school years. But I put myself in some precarious situations that fateful summer before high school that would forever change how I viewed myself and the world around me.

I was date raped that summer. I was fourteen years old, and I blamed myself for being stupid enough to place myself in a situation that would allow it. I had agreed to sneak out of the house to meet a boy that I didn't know well at all. There was quite a bit of pressure to go all the way. I said no, and I meant no, but I wasn't sure enough of myself to say it in a way that let him know that I meant it. I said no repeatedly, with tears streaming down my face, but I never said it with force. I gave up. I laid there with tears streaming down my face, saying no over and over again in almost a whisper. It was my first experience with sex, and I didn't tell a soul. I was ashamed and embarrassed.

I did, however, change how I viewed my body, myself. I didn't find myself worthy of treating myself with respect, and, in doing so, I found myself again in a situation for which I blamed myself.

Mere days after that first experience, at only fourteen years old, I found myself in the arms of a twenty four or five year old man. I was again horrified that I was stupid enough to carelessly place myself in such a situation. I was foolish enough to think that he cared about me, but was even more embarrassed and ashamed when I found out that I was just the night's diversion and didn't mean a thing to him. It was the beginning of years of promiscuity.

I went through high school going from relationship to relationship with intermittent one night flings in between, searching for someone, something that could fill that emptiness. I used sex. I always thought that it would make me feel worthy, loved. What it actually did was make me feel even more worthless and ashamed.

I tried alcohol during that time, and did have a couple of binge drinking experiences, but found that I didn't like feeling out of control in that way. I felt out of control enough without that.

I was a good student and planned to graduate at the end of first semester of my senior year of high school. With only a few weeks of classes left, I discovered that my boyfriend was cheating on me. About a week after breaking up with him, I found out I was pregnant with his baby.

During this crazy time, the universe brought a wonderful man into my life. Somehow he was able to see me through all the nonsense and to love me in spite of myself. That poor, loving soul married me, not really knowing

Beautiful Seeds of Change

what he was getting into, but he has stuck around through it all.

That same loving guy, after years of my insanity, of unpredictable mood swings, of seeing me at the highest of highs and at the depths of agony, finally convinced me to go see a doctor, a psychiatrist.

I went to the psychiatrist after years of cajoling, and only because I was in a period of really bleak and dark days. I think this is why my husband was able to convince me to go at that time because I just wanted to feel better. But I felt I was going just to basically admit that, yes, I was really crazy after all.

I remember sitting in the small, cramped office and having tears roll down my face as I described how hopeless I was feeling. I told the psychiatrist how tired I was, and that I knew I shouldn't feel this way, but I just couldn't see the light at the end of the tunnel.

I told him that my head hurt, but I was very careful not to tell him that what I described as a headache wasn't a "normal" headache, but that my head hurt because it was just so LOUD in my head. I wanted help, but I didn't want him to know just how crazy I really was.

The doctor diagnosed me with major depression – because I withheld information, and he didn't ask enough questions about historical behavior. He prescribed a wonderful little pink pill that boosted my mood to very good within a week. It then began to become less effective as my body became acclimated to it. I called up the doctor and said that I was beginning to feel that it was becoming less effective. He called in an increased dose.

Within two days of the increased dose, I was flying high. Really high. I began to have some incredibly grandiose illusions of who I was and what I was capable of doing. I did some things that hurt those that loved me the most. I decided that I didn't really need medication, because I had this under control, I had life by the reins, and I was invincible! I abruptly stopped taking the medication.

In just a few short days, I was more depressed than I have ever been in my entire life. Not only did I feel like giving up, I did. I didn't try to kill myself, I didn't even have the energy nor did I care enough to try that. I simply just gave up.

I started walking. I dropped my purse. I left it where it fell, and I kept walking. I came to a fence and ripped my shorts climbing over it so I could keep walking. I lost a shoe. I kept walking, right down the side of the highway. Some random guy in a van pulled up and asked if I wanted a ride.

I just shrugged. I didn't care what happened to me. I got in the van.

Someone must have been looking out for me because this random guy in the van was so very nice. He talked with me, or at me, I guess, because I just sat there glassy-eyed. Eventually he got me to say where I lived, but I'm not really sure how, or how long it took because I was so depressed that I didn't care. I didn't cry, I just didn't want to feel anything. He took me home and gave me the *Book of Mormon* that I still have to this day.

My husband was there at home, because, again, the universe was looking out for me. He should have been at work. He didn't even let me come inside the house. He put me in the car and took me to the hospital.

"How in the world did I end up here?" I thought. "And how will I ever get past this?" These thoughts raced through my head as I sat there, locked in. I looked around me, at the others in their pajamas and robes and slippers. I looked down at myself, wearing ripped shorts and a wrinkled and unkempt brown man's tee with little Warner Brother's Tasmanian Devils twirling about in rows of green. All I wanted to do was cry. I wanted nothing more than for the pain to stop … just stop. All I could envision, though, was it getting worse and worse.

I sat there in the psych ward and looked at the doors. I was locked in. I couldn't believe it. How could I have felt so on top of everything just days before? I was now diagnosed with Manic-Depression (Bi-Polar Disorder, as it is now known). I was given medications, a whole cocktail of them, which left me feeling flat. I didn't feel as if I had any emotions at all.

I was visited by the on duty psychologist. I don't remember his name, but I remember that he wore a ball cap and spoke in baseball analogies. He met with a group of us, and then individually. I spoke with him and told him about the noise in my head, that sometimes I got what I called headaches, which were just noise in my head. It was like a cacophony of people talking to each other, a thousand conversations all going on at once in a huge gym where the acoustics just echoed.

I told him that I hated feeling like I wasn't "normal" and that I was being forced to take medication that left me feeling like I had no emotions.

He was so kind. He just let me ramble for quite some time. When he finally spoke, he asked if I had any knowledge of the disease that I had been diagnosed with. When I told him that I didn't, only that I knew that I was crazy, he gave me a book. It was an average sized book that described the disease and how others had found ways to cope.

He then told me, "Shellie, you seem like a smart girl. I'm betting you have a fairly high IQ. You will figure this out."

Sometimes you know when you have a moment that is life changing, and other times you are just too involved with all that is going on to see that moment for what it is. I missed it. I had no idea how much those few words would impact my life.

After being released from the hospital, I simply got right back into "real" life. I read that book. I started taking charge of my life. Over and over again I would go back to those words. "You are a smart girl … You will figure this out."

Several months after being out of the hospital, I decided, against my husband's advice, against my doctor's advice, to wean myself off of the medications. I was determined to live my life feeling my feelings, but not only feeling them, but managing them.

It was rough going at first. I learned to journal. This helped me to determine things that were triggers for me. If I started getting down, I learned through journaling that I needed to adjust what type of music that I listened to, to fight the urge to stay in bed, to tell myself positive things, to get out and enjoy nature.

If I started getting too high, I learned to rein myself in. If I felt too high, I would put off purchases until I had a chance to discuss them with someone instead of just spending the money right then. I learned that nature was also beneficial when I was feeling too high. It was a little harder to control, because feeling high feels really good, but can lead to agitation and other self-destructive behavior. Through journaling, though, I was able to adjust my behavior.

Once I was doing better at self-regulating my moods, I was hooked on improving myself. My life was already much better than it was before. I began reading Dr. Wayne Dyer, who I had found through a PBS program. I read Louise Hay and began devouring books from other Hay House authors.

I began learning about the Law of Attraction, first through *The Secret*, and then Esther and Jerry Hicks and Abraham.

People began appearing in my life that would lead me to other things that were important to me. I learned about Neuro-Linguistic Programming via a special on TV with Paul McKenna. I joined a "Paul McKenna" group on line to have support in using the techniques and met a wonderful friend, who then introduced me to Emotional Freedom Technique (EFT) and to the works of Andy Dooley and his brother, who may be a bit better known, Mike Dooley. I started getting "Notes from the Universe."

I was introduced to a wonderful Zumba instructor, who invited me and several of her other friends who had similar ideas to begin meeting to explore the works of Louise Hay. It was the beginning of a special and wonderful group of friends that still meets and co-creates to this day, and has been instrumental in me finding my joy. We still love Mamma Hay, as we affectionately call her, but we have expanded and are open to learning from whatever and whomever the universe leads us to.

Out of all of this, the one thought that keeps coming back to me, is hearing that I am a smart girl and that I will figure this out. That thought has taught me responsibility.

I am responsible for me. I am responsible for everything that has happened to me.

This may not be a popular thing to tell a victim of rape, or someone who has a disease, but it is true. It is all in the perspective, though. If you are telling a victim of rape that she is responsible, and she takes that on as blame then it would not be productive. However, if you tell a victim of rape that she is responsible, and she takes it on as empowerment, it can be very cathartic.

I had no responsibility for my rapist's actions. I did, however, have responsibility for placing myself in harm's way. I can change that in the future. I can be more selective about with whom and where I go. I can take charge of my reaction to what happened. I do not have to be a victim. I choose to be not only a survivor of my past, but a THRIVER. I didn't survive a horrific event, I learned from it. I learned not only to protect myself, but I learned about myself.

The same can be said of everything in my life. I can CHOOSE what I take from it. Do I choose to take on a victim role, do I wallow in the depression, or do I learn from it? Do I curse it happening, or do I give thanks that this experience shaped the person I have become? I am RESPONSIBLE for making that choice. Responsibility equals empowerment in my book. I am empowered by knowing that in every situation, I am responsible for where I am, for how I react, for what I gain from it.

I feel responsible now to let you know that your moment that changes everything, your beautiful seed of change, can be something as simple as a few words. Your words, something that doesn't seem that profound to you, could be someone else's seed of change. As you go out about your daily business remember to make your words matter, make them kind. You could inspire huge change and growth in someone and never even know it. Sometimes just being given a tool or two and the permission to figure it out for themself is all someone needs.

I am sure that baseball cap wearing psychologist has no idea the impact those few words had on me, but if he is reading this, I want to take this opportunity to tell him that I truly appreciate him.

You, my dear reader, YOU are smart. You will figure this out.

About the Author

SHELLIE COUCH is creator and owner of Practice Living Joy, where she provides group and individual coaching and workshops for living with joy in the present moment. She is often called upon as a speaker on the topics of the power of joy and overcoming personal obstacles.

Shellie resides in rural Inman, Kansas with her husband. She enjoys spending time with her three adult children and her two grandchildren. She also enjoys travel and time with friends and enjoys them even more when the two can be combined.

shellie.couch@practicelivingjoy.com
www.PracticeLivingJoy.com

Acknowledgments

I would like to thank all those that have been a part of my transformative journey: My husband and children who have stuck by me through it all, and my "Saturday Sistas" without whom I would still be floundering. Thanks for everything, I love you all!

Robyn Podboy

Dedicated to all of my mentors who have inspired me.

Chapter 8

HARVESTING AUTHENTICITY

As I was heading out the door to catch my flight to Arizona, I just grabbed "the book" I had bought it many months ago, but never found the time to read. This particular flight would be six hours and was the "perfect" time to be able to read it.

Sometimes I find that I am drawn to a book, and I'm not sure why. Did I hear something about the author? Or maybe it was because I thought the cover was beautiful? When I was glancing at the description it explained four simple agreements to apply to yourself to live your best life. I have been on my spiritual journey since I was very young and am kind of a junkie for the secret knowledge I believed this book was going to give me. So I had quickly bought it to add to my library of the many books I have read and applied over the years. I have enjoyed and learned from so many authors who have shared their knowledge (aka secret) to live a more authentic life.

I am a seeker for hidden wisdom and just love sharing the knowledge and methods I have been taught. When I share what I have learned, it is the most rewarding experience. Helping or guiding someone to the direction they are seeking is when I feel that I am most authentically living my life. Before leaving for Arizona, I was looking for more tools to help me deepen my knowledge on the subject of my *perception* along with enhancing the workshops which I facilitate.

I knew this book was a perfect read for me. The timing couldn't have been more ideal. The impression I had was that with only four simple tools, it would be pretty easy to apply to my life, so I began reading.

The book started speaking about *domestication* and what that suggests. To me, *domestication* is the behaviors and habits we learn as children from our parents, siblings, kids in school, people at church, along with other adults as well as our neighborhood friends. The impact from other people's opinions and reactions become really convincing to us. This is how we create in our own mind the perception of *who we are* as well as what we think *we should be*.

It turns out that the choices we make and the life we choose to live are driven by the opinions we learn from others which subsequently change what we would have chosen on our own. When I was younger this was very true for me. But as I become more authentic with who I am, I realize that I do have a choice and understand that no one can influence me, unless of course I want them to.

As I was getting deeper into the book, I was finding it a much harder read than I thought. What was the author trying to explain to me? My mind was not grasping it. How was I going to apply these "agreements"? I honestly thought I would need a private workshop to actually understand just how to do it!

These four agreements may be simple, but the author never said they were easy to do or to be able to keep as a mainstay. As I turned each page I was reminded of behaviors that I wasn't particularly proud of. I knew this insight would help me, but how was I going to do it? These are important tools I needed for my tool belt. A must have! I was excited to apply these to my life, so – "Let's roll!"

1. Be Impeccable with your Word

Speak with integrity. Say only what you mean. Avoid using the Word to speak against yourself or to gossip about others. Use the power of your Word in the direction of truth and love.

~ don Miguel Ruiz

I certainly did not speak very kindly to myself. I didn't even pay that much attention to how I spoke, or the words I used. I would, in fact, actually whisper my thoughts into words just to hear it out loud! I have said things similar to: "I'm not intelligent enough," or "not worthy enough" or "slender enough" – Blah, Blah, Blah. I could go on for 10 pages reciting my negative self-talk. Have you ever done that? Say dreadfully cruel things to *yourself* about *yourself*? This is something I have done since I was a child.

I certainly had stages in my life when I was a gossip queen, talking about "the latest" revealing things about others not thinking twice about the effects. To tell you the truth, that never did feel very good. At this moment I am thinking of all the times my words have hurt someone else, or how I have hurt myself. What a powerful affect they had on me and the others around me. Why hadn't I ever paid closer attention to how it was making me feel? I loved this insight and started to pay attention towards the words I chose to use. In my opinion, this should be taught in our schools as a required course! It would be an amazing class.

As I started to be mindful of the words I would use, I would replace "I hate" with "I'm really not into." Or, "that is so stupid" to "that's interesting."

They sounded so much nicer to say and also to hear. I could feel a different reaction or vibration, as some would say, in my body. That feeling was my gauge for using loving words and speaking truth.

I had always been a people pleaser and although I really love seeing people happy, I would not always come from a place of truth or love. I would lose my integrity and become something other than myself, all the while hating myself for not speaking my truth. Why was other people's happiness more important that mine? It seemed easier to me not to tell the truth, along with losing myself. I didn't actually know that I could speak with love and stand in truth and with that, I would be impeccable in my word. Amazing!

I remember the first time I did speak with the direction of love and truth. You see, they go hand in hand, you can't separate them. I needed to have the conversation with a friend so, before I was to meet with her I began by taking big deep breaths thinking of all that I had read.

I needed to be faultless with my words, come from a place of love, and then the truth would be revealed. I needed my words to be clean! Just breathe and send it out in love.

Doing this was so frightening to me that just the thought of it made me feel sick. I could feel my body shake! My voice would quiver. Why was I so afraid to speak from a loving place? You cannot go wrong with love and truth! Okay, so here goes….

I told my friend that I thought our friendship had outgrown itself. I felt grateful for our time together and for the laughter we had shared. I had learned so much about myself from her, but I needed to move on from the friendship so I could grow and become more of who I wanted to be.

There it was … MY truth said in a loving way! My words were not about her, they were about me. They were clean. I said them with love, and the truth was out there like a butterfly... FREE. I felt free; an exhilarating sensation came over me. I was feeling a deeper authenticity than ever before. I became more of myself than I had ever known myself to be… Awesome! I can do this!!

Words have the power to destroy or heal. When words are true and kind, they can change the world.

~Buddha

2. Don't Take Anything Personally

Nothing others do is because of you. What others say and do is a projection of their own reality. When you are unaffected to the opinions and actions of others, you won't be wounded from unnecessary suffering.

~ don Miguel Ruiz

I have to say that this agreement was a tough one for me. I had always thought that in one way or another, it's always about me. I was very insecure and vulnerable with my thoughts. I constantly felt personally responsible for the behavior of others. I took everyone and everything personally. This must have come from my *"domestication"* the author spoke about earlier. When I became aware of what people were saying paired with the words they were choosing to use, it clearly made a distinct impression of them.

One occasion in particular comes to mind which opened my eyes to help me navigate out of taking things so personally. I was facilitating a workshop with a friend of mine who lives out of state. We always work to create workshops together with a mesh of our ideas as well as our vision for what we see the end result being. This method has been working beautifully for years. It's a wonderfully creative game of ping pong producing magnificent gatherings. I believe that it works so well for the reason that we are impeccable with our words. When we speak our truth in love, the magic is revealed, then everyone benefits. There is no doubt about that!

We were working on our latest gathering when I could feel a shift in her attitude. She expressed that she felt a disconnect from me, and felt that we were not on the same page regarding the time importance. As I listened to her, I did feel personally attacked, then felt sadness combined with anger. I didn't have a chance to respond because she was interrupted and needed to "call me right back."

Wow! I thought, "Where was that coming from?" As I went back over our conversation, I could see that she was speaking about herself. She was the one feeling disconnected from the gathering, and she was the one who felt the scarcity of the time. This shift had nothing to do with me. I was very grateful for the time to actually reflect on the conversation and be able to recognize what was really being said and what was real for me. Having that interruption gave me the time not to take it personally and then to respond accordingly. If I had reacted in my old ways, I would have been very upset and wallowed in it for days. I did not react, I responded. That was a huge difference in my behavior.

To respond is positive, to react is negative.

~Zig Ziglar

Stop and take the time to really listen to what someone says or does. You will see them with a different pair of eyes. Free yourself and step into your authenticity once again!

Believe it ... It's not about you!

~R. Podboy

3. Don't Make Assumptions

Find the courage to ask questions and to express what you really want. Communicate with others as clearly as you can to avoid misunderstandings sadness and drama.

~ don Miguel Ruiz

Assumptions are usually based on our own perceptions, which can simultaneously cause us to **take things personally**. Perception is a funny thing since everyone has their own personal view about how they see life. We tend to assume that everyone else sees the world the same way we do. I know I did. Making general assumptions is hard not to do.We make assumptions when we don't understand a situation.

It is a genuine reaction to instantly fill in the missing information by making up our own story. We do this because we have to try to make sense of people and the situation. Most of the time our "made up story" is untrue which causes all kinds of misunderstandings and drama. As much as we would like to think we know what others are thinking, we simply don't know the reasons why people do the things they do or think the things they think. We know nothing until we ask them. How simple is that?

This agreement is a challenging one, and it is constant test for me. It's ironic when lessons in life that you need to master seem to come into your life over and over in different areas until you "get it." I grew up in a house which, as I look back, seemed to be a very critical one. I know that we were not aware of our behavior. We seemed to think we knew everything about everybody else lives. Even when they would tell us their truth, we would change the story to what we really thought was "the real reality." Perception is something of your very own.

You cannot wake up to any other truth than your own,
what suits one man may not suit another; therefore you
can't truly understand a person until you consider things
from his point of view.

~ Harper Lee

I was attending a seminar in California for a week. My flight arrived quite early in the morning while the seminar did not begin until late in the afternoon. I spent the day walking around the town, down to the beach, even taking a nap on the cabana lounge chairs. I was feeling that nervous excitement about what this week would bring. Periodically I would check back in at the hotel to see if I could get into my room, but no such luck.

I began to notice people doing the same as I was doing, floating around the hotel waiting to check in. I decided to devour a late lunch in the hotel's beautiful courtyard listening to soothing water fountains while the sun was shining. I noticed a woman that I had been seeing throughout the day sitting at a table in the courtyard as well enjoying her lunch. As I walked by I smiled, as I had done many other times that day when I had seen her, trying to get her attention thinking to myself, "I bet she is here for the same seminar as I am." Looking her way while smiling, I thought she would receive this as a gesture to join her, but she was not interested. So I sat alone.

As I sat eating my lunch, I kept looking over at her and started to create a whole story about the reason she was not engaging with me. I mean really, how can you not smile at someone who is smiling at you? I went into what I call the "assumption zone." I was creating a story to fit into what I assumed to be the truth. Now I was hoping that she was not attending the seminar because, after being in my assumption zone I didn't want to have anything to do with her. Huh!

It turned out to be no surprise to me that she was indeed at the same seminar (see I know everything).

Throughout the week I didn't have much to do with her during our meetings or breakout sessions until the last day of the seminar when we were paired together to work on a presentation. In my assumption, this was not going to be fun. However, as we worked together, I started to see her with a different awareness. As I was hearing her truthful, inspiring story, I realized I knew nothing about her, and my story of her that I assumed to be "spot on" was so "spot off"!

Beautiful Seeds of Change

I had created this whole "truth" for myself when all I would have had to do was ask her if she'd like to have lunch, speaking with loving, truthful words, and not take it personally that she didn't smile at me! Booyah!

I had missed out getting to know this magnificent woman all week due to my assumption – a lesson I was grateful to have learned.

Assumptions allow the best in life to pass you by.

~John Sales

Another example of this lesson for me was learned through my older brother. He has been a friend to me as well as a teacher. One time he had been suffering from a flare-up of ulcerative colitis and along with an ongoing battle of MS. During this time in his life, he spoke his words like he was trying to hurt me with them. Everything I would try to say would be returned with a slap of words!

I was convinced that if he would take care of his eating habits, this terrible condition would go away. I assumed that with all this wonderful advice I was giving him, he would surely follow it! I never had such an illness, but, of course, I knew everything about how to cure it.

Weeks turned into months as he was slowly dying. He was following his doctor's advice, taking many different medications with a few dietary changes. I was feeling very frustrated, and it was very hard for me to talk to him with the state of mind he was in. So, as a result we stopped talking for a few months. I assumed that he had enough of my advice and really didn't want to hear from me. I created a story to match my beliefs on what was happening with him and why.

Are you are coming to realize as you read this that my story was an assumption and the furthest thing from the truth? The doctors he was trusting to help him were not doing such a good job, so he and his wife took matters into their own hands. Off to the Mayo Clinic they went to find the answers. I had called to see if I could help and join them if they needed me. They received that request with loving, open arms. But I was afraid to go due to my made up story in the "assumption zone."

This was a very emotional time for them as a couple and for me as his sister. I became aware of the reasons for his behavior: He was coming from a place of absolute fear along with frustration. He was slowing dying without any doctor really taking an interest or helping him. Once again it had nothing to do with me!

I had assumed that it was all about my pushing to try helping him find the answers - my answers not his. I was taking everything personally. This situation was illustrative of agreements two and three - a double whammy! I am grateful for this lesson because it made my relationship with my brother real. We have grown into adults that love each other and understand each other on a higher level of truth than before. It's easier for us to ask without assuming, to speak in loving words and understand what each of us needs from each other.

Assumptions are the termites of relationships.

~Henry Winkler

I do want to point out that not all assumptions are bad in terms of survival, but when you are talking about what you think you know regarding other people, you need to be aware that you don't!

4. Always Do Your Best

Your best is going to change from moment to moment; it will be different when you are healthy as opposed to sick. Under any circumstance, simply do your best and you will avoid self-judgment, self-abuse and regret.

~don Miguel Ruiz

This agreement may be the one that seems to be the simplest, but it can also be a bit challenging. I used to say to my kids all the time: "If you do your best, then you can feel confident in knowing that you gave it your best shot. You can't do better than that. So let the test scores be what they will be! Your best!"

To me, doing your best doesn't mean comparing yourself to others. And by this I mean, no one else! This agreement is about "the best" for you. My best might be walking two and a half miles; yours may be running five miles. It is different for all of us.

Wake up each morning and make that commitment to yourself that you will do your best in everything that unfolds throughout this day. Perhaps doing your best means giving more of yourself at your job, or in your home life rather than watching time tick by while playing on your computer 'til the end of the day. Doing your best might mean accepting your spouse or other family members for who they are rather than being overcritical of them. This could apply to everyone you know. Accepting that they are doing the best they can for **themselves**.

One way I have found to do my best each day is waking up with this commitment that I will do my best today! Some suggestions I would like to share with you are: make better choices, be more accepting of others, and take some time to quiet your mind by meditating even if it's for five minutes. For me, it helps focus on what doing my best is. You don't have to be in a room for long periods of time - just take "a time out" and be still. Stop complaining or whining, which wastes so much time along with energy and doesn't help you get where you'd like to be. Think instead how to move forward from these thoughts.

I include using agreement number one, this keeps me moving into the direction that I want to go, instead away from it. Bring more music into your life. I love the words of "The Middle" by the artist Jimmy Eat World. Play that and dance! Take care of your body by eating healthier foods. Be grateful and feel appreciation for all life has given you. Gratitude is the most important detail to help you do your best. Don't forget to laugh! Laughter can help you see life with a different perspective and guide you to do your best. Try to see what is funny about the situation or how you are behaving about things…. it may make you laugh.

There will be many things you will be able to shift with this new awareness. Stop for a moment and think of a few that will be fun to do. These new ideas will bring you to a place of doing your best!

*Always do your best. What you plant
now, you will harvest later.*

~Og Mandino

I read a quote once that *"Reading a good book is like finding a new friend!"* I discovered that this little book with such a beautiful cover which I was so drawn to read has become a very important friend to me. In the beginning, I found that I could not wrap my mind around applying these agreements, they seemed so challenging for me. I needed to read them many, many times. don Miguel Ruiz's *The Four Agreements* has been the "Beautiful Seeds of Change" for me to live my life in the most authentic way. This magnificent book planted the seeds for me, and with just a few small changes, along with my awareness of these agreements, every day I can see the magic of perception! I am eternally grateful. I am growing, forever learning and becoming more authentic every day. I know when I change everything changes!

I change the world by changing myself. I am changing the world by loving myself, by enjoying life, by making my personal world a dream of heaven. I change myself, and just like magic, other people start to change.

~ don Miguel Ruiz

About the Author

Robyn Podboy is the Owner of "Shine Your Light Now." She is a Personal Growth Facilitator, Motivational Speaker, *Heal Your Life*® licensed workshop leader and teacher, author and poet. Robyn creates and facilitates empowering workshops and retreats to unlock your authenticity for personal growth. Robyn lives her life through the eyes of optimism and humor, helping others shine in their own light. She grew up in the northern suburb of Chicago, Illinois and now resides in Ohio with her husband and two sons.

robynpodboy@aol.com
www.shineyourlightnow.com

Acknowledgments

With much love and appreciation to my husband, Tony, for always supporting and encouraging me. To my sons, Alex and Nate, for the wisdom and grace you both have to live your life authentically. To my friends for their unwavering love and support. To Lisa Hardwick and Nancy Newman for their amazing talents and dedication to creating magic.

Lisa Hardwick

Dedicated to Christopher, Aaron and Austin - My treasures.

Chapter 9

AN AWAKENING TO CHANGE

This morning I walked outside and sat on my step with a cup of coffee as I peered into my garage at the enormous stacks of packed moving boxes. I mentally start counting - *One, two, three … forty nine, fifty.* Over fifty packed boxes were all neatly lined and ready for the big and final move on Saturday. More than half of those totes were my treasured book collection – books I have had throughout my life's journey and many which were given to me as gifts from some of the most amazing people I have had the pleasure to meet.

"My sons are going to have a FIT when they realize how heavy those are!", I thought with a grin – knowing I would probably be told that since I packed them – I was to carry them. I sipped the steaming cup of brew while I thought of all I still had to do. *Pack the guest bath, touch up paint, wash the windows ...* The list continued to grow in my mind and I felt myself experiencing a fairly powerful bout of anxiety.

I made a choice to sell my home quite a few months ago. It wasn't an easy decision to make because I love my home … but I love living my passion so much more. To continue to keep my beautiful, spacious house I would have had to sacrifice my "calling," and that was not something I was willing to do at this point in my life. Now as I looked at all my personal belongings boxed up and neatly labeled – I remind myself that all my choices are divinely guided and these major life decisions are for my best and highest good.

As your understanding of life continues to grow, you can walk upon this planet safe and secure, always moving forward toward your greater good.

~Louise Hay

Another sip of coffee and I stand up to begin another day of preparations for the upcoming big moving day. As I stood – I noticed something jumped off my jacket onto the ground in front of me. A praying mantis! OH GOSH! I was startled, and I wondered if my neighbors had heard my scream. That mantis had been crawling up the front of my jacket! I sat back down for a moment and watched the mantis. It stood and looked at me in such a calm manner. *"Wish I could feel that calm right now,"* I thought. I stood up again, told the mantis goodbye and headed back into the house.

After a couple of hours of work, I decided to go back out outside and check the mail. As soon as I opened the door – there lay the mantis on its back, directly on the step where I had been sitting just two hours before. My little friend had transitioned. Though some might think it is crazy – I gave this newfound acquaintance a proper burial right behind my home in a beautiful wooded area. The fresh air and the beautiful trees seemed to revive me. My mind seemed to become much clearer. It was as if this small mantis decided to move on at this time to help me to get myself outside and soak up some sunshine and breathe some much needed fresh air.

Later in the day I researched the praying mantis. What I found brought me such peace and clarity. I learned the praying mantis comes to us when we need serenity, calmness and peace in our lives. Needless to say, it hadn't been very serene the past few weeks with all of the negotiations, packing and simply the sentiments of change I had been experiencing.

An appearance is usually made by the mantis when our lives have been saturated with such an excess of commotion, pandemonium, and professional responsibilities that we tend to lose touch with the inner voice because of peripheral mayhem we have created for ourselves.

Upon watching the mantis after she had jumped away from me, I could clearly see the reasoning of the symbolism of the praying mantis as she conveys tolerance, fortitude and tranquility. The praying mantis is ever-steady in taking her time and goes about her life at a hushed rate, and these mannerisms attributed to her being a representation of contemplation as well as meditation. Ah – now I understand. Through all the present chaos of change, how long had it been since I had practiced a deep meditation? I actually wake up every morning and go to bed each evening in gratitude – however for the past couple of weeks, I was leading a life of "busy-ness" where I didn't devote that important time for deep deliberation.

Learn to become still. And to take your attention away from what you don't want, and all the emotional charge around it, and place your attention on what you wish to experience.

~Reverend Michael Bernard Beckwith

Upon further research I learned the praying mantis on no account attempts movement until she is absolutely certain it is for her best interest. She has been extensively respected in China due to her mindful behavior.

I realized my encounter with the praying mantis was a significant point for me to examine my life balance and to ensure my mind, body and spirit were all in agreement together so I could be at my ultimate best during these days of alteration. I knew it was in my best interest to be aware, become calm and devote time for deep meditation while being more mindful of the choices I was making with my thoughts as well as my schedule.

Today, I am grateful I was reminded to be mindful, to enjoy the sun and the fresh air, to call on my inner spirit even more so when I am in the middle of commotion and disorder which seem to take my focus off of what is really most important – a deep relationship with Spirit.

There was a time when I prayed to a Spirit I did not know.

I was always front and center at church. I was also known to be the "special music" performer a few Sundays each year, and was typically known to be one of the first to sign up for small group participation and volunteer work. I prayed reverentially for gratitude and for divine guidance. But it wasn't until an amazing awakening that I actually knew "who" or "what" I was praying to. This was the day that my life changed.

I remember that day clearly and I am certain it is an event I will never forget. I was in the midst of abysmal depression, and I was quickly losing ground with this particular episode. I hadn't showered in days, I was depleted and I felt defeated. Weeping uncontrollably while kneeling in front of my fireplace with my forehead against the floor – I "felt" it. "Felt what?" you ask.

I felt the most amazing calmness I had ever experienced in my life. I lay still for a moment longer and then I "heard" the words to guide me to an interventional awakening. I "heard" for the first time in my life the Spirit I had been praying to since I was eight years old. The "voice" wasn't at all what I expected – I suppose I predicted something deep and masterful like a "Morgan Freeman" type voice, but it wasn't like that at all. No, the feeling and the voice was calm and serene. It was a feeling like the deepest most unconditional love imaginable. I knew at that moment my life was about to change. I was about to experience a path which I had unknowingly been preparing to travel my entire life. I knew without a shadow of a doubt I was chosen to make a difference in the lives of many people who would be presented to me in the not so far off future. I became filled with gratitude.

The enlightened give thanks for what most people take for granted. As you begin to be grateful for what most people take for granted, that vibration of gratitude makes you more receptive to good in your life.

~Reverend Michael Bernard Beckwith

On this particular day I experienced more ambition, determination, motivation and hope than ever before. This day led me to many tools and teachers where I was able to regroup, revise and rebuild. What I built was a beautiful life and the opportunity to assist others in building a beautiful life for themselves as well.

The Three Core Seeds to Transformation

Awareness Seed

As I was catapulted into this new energy, my journey led me to different corners of the planet where I was educated, began healing and grew. I could feel the old belief system breaking down and the newfound enlightenment taking over. I began writing and teaching while continuing to learn and flourish. When I would find myself reverting back to old behaviors and beliefs – I would become aware of it and utilize the tools that had been taught to me by some of the masters I was fortunate to have been educated by. Many times, the awareness alone would be enough to change my thoughts and actions. Other times I had to actually stop and choose to perform a cleansing meditation or execute a healing writing exercise to bring myself back into balance. The more I practiced simple *awareness* – the easier it became to convert back to a higher energy vibration.

High Energy Vibration Seed

The goal is to raise our vibration so we feel better, and when we feel better, life is better. Right? We all want to feel good. Many of us have felt so bad for such a long period of time that we don't even realize that there is another way of living. Some of us just think we've been handed a misfortune and resign ourselves to accept it. There was a time when I felt that way until I learned the reason I was living such an unfulfilling life was because of the choices I had made after situations that would directly involve me.

Today, I am aware of how I feel, and what my options are. I learned to no longer stay in a space where things make me feel less than good. This includes people, environments and activities. Have you ever spent time with a really close friend, and when you left, you realized that every time you are with that friend you feel completely drained? Perhaps that friend is always in distress or likes to gossip about others or doesn't like to discuss positive things in general.

There was a time I surrounded myself with people such as this. I was a sponge, and I would allow them to take every ounce of energy out of me and send me on my way. I would even be one to participate in their pity party and I would end up feeling worse when I left than before I got there. Isn't that crazy? Time is valuable, and when you allot your precious time to spend with a friend, it is supposed to be uplifting – right? But you end up feeling bad? Insane. Yet many of us do it consistently.

I learned that when I don't feel good about myself, I attract those who don't feel good about themselves. Who are you surrounding yourself with? There are times I still find myself in the presence of those who are living at a low energy vibration; however, now I am aware of those feelings, and I remove myself from consistent contact. If my higher energy vibration is affected – I now set boundaries and move on with love. We must take care of ourselves and protect our high energy vibrations so that we are able to share ourselves with those who are ready to receive our gift. Otherwise, if we lower our vibrations, we are not at our best and highest good for ourselves, our families and for those that can benefit immensely.

When we move towards people, places and things that make us feel great – we thrive! When we stay around unfulfilling beings, environments and situations that make us feel awful – our soul deteriorates. So it's pretty simple – move towards those that make you feel good, and step away from things that make you feel bad.

Checking In Seed

"Hi, uh … God. It's Lisa … do you have a moment?" Little did I know during all those years of adamantly praying for divine guidance that God was ALWAYS there. Many choose to call God by other names (Source, Spirit, Jesus, Universe, Higher Power, Inner Voice, Intuition, Consciousness, etc) depending on their belief system. Now that I understand that I am one with Spirit, I no longer care about what others choose to *name* Spirit for identification. And, there was a time that I was so into my religion, that if others didn't use the same name for God as I used, I would become very disturbed. I mean really, is it tomato (toe-may-toe) or tomato (toe-mah-toe)? Either way you say it – you must have it to make a great salsa – right?

Think of all the wars created over "religion." Do you really think there is a "Loving God" who would want us to kill our brothers and sisters because they didn't use the same name? In almost all religions – there is one teaching that is obviously consistent. God is love. Therefore, I know if we act in love versus acting in ego – the world would heal. Now if someone could simply direct me to an entity that could create this message and place it on billboards throughout the planet – I think we may have something here!

*If I want to be loved as I am, then I need
to be willing to love others as they are.*
~Louise Hay

I check in with Spirit throughout my day. I no longer fly on "Lisa-Pilot." Each morning when I wake up and before my feet hit the floor, I give thanks for all I am grateful for and ask for Divine Guidance in all I will encounter this day. Doing this immediately jump starts my day into a higher vibration and a knowing that all that is presented to me on this day are for my best and highest good.

You don't have to experience an interventional awakening with Spirit like I did to be able to "check in" with God throughout your day. I believe I was gifted the awakening because my voice was so loud that it was nearly impossible to hear Spirit's soft, wise and comforting voice all those years. I refer to my loud voice as my pain. When I was able to heal much of the pain, I was then able to hear Spirit. The more I heal – the more I hear.

Do you ever call a friend or a mentor for their opinion or to discuss a matter that may be confusing to you? Yeah, at times I do, too. The friends and mentors I surround myself with today are all high energy vibrational beings. Therefore, I know our conversations are Spirit guided, and the outcome will always be in love and for the best and highest good. In most instances, I communicate with Spirit when I am searching for answers. There are times I converse in a simple format and other times through deep meditation.

If you were to eavesdrop on one of my simple format conversations – you would hear something similar as to one person simply speaking with another friend:

Spirit God, I am asking you to guide me through this decision. I feel as if I am trying to control the situation, and I need you to take over because frankly, I'm feeling tired. Okay? Great! Now, would you like to go for a walk?

Or, perhaps:

Hello Spirit, I'm trusting that I am right where I am suppose to be, doing exactly what I was created to do. Thank you for guiding me. I am grateful for our Oneness. I am grateful for this life. Isn't this awesome!? Now, what would you like for dinner?

Then there is the deeper connection exercise I practice through meditation. This level of correlation is filled with so much unconditional love, peace and serenity, it is challenging to explain through mere words. During these measures I set a comfortable space for myself with calming meditation-style music and oftentimes light candles for ambiance. This is when I connect and am able to listen and hear Spirit. The more I exercise this practice – the more I am able to tap in and receive amazing guidance.

The most effective methods for deep meditation begins with setting the space and then focusing on my breath. I will focus on my breathing for a few minutes, then I will visualize with my mind's eye all of my thoughts leaving my mind. The goal is to have a mind that is free from all thoughts and is clear and calm. When a thought creeps up into my mind (*you have laundry to do, an appointment at 5, did you turn off your cell phone ....*) I simply acknowledge that the thought is there and lovingly whisk it away and concentrate on my breath again until my mind is virtually cleared.

I then visualize my body being filled with bright, glittery, gold light. I start at my feet and bring the light through my body out beyond the top of my head. I am calm and filled with divine light. During this time I continue to concentrate on my breathing and relaxing all areas of my body while I "listen" to words of wisdom from Spirit. Learning deep meditation took fortitude – however the practice reaps magnificent rewards.

During one of my deep meditation sessions, Spirit spoke to me concerning the creation of a career through assisting others in regards to writing. I never question Spirit's guidance. Never. There may be times I don't understand the messages, or even times when there seems to be some enormous roadblocks; however, I follow the divine messages knowing that when I choose to follow "the voice," the gift from Spirit is always given in love and for my best and highest good.

I have learned to trust the divinely guided process. I know I am right where I am suppose to be – helping others from all over the world turn their dreams into a reality by giving water and sunshine to their seeds then I wait in anticipation to view the field of vibrant colorful blooms.

Your thoughts and beliefs of the past have created this moment, and all the moments up to this moment. What you are now choosing to believe and think and say will create the next moment and the next day and the next month and the next year.

~Louise Hay

And so it is.

About the Author

Lisa A. Hardwick is a Best-Selling Author, Speaker, Workshop Trainer, Publishing Consultant and an Advocate for Self Discovery. She is passionate about sharing tools to empower others to live their best lives.

Lisa lives in the same small university town where she was born, Charleston, Illinois, to be near her three adult sons and their families. After years of extensive travel, Lisa has learned that her treasure always resided where her journey began.

lisa@lisahardwick.com
www.lisahardwick.com

Acknowledgments

A very special thank you and acknowledgment to my dear friend and business partner, Nancy Newman, for her dedication, devotion and sharing her many talents with me and with all the clients we are so honored to work with. You are an amazing being.

To my dearest supporters Ken Peplow, Debbie Bosler, Linda Ghent, Beverly Newcomb, Andre Lee and Robyn Podboy. Your friendship, laughter and love is what kept me going. I will forever be grateful for our connection.
To my parents, Monte and Linda Nugent, for your encouragement and love.

Zina Bulbuc

Dedicated to my father who dared to dream when dreaming was forbidden.

*A dreamer is one who can only find his way by
moonlight, and his punishment is that he sees
the dawn before the rest of the world.*

~ Oscar Wilde

Chapter 10

IT IS THE BEAUTY OF THE JOURNEY

They must often change, who would
be constant in happiness or wisdom.

~ Confucius

CHANGE IN ALL THINGS IS SWEET

Most of us have had a 'life *changing*' experience, or read a book that *changed* their life, or had an a-ha moment that *changed* everything. There are changes that happen against our will and changes that we want to make happen; there are changes that we don't even notice they happen; and there are changes we resist. They may be good, they may be bad, and sometimes they happen in our lives all at the same time!

We should be masters of change, and still, most of us are afraid of change.

I remember when I was little, my father used to tell me a riddle about a king who had a crystal ball. Every time he looked at it, his mood would change. If he were happy, he would become sad; and if he were sad, he would become happy. What was the message in that crystal ball? The message was: 'This too shall pass.' So, whatever is happening in your life right now, just remember: *This too shall pass...*

Change in all things is sweet.

~ Aristotle

Change is life: every day, every minute of our life is different than the one before. An hour ago, your body was different than it is now. Nature changes every day, like we do. All living things change continuously; planet Earth and the Universe change continuously... But this is just the 'seen' part of change; the physical world's change.

What about the unseen? What about our thoughts? We have anywhere between sixty and eighty thousand thoughts every single day. I am amazed how can we keep up with such a changing pace! And what about our emotions? How many times a day do they change? Does the change come from within, from our thoughts, or does it come from outside, something that someone else said or did to us? Many other subtle things like self-esteem, self-love, confidence, determination, or even the joy of living can be subject to change either spontaneously or through a long process. They are all part of our own self, they have their own power on us and on our lives, and yes, they can be changed to our advantage.

There are also our core values and our beliefs. How 'changeable' are they? The core values like love, fairness, justice, good and bad, sense of oneness / community, protecting the weak and helping the needy, are probably universal and exist in any culture. Not even under extreme conditions and circumstances can we change our core values. They come from within. They come from that place in us that is not material, cannot be seen, is eternal and doesn't change. Our core values have something to do with our souls. We just know when something is right or wrong, we don't really need somebody else to tell us.

Love is not love that alters when it alteration finds.

~ William Shakespeare

But our beliefs are crafted during our first years of life: when we discover the world, and we discover people, and things, and ourselves. Everything that we hear and see, everything that we are told then – especially by our parents, family or teachers - we take as true. We really, really believe it. At a young age, we are trusting and innocent. We are not aware of what suspicion is, or why people need to lie to each other. We don't have those notions.

So, we believe everything and little by little, some things will leave a print in our memory, in our thoughts and in our emotions. We will take that information with us to adulthood, and never question the validity of it. These are beliefs. Can they be changed after years and years of being part of and defining our persona? The answer is: 'Yes, they can be changed'! Would it be easy? Most likely, there would be a lot of resistance in the beginning. But the more willing we are to change beliefs that don't serve us anymore, the easier the change will happen.

The universe is change; our life is what our thoughts make it.

~ Marcus Aurelius

Beautiful Seeds of Change

MY STORY

There are seven billion stories of life changes on this planet. Mine is just one of them. I wish I could tell you a success story about myself, and how I had a sudden big breakthrough and became a different person, but the kind of change I want to talk about is not happening overnight. It is rather a process that may take months, or years, depending on life's events and history, and the desire to change.

It is a process that sometimes is so subtle, it is hard to be noticed while it is happening. This was my case. I went through some big changes in my life, without being 'aware' of the need to change my ways or my response to change. Later, as life is change, I went through some more dramatic changes, but this time I knew better: it was up to me how I reacted to what life had to offer me, and still, every big change caught me unprepared. Or so I thought…

My first trip to America was a gift. In 1998 it fell in my lap just like that, without even trying too hard. It is fascinating how things we do sometimes on a spur of the moment can change our life in a big way, many, many years later. Let me first go back in time and tell you how it all started.

In 1978, I was studying chemistry in Romania. I had a group of wonderful friends, the party-nerd kind, and we liked to do everything together: study, party, travel, mountain trekking, everything. In the first year when we discovered each other and formed our group, we were in different classes, so our schedules didn't allow us to spend as much time together as we wanted. In our second year of study we had a choice of being all in the same class, but that meant we would all have to take the same major and graduate with the same specialty, and that was in leather chemistry. For us, at the time, it wasn't a big deal. Romania was a communist country, which meant, we didn't have to worry too much about our future. We would all have a job with the government after graduation. Everything in the country was government property; there were no private companies and no competition. It didn't make a big difference if we were specialized in polymers, or organic chemistry or leather chemistry, our jobs were paid the same wage as engineers. So, we embraced the idea of being all in the same class and being able to have exams on the same day, so we could party together afterwards. This is how I became a specialist in leather chemistry. It was a seed that I planted without knowing what it would later grow into…

Twenty years later, in 1998, I was living and working in Australia. I had had a stable job for seven years with a leather company. Everything seemed to fall into place, and I was trying to make myself feel at home in a country that was so far from my own, both geographically and culturally.

1998 was a very intense year for me. The year before, I lost my mother who was the last close member of my family. I still had a few cousins back in Romania, but no parents and no siblings. When I returned back to Adelaide, after her funeral in Romania, it hit me: I was alone in this whole world. And that is how I felt. I tried to talk to God, but I couldn't. I was so angry with Him for what He did to me. I was never a religious person, and I had a lot of questions about His existence or powers. Not knowing how to deal with grief, I slowly fell into depression.

Most of my friends in Australia were Romanian immigrants like me. We had a loud and happy group, with lots of barbeques and parties. There was a lot of laughter and jokes every time we met. But we had all grown up in a culture where laughter was also our way to cover up pain. So, nobody was eager to talk to me about what I was going through, and I shared the same attitude. I felt ashamed for having such a burden on my shoulders. I tried the best I could to remain the heart of the party and be funny, loud and outgoing, as they knew me.

But inside, I was bleeding. I was confused, didn't know what I want or what to do, bottling up a lot of fear, grief and anger. I was terrified and didn't even understand of what. I kept going twice a week to my aerobics and step classes, and I still took my long walks on the beautiful Australian beach every night. I didn't know at the time, but this was the only treatment I had for my depression.

My love life was a dysfunctional relationship with a man who didn't have too much to offer, but I was in love with him, I was blind and I was scared to let him go. Alex was a tall and handsome man, with sun-bleached blond hair and blue eyes. His skin was always tanned, and he had beautiful hands. He was funny, witty and always challenging me, which I liked.

He had been my next-door neighbor for a couple of years, and we used to share stories, food and sometimes borrow money from each other. He would tell me how his girlfriend asked him to bring her beer rather than flowers, and I would tell him about my yuppie and really boring boyfriend who worked on his Ph.D. and took me to restaurants where he expected me to pay for my share.

Alex tried to court me for almost a year, but I resisted and made fun of him. I knew he liked me. What was not to be liked? I measured up to him: I was tall and slim, with a smile to die for, funny, kind and intelligent. I had it all. I teased him that he was just a puppy, he was too young for me (he was a few years younger), but I was flattered at the same time. It was a nice friendship that changed when we took it to the next level.

I learned that Alex was cheating on me on a regular basis. At first, I tried to win him back (although he made me believe we were still together), and I tried to make him love only me. Then, I took heart and confronted him, but he told me how natural it is for a man to have many women, and even gave me examples of animals and nature itself. Then he told me that we didn't owe anything to each other, so we were free to do what we want.

My self-esteem was so low, I believed him! I thought I would have to be even smarter, funnier and more beautiful, so he would not want anybody else. The harder I tried, the more I suffered. He didn't change a thing.

I tried to break up with him and date other men, but all of them were boring and not smart enough, and not tall enough. He was the only man for me in the whole world. I didn't want to be with anybody else. When the phone rang, I would drop everything else just to be with him.
Our rocky relationship went on and off for five years. I was miserable inside, but I had no clue how to get out of this whole charade.

At the time I wasn't aware of my self-esteem. It was a concept that was not in my vocabulary. I was interested in UFO's and pyramids, I used to read about how the mind can heal the body, but I understood it from a strictly scientific point of view. I was a scientist after all. I found a book shop in Adelaide called Cosmic Pages which had a lot of interesting New Age books. And, because in 1998 I also found out that my vision was fading and I needed to wear glasses, I went to Cosmic Pages to find a book with eye exercises to improve my vision.

I asked the shop assistant to help me find a book about how to heal my eyes. I used the word, 'heal,' for lack of a better word. She brought a book called *You Can Heal Your Life* by Louise Hay, and told me that it is a very good book. It had been selling like hot cakes for more than ten years now, and everybody likes it. She hadn't read it, but she told me I would love it. No, this was not what I needed. I was looking for a book for my eyes, not my life. We found a book for eyes, and in the end I bought both books.

Of course, I went home and immediately started to read the book I didn't want. It was very easy and pleasant to read, and it was talking about self-love. This was a little in contradiction with what I learned growing up: Sacrificing yourself for other's needs, treating your friends better than you treat yourself was something highly valued and which showed integrity and a noble character. Self-love was perceived as selfish or even arrogant. Still, everything Louise said made sense to me, and I agreed with her.

I tried to do the mirror exercise she recommended. I had to look into my own eyes in the mirror and say out loud: "Zina, I love you, I accept you, and I approve of you just the way you are." I hardly started the phrase, and I choked crying. I tried again. Again, I couldn't say it because I cried. It took me a few months until I was able to do it. That was my a-ha moment when I realized where my self-esteem was. I didn't know then, but many years later, this book was going to change my life. For now, a little seed was planted.

And then, the same year, 1998, the news came out: my employer was going to close down within the next year. We were encouraged to look for jobs elsewhere while still working there. I was in no mood to start looking for a job, but I had to. I contacted a couple of agencies, and sent a good number of applications, to no avail. I started to lose faith, then the Universe smiled at me.

A friend and business partner from Germany told me there was an American company looking for a Research and Development manager specializing in leather chemistry. Leather chemistry is a rare specialty, and there is no such school in the US. I found out later that all highly educated specialists were brought from Europe.

United States!?... I was hesitant to move from Adelaide to Brisbane, let alone moving across the ocean. No, this was too far, and I couldn't bear to move yet again to another foreign country where I didn't have anyone to call on weekends, and where I had to start again to read all labels in a grocery store. But then again, sending my resume didn't cost me anything, and I could test my value on the American job market. I sent them my resume and after a few phone calls at small hours due to the time difference, they asked me to come for an interview.

A big opportunity had fallen into my lap, but instead of grabbing it with both hands, I was hesitant. I didn't see the big picture. I was too caught in my depression and my old fears, lack of trust in myself, and my old beliefs. I thought that such spectacular things always happened to other people; as an immigrant, I was supposed to live an anonymous life and watch others succeed.

Still, it struck me that because in 1978 I loved my friends so much I didn't care what my major was in school, I was now flying to America for a job interview! What were the odds? Sometimes, we choose to do things in life that don't make too much sense. Years may pass, we forget about them and then, boom! Something happens, and the puzzle comes together. Twenty years later, I understood the reason I made that almost childish decision. I had to come to America, and this was my only chance: my specialty.

Yes, my first trip to America was a gift. I had my plane tickets, a nice hotel room and a rented car for the whole week, everything paid for, and I was 30 miles from Washington DC. The interview went well, but I didn't think I would move across the ocean for the second time in my life. So, I made sure to visit all the historical monuments and the White House. I took lots of pictures and bought presents for myself and for my Australian friends. After all, it might be many years before I came to the US again.

But after returning to Australia, all my pain, fear and loneliness re-surfaced. I felt that I had nothing to look forward to if I stayed. I knew I needed a big change in my life, a fresh start, to find the right way. So, one December night in 1998 at 1:00 a.m., when I got a phone call with the job offer from US, half asleep, I said "yes."

When I broke the news to my friends, everybody was envious of me. They told me that this was a once in a lifetime opportunity, how lucky I was! I knew I should be happy and excited, but all I felt was fear. I realized by now that I was depressed, and thanks to Louise Hay's book, I knew that my self-esteem was very, very low. I didn't know what to do about it, and I enrolled in a Stress Management class, paying the $200 tuition which seemed very expensive at the time.

During the first class, our instructor listed all the big stressors in someone's life: changing your job, moving houses, losing a loved one, breaking up a relationship and not having support from your family or close friends. Then, she went around the room, and each one of the participants had to identify the one or two issues that applied to their situation. When my turn came, I had them all.

Five months later, I packed my things, I took my depression, my low self-esteem and my heart, and moved to America. This time, I wanted to make it right. I still didn't know how, but I trusted in my strength and resilience. I thought that being smart and hard working would be enough. Little did I know what was ahead for me.

I settled in Maryland, and life was good. My American employer brought me here on a well-deserved H1-B visa for professionals. My specialty was sought after, and there was no American university offering such classes. The only problem was that an H1-B visa was limited to three years with only one extension of another three years. After that, I would have to return to Australia.

The solution was for my employer to apply for a green card on my behalf. This was the only way I could receive a green card: employer sponsored. We agreed at my job interview that the company would sponsor me to obtain a green card, so I didn't have to worry about moving back and forth between US and Australia.

The first couple of years were like a dream for me. I was driving to work with a big smile on my face and kept saying, 'I am in America!' I was often thinking about my father; his dream was to flee Romania and bring us to America. He had been arrested and spent years in a political prison in communist Romania for such a daring dream. He died in a car accident the year of my graduation. And now, almost 20 years after I lost him, I was here! I secretly liked to believe that this was his work from up there, to help me come here. I was happy.

This was my story of going through big, really big changes in my life, without being aware. I lost my last member of close family, I broke up a long-term relationship, I changed jobs, I moved to another continent. I was so overwhelmed with all of this that I was living one day at a time, and had no idea of how to deal with it. I was on automatic pilot. I was on survival mode. I had my new job in America (!), and hoped that it was a new beginning, but I had no tools and didn't know how to really enjoy and take advantage of it. I was caught in my old thinking patterns, and everything I was afraid of was still part of my daily thoughts. I didn't really change, and I wasn't even aware of it.

THE AMERICAN DREAM

But, the show must go on. My life in Maryland was pretty much the average American dream. I had a good job, I started to date and go to different events to make friends and get to know people. I really enjoyed my first real Christmas tree after eight years of plastic Christmas trees in Australia. Christmas was too hot there, and real trees wouldn't last. So the smell of a pine tree in my house was such a treat, and brought back childhood memories from Romania. I started to do Louise's mirror exercise without crying. I even created a few affirmations which I repeated every day. Soon after, I discovered books by Deepak Chopra and Wayne Dyer. I didn't have many friends, but my job kept me busy, and I loved it. I enrolled in an MBA (Master in Business Administration) program, and I was enjoying it tremendously.

But in 2002, everything was going to change. Yes, change again, and in a big way. I was diagnosed with melanoma, the fastest growing cancer, resistant to chemotherapy and to radiation. There was no treatment for it. I was alone (again!) and petrified with fear. My old thinking that I have to do everything alone, that I have nobody in this whole world, was still at work.

Despite that, I had learned a few things, and I was more aware and knew that asking for help is okay. So, I asked for help from friends, relatives, everybody I knew. The help came over the phone, in the form of advice, opinions and moral support. But every night I went to sleep alone with my fear. I knew that any decision I would make would be mine and only mine. Nobody could choose for me.

This was probably the first big change in my perception of life and what life is about: Responsibility. We are responsible for our own decisions in life. We don't need to blame anyone for anything. It all comes down to our own decisions, and the best decisions are made when we have the time and clarity to listen to our intuition. Our intuition is actually our Inner Wisdom talking to us. Although at the time I couldn't see this, I made all the right decisions. Being so scared that I couldn't think straight, I went with my intuition.

I immediately underwent surgery, a few months of strict diet and detox, and for the next few years I learned how to let go of that fear: fear of staying in the sun, fear of going to the beach, fear of eating meat or having an ice cream; *fear for my life!* I still go for checkups every six months, but now I know I am well and it will never come back.

I didn't have a magic rule of how to let go of the fear. I just let life happen, and little by little, I got caught in daily events, and plans, and hopes, and I just realized one day that I am not afraid anymore! I actually shifted my attention from fear to better things that were coming into my life. I let go of the past. My scar was healing, and my life went back on track. I was working hard at my MBA degree, and planning to buy a town house. My green card was still in process, but I had hopes to have it really soon.

But in 2003, change came back into my life. I moved some furniture, made the wrong moves and dislocated three discs in my lower back. I was in bed, unable to move for ten weeks. I needed my neighbors' help to take me to the bathroom and to change my underwear. This time, it was not fear, but pain that brought my life to a halt. I didn't know such pain could be endured by a human being.

I had to re-learn how to walk (first in a swimming pool), and my first victory was when I could walk for a whole minute on a treadmill, at the lowest speed. I was in excruciating pain when I prepared my thesis for the MBA class, and I had a neighbor taking me to school for my final presentation. I couldn't sit down, so I had to stand during the whole class, holding on to the backrest of a chair.

Shortly after graduation, I closed a deal to buy the most beautiful town house ever. It was brand new, very spacious and with lots of windows and sunlight. I watched it being built for a few months before moving in. It was so beautiful, and so perfect, and still there was something in me that stopped me from being really happy. I couldn't tell what it was, but somehow, I felt a little guilty for having such a big and wonderful house, all on my own. I was not sure if I deserved something like this. Yes, my low self-esteem had found a way to express itself again! Even after so many years of reading and learning about myself and what life is about, I still didn't get it. I felt I *didn't deserve* what other people *could have*.

Anyway, these were just little thoughts I didn't share with anybody. This was my American dream. I was recovering from my back injury, I received my MBA, and I bought my dream house. Well, you guessed it: change was going to come again. And, although I thought I learned a little about fear and pain, and about changing my way of thinking, and changing my old patterns, I was (again!) not prepared for this.

My employer was going to close its American facilities and move to Mexico. Even though my job was in jeopardy, I started to make business trips to Mexico to help with the transition. But this time with this change, I thought I had the tools to face it. I started to do daily affirmations (as I learned from Louise Hay's book) that I have my green card, and my job is secure, that I have a nice job, and it is close to home, and I earn $90,000 a year (which was much more than I was actually earning at the time). Every morning, I would say out loud these affirmations, like a prayer, even though they seemed a little exaggerated, and hard to believe.

My green card was still in process (after more than five years of waiting), and my hopes were that I would get it before my company closed down. If the company closed before I received my green card, I would lose it. And then, the day came when I was given a choice between moving to Mexico and keeping my job, or staying in America and losing my job. If I moved to Mexico, I could not return to the US, I would lose my green card. I could work in Mexico for a year or two, or five, and then ... what? Moving to Mexico, meant for me that I knowingly and willingly said good bye to America for good. I couldn't do it. I couldn't tell why, but what *I really wanted* was to stay here.

So, I lost my job and with it my employer sponsored H1-B visa, my soon-to-be-received green card, my income, my insurance, everything. I had no savings (I put them all in my dream town house), I couldn't pay my mortgage, and had nowhere to go. No family, no old friends to turn to, nobody. I realized then how important it is to have somebody in your life that knows you, really knows you. As an immigrant, you don't have the luxury of your old friends from childhood, high school or university, who know you and trust you. Who would take you in, not knowing for how long, not knowing if you will be able to get a job without a green card or even a valid visa?

On October 28, 2005, the day I lost my job, I drove home in disbelief. I couldn't believe this *was actually happening!* All my prayers, and my affirmations and hopes didn't do anything. I was not supposed to go through all this! I stopped at a gas station to buy cigarettes, although I had quit smoking a few years back when I was diagnosed with melanoma. I went home to my beautiful town house and didn't know what to do.

I smoked, and cried, and didn't know what to do... Should I call somebody? But who? What should I tell them, or ask for? I couldn't ask anybody for the only thing that would give me some security: a green card. Security kept escaping me. For the past seven years I had tried to build a life for myself, I tried to create a secure environment that would make me feel 'at home,' but I was cheating myself. For someone with no family who moved from country to country, there is no such place.

My life was a failure; I wasn't able to 'have a life' at all! I was just surviving from one crisis to another, just trying to catch up with everybody else who had a life... What was I doing wrong!?... If I only knew then what I know today! It was my old beliefs and my own thoughts that kept me in a place I didn't want to be.

> *When we are no longer able to change a situation*
> *- we are challenged to change ourselves.*
> *~ Viktor E. Frankl*

Losing my job meant losing everything: my income, my close-to-completeness green card, my H1-B visa, my insurance, and my house. But what I didn't realize then, was that I not only lost everything on a material plan; I lost my faith and my hopes. Everything I thought I learned about the power of prayer, and about doing affirmations, everything I thought are good tools to help me survive and deal with crisis and hardship, was gone in a moment. It was almost like I forgot everything I learned. I let go of my strengths. I lost my soul. Fear took over and it was stronger than me. *I allowed it to be stronger than me.*

My birthday was coming in two days. Just a week before losing my job, I had plans to make a party in my new house, to celebrate both Halloween and my birthday, and invite some friends over. Now, it didn't matter anymore. I cancelled everything.

Some immigration lawyers told me I had 48 hours to leave the country, others more optimistically promised to change my now useless H1-B visa into a tourist visa, which would give me three more months to sell my house, and ship my stuff to Australia. And all this, for fees I couldn't afford. I had nothing in Australia to return to. When I left, I left for good, knowing that I would settle in the USA.

Within a few weeks from losing my job, I developed pneumonia. No wonder: lungs represent taking in life, but what life was left for me to take in?... I started sweating really badly during the night, and the next morning I was lucky to be able to drive to my family doctor and get a prescription for antibiotics. By the time I came home, everything became a blur. And it stayed like that for the next week. After a few days, the sweating stopped, I was able to get out of bed, but felt really weak and sick.

As soon as I could walk, I took a chance and drove to the nearest 7 Eleven to buy cigarettes. I didn't know how bad pneumonia was. But scared, afraid of my own future, disappointed with life, and miserable as I felt, I didn't care anymore. I had to move out from my own house and had no place to go!! I took the antibiotics, ate nothing for days, felt sick, drank tea, cried and smoked.

And, this is how I spent Christmas, when all my friends were partying together. I had called them, not really knowing why, and they reluctantly asked me: "Do you want us to come and bring you something?" Of course I did, but hurt and pride took over, and I answered: "No, I'm fine, I'll survive." And survive I did. Nobody was coming to visit me. I even found an excuse for them not to come and see me. I thought maybe they believed that pneumonia is contagious... Maybe.

THREE MIRACLES

I called every acquaintance I had, to tell them that I was looking for a job. Without a green card, getting a job was mission impossible. But I did it anyway.

I did it because I wanted to have the peace of mind that I tried everything I could try to stay in America. One day, a friend from Romania told me to call Eve – an American friend of hers who was a lawyer in Washington DC – and ask her to help me find a good immigration lawyer. I did call, and left a message, but I had no money to pay for a good lawyer.

Eve called me back, I told her briefly my story, and she asked me if I had a nice long evening gown. I said 'yes', and at that moment my life changed (again!). Their law firm had a late Christmas party, and she managed to sneak me in. I didn't know anybody but her, and it didn't really matter: I had nothing left to lose. I was so saturated with fear for what was ahead of me, that I was beyond fear: I was calm... It was one of those moments in life when everything seemed to unfold in slow motion. So, I made a grand entrance, in my royal blue long evening gown and red lipstick. I smiled around and gave everybody my business card, which I made up the night before on my home computer.

The next morning, a miracle happened: a lawyer I met at the party called me. He was not an immigration lawyer, but he needed help in his office and was willing to hire me for a few months. I didn't care what kind of work I had to do, as long as that would help me extend my working visa in US.

We made the deal: he would legally hire me, and sign all papers to have my visa extended. In the mean time, I could work for him while still looking for a job in my profession. Chances were very slim, but I had no money to move back to Australia, and I had to stay in Maryland until I could sell my townhouse. To me, at the time, this was the only option I had.

And once more, the puzzle of my life came together: I had received an MBA just because I wanted to prove to my employer that I was there to stay and grow with the company. My MBA degree didn't impress them, and I had no benefits out of it. Years later though, when this lawyer hired me, it was the MBA that saved me: I couldn't work in a lawyer's office as a chemical engineer. But I could be hired as a business manager.

And then, the second miracle happened: a former neighbor of mine, finding out what I was going through, offered to lend me $10,000 without interest, to help me pay my mortgage until I sold the house. Within a few days I started packing, moved everything into a self-storage unit and rented a small, one bedroom apartment in Silver Spring, MD. I worked for that lawyer for about three months, living out of boxes, and desperately applying to all jobs I could find on the internet regardless if they fit my education or not. I managed to sell my home, I was lucky to make a small profit, and paid back my debt of $10,000.

I had now enough money to move back to Australia, but just the thought of moving back gave me chills. I would find myself in the same situation I landed in Australia fifteen years earlier: alone, no money, no job, start from scratch. I wondered what the fifteen years between then and now were about?... (Now I know: they were my time to learn, and grow and change. But I couldn't see the change, not yet).

By the end of the third month in my temporary job, I was depressed, and lost any hope to find a company willing to hire me and sponsor my application for a green card. I was crying every day trying to say good-bye to my American dream. I felt that my life was a total failure, and I was not worth living. Why did God bring me to America, keep me here for seven years and make me go through a lot of trials and hurts, just to send me back to Australia? It didn't make any sense.

One day, on my way home from the lawyer's office, I stopped at the National Cathedral in Washington DC, my favorite place to pray. I went in, but couldn't pray anymore. I was dry inside. I just sat there, and asked God to do whatever He wanted to do with me. To take me wherever He wanted, I didn't care anymore. There was nothing else that I could do, I completely surrendered.

I went home feeling that a burden was taken off my shoulders. I had nothing left to worry about, I totally gave up. The next morning I went back to the office. Before lunch, I got a phone call from a company I never heard of, asking me to come for an interview. I was so embarrassed because I didn't even know what job I applied for. I asked them to give me their website, so I could find their location and what they did.

I went to the interview, and it turned out they were in the energy saving business. We talked and had a good time, but I apologized and told them it was a mistake, I didn't realize they were not in my field. A few days later, they called me back and asked me to come for a second interview. This time, they asked me if I could make presentations and do public speaking. I said yes, I had done it before and loved it. But, again, I backed off: I asked them if my accent would not be a problem for such a job. After all, English was my second language and when I spoke, this was very obvious. Their Executive Director smiled and said: "no, this will keep everybody awake when you speak."

They agreed to sign my visa extension, and they asked me if I would be happy with a salary of $90,000 a year. I almost fainted. One year ago, I was doing affirmations driving to work every day, saying out loud that I would find a good job, close to home, which would pay me $90,000 a year. This company was a 10-minute drive from my apartment.

This was another big lesson I learned. You may pray for something, and do affirmations, for many months, and nothing happens. Then, disaster strikes, you forget everything you have done, and totally give up. *You surrender to a higher power; you let it go.* Without being aware, what I really did was this: I prayed and did affirmations for a long time, and then I let them go (that day in the National Cathedral, when I surrendered). *Only when I detached myself from the outcome of those prayers and affirmations, did they come to life.* So, if you really want something, and pray for it for a long time, it comes a moment when you have to set your prayers free.

Let go and let God.

~ Wayne Dyer

I understand now, that what I thought to be the most disastrous situation in my life, was actually a blessing: I learned trust and surrender.

The following week I traveled to Canada to change employers on my visa, and a week later, I was the Director of Education of a non-profit organization in Washington DC. This was the third miracle. I was meant to stay.

LESSONS LEARNED

My story didn't end there, and I didn't live happily ever after… Some years passed since then, and I went through other trials and tribulations. But today, I have my green card, I have a good job and I am grateful for my health and for my life. I learned to face my fear, go through it, and do what I have to do anyway. Did I change? Yes! Little by little, with every event, good or bad, I learned something about myself and about life.

Do I still have bad days? Yes! Do I still have fears? Yes! I am still a work in progress. But the difference now is that every challenge becomes an opportunity to learn, to trust and to let go. I noticed for the past few years that even if I am facing impossible situations, and I am overwhelmed with fear or frustration, I allow them to consume for a few hours or a few days, then I let them go and find my way back to reality. And the reality is that every time I went through something 'bad', a miracle happened, God patted me on the shoulder and told me: "Now you see that I take care of you, and I help you?" Yes dear God, now I see it.

Miracles do happen, but we have to learn to recognize them. They may come in the form of a neighbor that lends you some money, or somebody that will hire you for only three months, or a job that comes to you from nowhere. But they do happen. Sometimes it can be a friend, sometimes it can be a stranger that makes them happen. Regardless, I like to call those people 'Angels' that came into my life. All my experiences taught me that I can overcome anything that comes my way. All the pain and fear was there to help me regain the trust in myself.

What I really wanted to tell you is this:

- You are never prepared for the change ahead of you.

- You don't need to be perfect and do everything at the right time, because what you think needs to be done, may not be the plan that a higher power had for you.

- Don't hold on to old hurts and don't hold on to the past. Learn forgiveness: for others and most importantly, for yourself, for your mistakes. Those mistakes had to happen, to bring you where you are today. Forgiveness sets you free.

- Be open to life's changes and go with the flow. Take one day at a time. Life is a river. You are swimming in it. If you try to resist it and swim against the current, everything becomes really hard and puts you in danger of drowning. If you just float on your back and let the current take you down the river, if you don't fight it, it will eventually take you to the safe shores. This doesn't mean you don't have to do anything and just 'let life happen.' It means that you can make plans and follow them, but keep your eyes and ears open to the signals and messages that you get. Stay open and trust your intuition. Do what you have to do, but if something doesn't 'feel' right, stop and ask yourself: "What is it that I really want?"

- Trust every day that you are in the right place at the right time. Let me say it again: *trust every day that you are in the right place at the right time.* Everything happens with a reason. You don't need to know the reason. Just accept what is happening right now in your life and know that it is happening to prepare you for the next step. You cannot connect the dots now, but you will be able to understand it in the future. You will look back and say "oh, now I understand why that happened!" It took me twenty years to understand why I took my major in leather chemistry, and four years to understand why I took the MBA course. The first brought me in America, and the second helped me stay here when I thought everything was lost.

- Trust your intuition, trust your heart. For over five years my green card processing dragged on, just to lose it when my employer moved to Mexico. I thought this happened to tell me it's time to give up and leave this country. But I asked myself: "What is it that I really want?" And, what I *really wanted* was to stay here. When you try to achieve something and it takes you years of effort, you reach the point where you ask yourself: "is this a sign that I should give up? How do I know when it is time to stop trying?" If in doubt, go back again and ask yourself: "What is it that I really want?" Trust your heart. You'll have the answer whether you have to keep trying or it's time to give up and move on.

- Your thoughts create your future. Your thoughts are shaped by beliefs that you learned and acquired over the years. Do you carry a belief that came from your childhood and still hold on to it? Maybe it doesn't apply anymore to the person you are today, but you keep believing it is still true. Be aware of your self-talk and watch what you are thinking about yourself repeatedly for a few days in a row. I would suggest you focus on things like self-esteem, trust in yourself, what you believe you deserve in life, but you can also observe what you think about the people you attract into your life and how they treat you. Do you see a pattern? Is there anything you would like to change?

- Everything is temporary. It took me eleven years to get my green card. Eleven years of anticipation, fear and hope. But eventually, I got it. When you are in a difficult situation, even if it is dragging on for years, just remember it will come to an end: *this too shall pass.*

- Trust that when you are ready, the right teacher or master will show up in your life. Keep your eyes and ears open. Sometimes, the teacher may be somebody or something you didn't expect: a job that is lost, a moment of despair, an unfortunate event, a passerby on the street, a dream, a book or a neighbor …

- Any time is a good time to make a change within. It doesn't need to be something big and spectacular. *Now* is your moment of power. You can take responsibility and start to change everything you want in this very moment. It is only up to you. Just ask yourself again:

"What is it that I really want?" Your heart knows the answer.

I like to think about life as a wonderful opportunity and a wonderful journey. It is after all, an experiment. It is a dress rehearsal. Just remember: the 'real' show is not going to happen. So, the dress rehearsal is about getting it right through trial and error. And this is okay. This is learning, growing, change. This is your change. It is never too late. Don't be afraid of anything that hasn't happened yet. *Just don't be afraid!*

Life is not about 'getting there'; life is about the beauty of the journey. I wish you love.

About the Author

Zina Bulbuc is a licensed *Heal Your Life®* Workshop Facilitator and Life Coach. She also holds a Master in Chemical Engineering and an MBA. In 2004, she was the first one to translate and publish Louise Hay's book, *You Can Heal Your Life*, in Romania. Her deep desire to help others combined with the curiosity of a scientist led her to the discovery that science and spirituality are much closer than we thought.

Zina lives in the Washington DC Metro area and enjoys the outdoors, travelling, reading and helping others finding their own true self and path in life.

zina46@gmail.com

Beautiful Seeds of Change

Acknowledgments

With joy and gratitude, thank you Patricia Crane, Nancy Newman and Lisa Hardwick. You are the three fairies who opened a magic door for me. This is the first step I took in bringing an old dream to life. To my dearest friends, Doina Serban and Linda Hellman, thank you for your support and honesty. To Louise Hay, thank you for writing the book that changed so many lives and opened so many doors.

Jill Haas

I dedicate this to everyone who has touched my life. You have influenced me more than you will ever know, and this journey would not be the same without you in it. I am grateful for each one of you, no matter how big or small, positive or negative our encounters may have been. Every moment has brought me to where I am now. Thank you.

Chapter 11

GRATEFUL FOR MY DIVINELY GUIDED LIFE!

Living a life of gratitude means not only being thankful for who I am now, but also giving thanks for my past experiences because they led me to where I am today – the good, the bad and the ugly. Others often tell me what a great life I have and how peaceful and calm I can be. Although I am grateful and flattered for them sharing these compliments, I also know this is their perception, or you might call it "judgment," since they don't know everything about me. Usually what comes after perception is judgment which is based on the perception. This is normal, since most of us probably don't know the history that makes up the lives of everyone we know, so we surmise on our own "who" someone really is.

Sometimes even those closest to us haven't shared with us their triumphs, setbacks or, heaven forbid, skeletons, and certainly this is not required. Sharing details can cause people to look at us in a different light. They might rethink our worthiness of association to them, and we're either drawn closer or pushed further away. So, as humans, we tend to keep darker things about ourselves under the radar and tell others on a "need to know" basis.

Life can be a roller coaster. You can either go with the flow, enjoying the ups and downs, or you can resist with white knuckles, shrieking the entire journey. For me, it was a little of both, but mostly the latter until I learned how much better it is to flow with the current, no matter how turbulent. I'd like to share with you a few select instances from my own personal roller coaster, in hopes it will help many realize they also can come out shining on the other side despite a myriad of challenges and obstacles. My story is one of manifesting my heart's desires, even though some desires weren't intended as aspirations. Or were they?

Certainly, I'm not saying I don't have a great life nor am I negating being peaceful and calm. Rather I feel it is important to share that I wasn't always this way, and it took some work on my part to get here. Ok, let me be honest, *a lot* of mental, emotional and spiritual work which is still on-going. Do I want everyone to know every detail I went through to get here? Probably not, but I don't mind sharing those gems that truly enriched my life.

Sure, some of those experiences were long, exhausting and demeaning. I felt unhappy and certain that I was truly a victim of circumstance. I would have sat you down to convince you how bad I had it compared to you or anyone else. I just couldn't feel or see the reason for any of the turmoil in my life, not even after it was over and done, and I was on the other side looking back at them. Most people don't realize the silver lining until after the storm has passed.

At the very least, I will give myself credit for expressing my feelings, even the negative ones. But, little did I know that this passionate articulation was manifesting more negativity. Each verbalization of my personal drama, done with passion I might add, was creating just what I didn't want. But I didn't know then what I know now.

Passion is one of my greatest gifts and being an Aries, the attribute of fire definitely fits when it comes to emotion across the entire spectrum. Even though I have not formally studied the Zodiac, I know enough to see the validity of the qualities associated with the astrological signs. For example, a friend pointed out how, after telling a story that happened years ago, I still harbored the irritation of the situation. It was as if the incident had just occurred.

He was right. I was still angry with that person for how they treated me. My anger was refueled and very real at that moment. "Let it go," he said. How could I let it go, even though it was years ago? Someone wronged me, and justice was never done. That's why I still felt so bad, right? Someone had to pay, or so I thought. Had I put such passion into focusing on the good things and feeling gratitude for those things, maybe it would not have taken me this long to get to where I am now. But life is all about the experience, right?

I was the greatest story teller when it came to talking about the trauma of my life. It didn't seem real until I started the personal broadcasts. Sometimes it was a way to receive attention to know I wasn't alone in the "knowing," and it seemed "healing" to tell everyone who would listen, including strangers, if conversation was even remotely related.

Now I don't want to paint a picture that I was crazed, looking to anyone and everyone, but I was looking for kind ears to hear what I had to say and hoped they would offer me information, even the smallest scrap, that would assist me in moving away from certain experiences that I would say were more than unpleasant. I remember sharing some very personal details almost to justify to the listener it was worth listening to me!

Some of the most upsetting times were in my adolescent and teen years where my family moved constantly from one state to another. Often people assume I'm from a military family due to all the moves, but my father was always open to an opportunity to make more money and develop his career. I found it difficult to maintain long distance friendships and make new friends always being the "new kid" in a new school.

The ages of 10-18 were pretty rough for me. Those years were the foundation for the low self-esteem in the years to come, which would be exacerbated by going through two marriages where reinforcement of a poor self-image continued. When I moved on to my second marriage, I found myself almost identically duplicating my first marriage!

In addition, my second marriage was a rebound relationship, and since I hadn't allowed myself time to heal in between, it was probably doomed from the start. But at the time, having a significant other in my life gave me an identity – or so I thought. It took some time for me to realize the fallacy of this belief, and how it contributed to the failure of both relationships.

I felt I *needed* these men in my life, but neither husband supported me emotionally at all. I thought they were totally different, but the way I felt as a person being with them was similar: I felt insignificant, unimportant, unloved and I was the butt of their jokes, especially in front of their friends and my family.

I recall when I changed career paths and decided I wanted to pursue nursing. My first husband said something to the effect of, "I don't know how you'll ever make it through nursing school. It takes a really smart person to do that." That was mild compared to other inferences he made. This is the same person who told me after we divorced that I would never be happy or find another person like him to be with me.

I started to believe the observations he made about me regarding my "stupidity," and at the time, I did wonder who would want me. I felt very ugly physically and very nervous emotionally. This continued the self-esteem plummet. What the heck made me stay so long with these guys? How does one continue to brush off emotional abuse, somehow making it okay? I look back now and know that the person I am today would never tolerate such talk, not even the slightest hint of it. Even though I resented it, I suppose I got used to it and so it seemed normal.

My second husband was an alcoholic. Things seemed fine in the beginning, and I have to admit I was enamored with him. I was so attracted to his charm. He was a cowboy from Arizona, and for me at the time, was exotic and thrilling. I was on an adventure in which I had a really great time. That is, until we moved in together, and I began to notice things changing.

He started to exhibit jealous behavior. It was more than subtle at first, as one night after work he accused me of cheating on him. Although the only thing he used as his gauge was that he had surprised me at work and saw me sitting in a booth with others while one guy had his arm resting on the booth behind me, he was quite convinced he had "caught me." I didn't even know the man, except that he was with a Detroit radio station and that night I was hosting an event which they were broadcasting. But, of course, my explanation did nothing to change his belief.

In addition, I noticed his drinking becoming more frequent. I think he must have just gotten more comfortable drinking around me, so to me it only seemed more frequent. After we divorced, a friend shared with me that he had seen him in the 7-11 parking lot dumping out a Big Gulp cup to fill it up with beer on a weekday at seven or eight o'clock in the morning! He was eventually let go from his job after several reports of having the "cocktail flu."

We tried to make it work after he agreed to attend AA. He had a sponsor for about two weeks then just quit, stating he didn't have a problem. I had no idea what was really going on with his drinking, his job or who I really was even married to anymore. Many details still remain a mystery today. I'm just grateful I was able to pull my head together and remove myself from yet another toxic relationship.

When my second marriage dissolved, I felt so free, and this time I really wanted to do things right for me. I was still working through my own personal identity. I had the best intentions to find the right person, but somewhere along the way I started listening to my ego again, telling me I needed that significant other in my life.

I soon found myself in another relationship, which started out as "friends" but moved into more after taking my ego's advice. We ended up engaged, even going together to look for a ring, etc. I recall crying shortly thereafter because I realized it just wasn't what I wanted. Instead of being true to myself, I allowed myself to remain in this relationship where it felt like I was engaged to my brother rather than a boyfriend.

Somewhere between the years 2000-2001, after that relationship ended, I remember seeing a psychic who told me how she met her husband after making a list of qualities she wanted in a significant other. I had personal readings before, but this one was different since she shared such interesting advice. I don't know what compelled me to start my list, but I figured what the heck, with two failed marriages and one engagement called off, I was still willing to try again. Maybe this woman knew what she was talking about, and what do I have to lose?

I had neither heard about co-creating your future or the "Law of

Attraction," nor had I taken the words "manifest destiny" to be something other than words from a fairytale or movie. "And they lived happily ever after…," seriously? You can really do this? What she said really resonated with me and aside from the ego, something else told me this was truth, and I wouldn't be disappointed. What a path I began to follow from there.

Some people dream of a fairytale story and at the same time think they know this could never happen because it is reserved for fantasy only. However, for me, I truly felt someone was out there looking for me as well.

So with eagerness and curiosity, I compiled the list over three years of intermittent dating, using the traits I didn't like as a guide to what I did want in a partner. I held nothing back and proceeded to jot down everything from physical features and spiritual beliefs to table manners and supportiveness. You name it, and it was on the list. Consequently, as if a magic wand was waved, and words from an ancient spell uttered "Poof!" Dave appeared! Somehow he manifested in my life on an internet dating site, and we've been inseparable since November, 2003.

We hit it off right away and did what many couples in love do, started talking about the future and our desires. By February, 2004 we were looking for homes or property to build a new home. Since I now had the skills to create my dream mate, why not use those same skills for our dream home? Dave was willing, so together, over the course of several evenings, we filled a blank journal describing what the new home would be like, including the surrounding property, neighbors, country, land, etc.

We fantasized about a beautiful property surrounded by deciduous trees and wildlife. The home would back up to something natural and not someone else's backyard. We affirmed our neighbors would be friendly and have well-kept yards and homes. The property was in the country on a quiet street with minimal traffic and noise, just to name a few things from our list.

We did find the perfect property in a small subdivision with only 20 lots and 15 homes, one way in or out, surrounded by deciduous trees, farm land backing up to our yard, and everyone keeping their homes in top form. Everything we described in our manifestation book came to life! This was so fun to see our creation erected from mere thoughts into reality. I vividly remember sitting on the kitchen floor of the old house, with our samples and swatches spread out, planning what would go where for paint, cabinets, fixtures, tile, etc. It was such an exciting time for us planning and visualizing our future together!

I was focusing so much energy and thought on the new home project that I neglected to keep the balance in other areas of my life. While the new home was in progress, I started looking for a new job, as I wasn't happy the way things were going at my current company. Reorganization was taking place, and my sales numbers weren't where I wanted them. I needed something solid where I wouldn't have to worry how to entice my customers to buy from me. I wanted a product that sold itself. Hence the job search ensued.

What I didn't do before or during my search was specify the details of the work. I visualized a solid job within medical/surgical sales and earning an income well over six figures, and that was it. I guess I thought that would cover it. I completely forgot to be specific on the rest of the details, so the Universe lined up what I was in search of and didn't ask me to double check anything.

After many grueling interviews, I got what I thought was my dream job – selling orthopedic implants to surgeons and earning a great income as the product did sell itself. Along with that great income was a requirement of many hours of my time, including being hooked to a pager 24/7. This meant weekends, evenings, nights and holidays.

As I started the new job commuting each day on 100 mile each way drive, my Great Pyrenees, Zeus, was diagnosed with a type of bone cancer called Osteosarcoma. Our vet knew we were slightly financially strapped at the time with the upcoming move and pending sale of our home, so he suggested contacting a charitable organization he had worked with in the past. We are forever grateful to both Winston CCF and Animal Cancer Center and Imaging. This was a great assistance to us at the time of transition, as we did not have the liquid cash needed for these treatments and euthanizing my darling, sweet Zeus was out of the question.

We opted to try chemotherapy and radiation, while the Foundation helped us with the costs. I was so exhausted with the new job, the new house project and the stress of dealing with Zeus' cancer diagnosis that I wasn't thinking very clearly. I understand bone pain for humans is unbearable with any type of cancer, and Zeus was going through a lot of pain. He normally never even barked, but when he would just lie outside, whining and crying, I knew he was in serious pain.

Following some confirming x-rays, the veterinary oncologist let us know that the cancer had spread into his leg. To reduce his pain, amputation was recommended by taking the entire shoulder as well. I look back now and see how much that poor dog endured, all because I could not bear to add one more upset in my life. Somehow amputation was better than euthanasia, and there was still some hope that the cancer hadn't spread.

I realize that other people have had much more traumatic things happen in their lives, but it is unfair to compare or diminish what I feel in relation to others' experiences. At this very moment, I affirm that I forgive myself for any of the unnecessary suffering I inflicted upon Zeus. I was doing the best I could at the time and holding onto guilt now serves no purpose other than being something else to drag me down or keep me from moving forward.

With everything I had been going through, it almost seemed as though he was taking on some of my pain and suffering. It was so ironic, but I don't believe in coincidences. I absolutely feel he was here to help me through this part of my life, and he did. Thank you, my sweet Zeus.

Louise Hay teaches us that it is okay to feel, express and release your feelings. If we hold in our sadness, then we are denying our own feelings and basically saying, "What I feel doesn't matter in comparison to this." This simply isn't true. Processing our emotions is important. In addition, holding feelings in or dwelling on negative problems or concerns may cause other issues within us, physical issues. What we feel does matter, however it is best for us to face our feelings and deal with them at an appropriate time so we are able to move on.

Eventually, resulting health issues forced me to resign from the job I worked so hard to achieve. This was devastating for me and sent me on a downward spiral only to be left with an all-time low of self-esteem, self-pity, fear and self-hate. I was so mad at myself for so many things – oh, and let's not forget the guilt and the blame.

How could I quit my job without finding another one first? The income from that job alone could have covered all of the moving, building and living expenses for our beautiful home. Quitting after such a short time was one of the hardest things I have ever had to do. In fact, when I made the decision, I don't even think it was "me" who was doing it.

My manager and I were standing in the parking lot of a Lansing hospital, and I was telling her I had been going through so much with my dog being sick, building the house, the new job and the stress that it had resulted in me beginning to experience panic attacks. I recall being outside of my physical body when I first mentioned these personal issues. I shared my fears and uncertainty that I really didn't know what all of this meant. I suppose I was giving her a heads up that I wasn't sure I could cut it. How embarrassing!

In addition, the look on her face was disappointment combined with relief. She must have known I was not on my game before I laid it all out on the table. Feeling vulnerable, I was stating my truth right then and there, and I could barely stand it. All of the long interviews, intense training and testing I was throwing out the window, what was I thinking?

I realize now that saying everything out loud and sharing my fears of the entire situation was me speaking my truth. This is what literally set me free. I appreciate now knowing it was my higher-self taking charge to assist me in removing myself from a situation that was not serving me, and I had no choice but to take action.

We had only been moved into the new home for a short time before I gave my notice. It seemed like a time for celebration, but I was struck with berating myself for adding more stress to our lives. For a long time, I felt as though I had made the worst mistake of my life, as we barely scraped by until December of that year. Guilt and blame became my best friends and hung around with me like a ball and chain for the next year or two, while I job-hopped to find something that would be enough to at least help pay our mortgage and other bills.

Dave was most supportive of the entire situation, although I know it was un-nerving for him to think of the debt we were creating then. Not once did he either question my decision or try to sway me into staying with a job that was obviously causing me anguish. Some might say how *lucky* I am to have such a wonderful partner, however I won't say "lucky," because remember, I affirmed for him! But, I will state and reaffirm that I am grateful for his unconditional love, support, and friendship which grow more in our relationship every day.

The time off was undoubtedly a gift. Despite feeling like a complete failure, I somehow found bits and pieces of guidance that came to me in spurts, lighting my path to a more positive life. Until I really learned how to tune into that guidance, things moved slowly and the guidance was dim so that I didn't even see much of a difference, except that after starting a job with a home care agency practicing nursing, I was earning income again.

I look back at pictures of myself and see how I just let myself go and not in the "set yourself free" sort of way. I can see the sorrow and pain in my face. Life just wasn't fun for me even though I was trying to fake my way through. Sometimes when sadness is around so long, it becomes part of you, part of your identity. The uncomfortable becomes comfortable, and we forget how to be happy. That was me, unhappy and it was beginning to become normal, and I hated it.

At times I was so upset with how I felt, and at the same time feeling angry with this sad sack of a person I was becoming. I didn't want the struggling experiences any longer, and I was tired of trying to get through it because I didn't know the answers or how to change it. With that same passion, usually in tears, I would ask for someone to just come tell me what to do, and I would do it. I noticed that thoughts of the mounting debt would set it off, so I did my best to avoid thinking about it.

Feelings of desperation and anxiety would overcome me, and I would sob while begging to be removed from this planet and go somewhere peaceful and easy. I wasn't suicidal. I didn't have it in me to devise and carry out a plan. However, I did wish at times for a car to just side swipe me. I didn't know how things would turn out, and I was at my wits end with worry about the mystery that was my future, our future. Leaving the picture seemed easier than working through it. I just didn't have any solutions.

What I didn't realize then was that all of these statements were affirming my outcome. Not surprisingly, an old back injury flared up and kept me out of work. The original injury had occurred about three years before I met Dave when I was out of work and between jobs. I was out dancing with friends at the Chicago House of Blues and fell backwards down some steps in front of the band, but still walked around downtown Chicago in heels until about 3:00 a.m. By then both feet were numb in the toes and my back was really sore. The result was two herniated discs confirmed by an MRI.

I mention this because I am a firm believer now that we create everything that is around us, and everything that is happening to us right now. It may not manifest instantly or even within a few days, but it does manifest. Louise Hay's teachings in her book, *You Can Heal Your Life*, suggest a probable emotional cause for many bodily issues. Back problems represent the support of life, fear of money, and lack of financial support.

All three of those statements resonate with me now, and may have back then had I heard them. Most likely I wasn't ready to hear something that pointed the finger at me. Funny how when living life as a victim, it's easy to blame yourself, but when it's someone else that doesn't go over as easily.

It's obvious to me now that I was not feeling supported, because in reality, for a long time I couldn't even support myself and for that I was ashamed. I've always been able to support myself and earn enough money to be independent. It's interesting to me during these two particular instances in my life where I had gaps of unemployment, I had been incapacitated due to a back injury!

For at least two weeks during this second flare up/re-injury, I was unable to be vertical, neither sitting nor standing, and that included difficulty even using the bathroom. I was bed bound for most of the short recovery, but it seemed like forever. I'm a very active individual, and I don't sit still well. Lying in bed on my back was more than frustrating.

One day I was able to make peace with it enough to surf the internet. I came across an email ad mentioning a movie, *The Secret*. With my laptop on my belly and pillows supporting my head just enough to see the screen, I was able to stream and watch the movie. I was so intrigued that I ordered a copy for myself right away. Thus began a whirlwind of events which are still affecting me in positive ways today.

What I learned about the Law of Attraction from that movie resonated so strongly with me. I recall sitting up in bed with my jaw dropped as I listened to all the philosophers, speakers and teachers share their beliefs on the "Law of Attraction." This term was new to me, but everything they conveyed made perfect sense to me. It had to be true! It was the biggest "Ah ha!" moment ever, asking myself, "What the heck have I been doing to myself all of these years?" It was as if I was given a celestial slap from the Universe, waking me to how life is meant to be lived.

I raced through my thoughts of the recent past all the way back to my younger years of being tortured by kids in school and realizing how I created all of it. The most exciting thing was knowing I had the power to change everything, and that power is mine today! It was all up to me, and I was in charge. Woohoo! Who knew? I was renewed with energy, enthusiastic about life again and eager to make any necessary changes – mostly with my thinking and beliefs.

How silly I felt to realize I had successfully manifested in the past exactly what I wanted when creating descriptive lists for my home and a significant other. Why didn't I even think about taking it further and doing this for everything? Before this, I don't think I ever made the connection to create these lists about my health, well-being or financial success. Maybe I wasn't ready? Perhaps I still had to experience these things for myself so I would be passionate enough to share these experiences with others so that they could perhaps avoid some of the struggle and challenges I went through.

All I knew was that everything in the past didn't matter because I could change it. The biggest thing to change that seemed the most obvious was changing my thoughts and my beliefs. More specifically were the beliefs about deserving money and all things good in my life. The many times I would beg for assistance to come to me, I was really hoping for a direct road map with directions, start here, go straight, turn there, etc. I didn't realize I had to discover the journey as it happened, especially since I have free will and freedom of choice. We all do.

There are so many paths which guide us to where we are now, and we may choose different directions along the way. You and I may walk the same path, yet our experiences will be entirely different depending on the choices we make, our personal thoughts and our perceptions along the way.

Knowing what I know now is so uplifting and encouraging, and I hope it will be for you, too. I'm not saying that watching the movie I watched or reading the books I read will help you, but it may be a start for you to see what resonates with you. I always tell my clients, there are so many authors and speakers in the world with similar messages. It just depends who we are drawn to for wisdom. You will most likely learn from whoever resonates with you best.

And, as I've grown, I notice how I have moved on from certain teachers to explore other styles and deeper knowledge. As Buddha said, "When the student is ready, the teacher will appear," and how true it is! Learning of others' experiences is inspiring and perhaps yet another stepping stone on your journey, but following someone else's path won't necessarily lead you to their same experiences.

If you have a desire to find your way out of an unpleasant situation, I would like to suggest for you to ask for the guidance from within, listen for it and follow where those suggestions lead you. We all have different roadmaps to follow with many different adventures to experience. Your guidance may come through differently than mine, but trust that it is there and allow yourself to be awakened to it.

You may have many desires to accomplish within this lifetime, please know they will happen for you if you believe in them. Things may not happen overnight or even in a few months, but don't be surprised when they do. When we start working on ourselves and remove the blockades that prevented us from moving forward, our speed of manifesting picks up as we get used to it and then becomes the norm.

You may feel you are too old for anything to change, but that is a belief you can change for yourself as well. Or, if your personal list of change is so long and you don't know if you can get through it, just know it will all happen in divine timing. Peeling off those layers takes some time. Just go with the flow. Setting a simple intention to bettering yourself is a step in the direction of freeing yourself. But remember only you can make the changes.

Teachers may offer guidance, but you have to do the actual work and go through your own experiences.

As for me, I am living the perfect life for me right here and right now. Yes, there are still things that I desire to make my life better and happier, and those thoughts are born each and every day as I'm living and breathing life. Ever since these wonderful realizations came to pass, my passion and dedication has become empowering others through teaching, coaching, speaking and writing, while sharing personal experiences to not only help others heal, but also myself.

I've enjoyed sharing some of the "beautiful seeds of change" from my Divinely guided life with you, and I invite you to affirm with me now, "I am willing to change. And so it is."

About the Author

Jill Haas is a compassionate nurse who has been using affirmative thinking and the law of attraction philosophies for many years. In 2010, she became a certified *Heal Your Life*® Workshop Leader, then continued her training becoming a certified *Heal Your Life*® Coach. Jill was awarded a grant at the University of Michigan Hospital and is looking to study the effects of these philosophies with a pilot population of patients.

In addition, Jill is a Reiki Master, Angel Therapy Practitioner®, spiritual intuitive and founder of Infinite Happyness. Her passion is empowering others to live life full of "happyness."

jill@infinitehappyness.com
www.infinitehappyness.com

Acknowledgments

With love and gratitude to my ever supportive husband who is always there for me as my counsel and guide. You're more intuitive than you know, and your advice is invaluable. To my family and friends, I am so blessed and grateful to have you in my life. Your love, support and friendship mean the world to me. A special thanks to Nancy Newman and Lisa Hardwick for this amazing opportunity. Namasté to all.

Elizabeth Candlish

To my husband, Martin, for his support throughout my healing journey and beyond. To my son, Steve, my daughter Cheryl and my beautiful and fun grandsons, Josh and Fin. I wish you all lived closer to me.

My story is dedicated to all women who have or are experiencing breast cancer. May my words bring you hope, encouragement and fulfillment in your lives.

Chapter 12

SECOND CHANCE: Life After Cancer

More times than I can remember, I have been told that I would write a book. Who, me? I would think, "What planet are you from? What would I write about?" But eventually I started to seriously consider, "What would I write about?" Several offers have come my way in the last few months, but when this particular opportunity was presented, it felt right for me. Now, I am in the company of some beautiful authors, women and men, all sharing their own stories.

My story begins in early 2004 with a viral infection that went on for months. At that time I was working in a medical office and did not like taking any time off, so I continued to work. I just didn't like to let people down; I have always been one of those people who dedicated themselves to their job. Although I loved what I did as an Office Administrator, interacting with patients, making appointments and generally organizing everything, it could be quite stressful at times.

After several weeks of feeling really ill and having no energy, I went to see one of the doctors at my office, although not the particular one I worked for. This doctor told me that my problem was a viral infection; therefore, no antibiotic would help. I was told to just "work through it." Despite my best efforts to "work through it," the more I worked, the less energy I had and the worse I got.

But I kept trying because I knew that taking time off from work would cause me problems, which would add even more stress. My job was already stressful enough and on top of that, my commute to and from work was nearly two hours *each way*. Luckily my husband, Martin, and I did it together, which made it easier as he did all the driving, but it was still very tiring and added to the stress.

Still convinced that I didn't need to take time off work, because after all, that's what the doctor told me, I decided to consult a Naturopath. I still didn't know a lot about the Mind and Body Connection and was looking for that *instant* remedy to take the viral infection away.

The Naturopath was really good. She took the time to listen to my whole story, then went through my blood tests, explaining what each one meant and how it affected my body. This was something I had never been told before! She was not in a hurry to move onto the next patient, and I did not feel rushed in any way. I finally felt I had been listened to – I had been heard!

During this examination, the Naturopath found a lump in my breast and suggested I have it checked out with my family doctor. Coincidentally, I had an appointment in just a few days for my annual check-up with my family doctor.

At the annual check-up, I told him about the viral infection, and how I had gone to see a Naturopath. The expression on his face was priceless, as he rolled his eyes to the ceiling as if to say, "Why did you go to see a Naturopath?" He did not question me further about my appointment with her, but my feeling was that he was not very open to my seeing a Naturopath.

In fact, it seemed to have put him right off, and I don't believe he took me seriously or examined me as thoroughly as he could have. Even though I didn't even look ill and still had good coloring, I had absolutely no energy. Frustratingly, when a person looks as well as I did, it is hard to believe what they are saying, and I felt that the doctor was not hearing or listening to anything I was saying to him. In fact, when I told him about the lump in my breast that the Naturopath had found, he performed a brief examination which took only seconds, and then he declared that there was nothing there.

His whole reaction to everything was not the one I had expected to receive since I had gone to him in good faith to try to find someone to help me. I was so tired, I didn't even have the energy to argue with him. All I wanted at that moment was to be back home so I could rest, and I knew that we still had to catch a ferry and travel a fair distance to get there. So I went home having received no help for anything.

Shortly after this, I began experiencing bouts of vertigo. Vertigo is not nice at all. The room would spin around me, and I would have to hold onto walls as I attempted to go from one room to another. I definitely could not drive a car. Along with the vertigo, I was still fighting the viral infection and still had no energy. A local doctor told me to take stay at home for two weeks and take things easy.

Looking back now, I can honestly think: "Wow! My body was telling me to slow down and take things easy, and I wasn't listening." The more I worked, the more the Universe was trying to tell me to slow down. Now the Universe was giving me something else to make me slow down and start taking care of myself. Was I listening? I think at this time I finally thought, "Enough is enough." I knew I had to take care of myself – if I didn't, who would?

My mind was in turmoil. Here I was finally slowing down, taking off work to try to get my energy back, get over the severe viral infection and the vertigo, only to have my boss phoning me at home asking when I would be back to work – and I had only been off a few days! With the vertigo on top of everything else, I literally couldn't work. I had no energy, I was dizzy all the time, I couldn't move quickly because the room would start to spin. When I realized that my boss EXPECTED me to work whether I was really sick or not, and did not realize the effort I made when I had worked anyway for such a long time, I felt distinctly unappreciated.

Of all employers, a MEDICAL PRACTICE should have had the most empathy, but they didn't. Because I felt guilty, I actually attempted to go back to work, sleeping huddled in a blanket on the ferry all the way there. When I got there, I discovered that my boss had taken the day off and not bothered to tell me. Within a couple of hours, I heard a voice in my head say: "Make this your last day at work." I was so upset, angry and sick that I typed up my resignation, left it on his desk and returned home. I knew that I had to take the time to rest and concentrate on getting myself well again instead of trying to please others.

A few days later I heard a voice in my head say, "Go get a mammogram." I remember thinking, "What a good idea!" and immediately picked up the phone and made an appointment. I had once again listened to my intuition, although I didn't know that was what it was at that time. It was just a small, wise voice.

The appointment for the mammogram could have been made for the following day, but my energy was low again, as I had just been over to the city for an appointment a few days before. It was just too much for me to travel back to Vancouver so soon. The next available appointment was in late June, which was five weeks away, but this seemed fine to me. After all, my family doctor had said there was nothing there, so there was no reason to hurry! I had no need to worry about that lump – or did I? I had this nagging feeling; there was something or someone guiding me.

I had no idea what was going on in my body, but whatever it was, I was feeling terribly frustrated with not having energy. Even holding a book to read was too much for me, so all I could do was rest. When my energy would start to return, it was such a great feeling, I would go in the garden or the kitchen intending to do just one or two things. When I would begin to get tired, I would think to myself, "Just one more thing, and then I will sit down." Of course, I always went past that point of no return and did too much. It would then take me a few days of doing nothing at all to start to regain my energy. All I could do was rest and let myself heal. Slowly, I realized it was the only way for my energy to come back.

In June, I went for my mammogram appointment, and everything went well; or so I thought. A week later I received a letter. It's incredible how a simple letter can change your whole life in just an instant. The letter asked me to contact my local family doctor. I now had changed my family doctor to one where I lived because I could not do all the traveling to my other one. Even though I was a new patient, she was great throughout that challenging time and still is.

She told me not to worry, that she thought it was just another cyst. About three years prior, I had had a benign cyst removed from my other breast, so my doctor and I both thought it was the same thing. She then gave me a form for a digital mammogram at our local hospital. On this form she had written: Medium Risk.

If only I had listened more carefully to my body instead of trying to "work through it," maybe I would have realized earlier what was happening. But I now know one thing for sure: I did the best I could with the knowledge that I had back then. Nowadays, I am much more aware of my body and understand that there definitely is a Mind and Body connection.

After the results came in from the digital mammogram and an ultrasound, the attending hospital doctor wanted to see me in his office immediately. Luckily, Martin, my husband, had come with me for the appointment. He is such a blessing to me, and I am so grateful for all his support and love throughout this challenging time.

The doctor showed me the mammogram and said he was 99% sure that I had breast cancer. As is the case with most people upon hearing those words, a dread fear went all the way through me, and I immediately began sobbing. In the past, hearing the word, "cancer," from a doctor meant that then you died. But that is not the case these days, as I quickly learned.

The hospital immediately made an appointment for a core biopsy, which happened about 10 days after the mammogram. Even though the core biopsy confirmed the diagnosis, in the back of my mind, I was still hoping that he had made a mistake - that he still could be wrong. The worst part was not knowing what was going to happen in the future.

It was a very emotional time not only for me, but also for Martin, my family and my friends. I was in this highly emotional state for several weeks, but these tears were long overdue. I realized that I had not cried for a very long time; in fact, it had probably been a few *years*. The emotions of anger and frustration plus the stress of the last 18 months had taken its toll on me. I had kept all of these emotions in my body without release, and now these unreleased emotions had turned into a disease.

Beautiful Seeds of Change

It was all beginning to fit together in my mind and made total sense to me. My immune system had been fighting the cancer cells along with the viral infection. No wonder I had been so tired and had no energy!

I am so grateful for all the good doctors and the Medical Health System that took such good care of me, and that things moved as quickly as they did. I am very lucky that they had caught the cancer when it was still small. On one hand, that didn't make me feel any better. But on the other hand, I suppose that it did in a way because deep down I knew that there were others less fortunate than myself, and I felt reassured because I was very lucky.

I was then referred to the Cancer Hospital in Vancouver to have more tests and for radiation appointments. There are so many decisions that have to be made when you have received a cancer diagnosis. No one else could make them for me, they were my decisions alone - I had to choose the treatments that I felt comfortable with and listen to what my body was telling me. The decisions also involved appointments after appointments and lots of traveling to and from Vancouver. If I wasn't going to the Cancer Hospital for radiation, I was meeting with my oncologist, and my life just seemed to go from one medical appointment to the next.

My friends and family would tell me to just do what the doctors said. I wasn't so sure about that, and I could see the fear in their eyes and hear the tone in their voice. The truth is that they really didn't know what to say or how to react. This is a natural and common response which I didn't realize at the time. In fact, talking with other people who have been through this health challenge, as I call it, all have said the same thing: "Some friends moved on and new friends came into their life." This was true for me as well.

Having worked for so long in the medical system, I had heard of a wonderful oncologist. One of my former bosses, whose judgment I trusted 100%, had always referred his newly diagnosed cancer patients to Dr. Klimo. Since I had heard other good stories about Dr. Klimo, I asked to be referred to him.

I soon understood all the good stories. He was great! He was open minded, and always made Martin and I feel welcomed by shaking our hands with a warm smile on his face. I felt strongly that I was in good hands.

Dr. Bernie Siegel's book, *Peace, Love and Healing*, had been given to me by an acquaintance. What an amazing book to give to someone going through a health crisis! This book gave me hope and also added a new direction to my thinking. I even purchased his meditation CD's which also helped a lot.

In addition to Dr. Siegel's book and CD's, I did lots of reading: Healing Books, Angel Books, Reiki books, Doreen Virtue, all of which helped me through this challenging time. Everything I was drawn to I would read. I found that by just opening up a book – any book in a store or at home – it would fall open at precisely what I needed to read at that particular time.

When I had to make an appointment with a surgeon, again my work history helped in that I knew a good surgeon and a date was set for surgery. Surgery to remove a sentinel lobe and lumpectomy took place in July, 2004, and went really well. I was thrilled to learn that the cancer had not gone into the lymph nodes, and I was able to go home later that same day.

I am a very independent person and dislike feeling that I have imposed on someone or put them out in any way. So, a week later when I had a follow-up appointment with Dr. Klimo, I insisted on going alone. I knew that Martin had a business meeting, so I told him I would be okay and would meet him later. After all, I was just going in to get some medication, or so I thought. How wrong I was.

What a shock and surprise when Dr. Klimo recommended a partial mastectomy to take away the margins! Although he reassured me that this was just to be on the safe side, it was not at all what I expected!. The thought that I would need another surgery had not even crossed my mind. Here I was thinking I was going in for medication only to learn that I needed additional surgery. The news was so shocking and unexpected, I think I stopped listening.

Martin was annoyed with himself that he had gone to his meeting instead of coming with me. But after all, I had insisted so he had nothing to be upset about. Besides, we had learned a valuable lesson. After that, Martin never missed another appointment. That way, if I stopped listening to the doctor, or my mind was on something else that had just been said to me, Martin was there to fill in the blanks.

But right now, Martin wasn't with me. Coincidentally, my surgeon was only about two blocks away, and I went there immediately even without an appointment. Luckily, nobody was in the waiting room so I was able to see him within a few minutes. After I told him what Dr. Klimo had advised and that he wanted to see me back in his office within two weeks, the surgeon said that he didn't think it would be possible to have surgery that quickly. I left his office, angry and upset at these unexpected events, and wondering what was going to happen next.

The Universe, though, had other plans, and by the time I left his office and went to meet Martin, I had a phone call saying the surgery would be done – not in two weeks, but within 48 hours. As I said before, I knew I had the best oncologist, and when Dr. Klimo requests something to be done, it is done quickly. He is highly respected by both doctors and his patients.

Following the second surgery, I was sent home the same evening about 9:45 – even though I was still feeling ill, dizzy, and was so sick I could not walk on my own to the washroom. When I asked if they could keep me overnight because I was so sick, they just said no. No reason, just no. Martin then booked us into a local hotel for the night so I wouldn't have to travel and where it could be cooler than at home. Fortunately, I slept really well that night, and we drove home later that day.

This surgery took me longer to recover. After all, my body hadn't had a chance to recover from the first surgery, much less the effects of the combined anesthetic of two surgeries in two weeks. Further, my immune system was not as strong as it could have been because of fighting the original viral infection and then fighting the cancer cells. Now it was fighting to help my body recover from surgery and anesthesia as well.

Shortly after the surgery, I went back to Dr. Klimo, who declared himself very pleased with the outcome. He also prescribed Arimadex, which I would be taking once daily for the next five years.

A few nights later I had a dream that I was standing at a bus stop, just waiting for the bus. But when the bus arrived, I decided not to get on and instead moved over to let others get on board. As I turned, a lady went past and looked right at me. I distinctly remember saying to her: "It's okay. I was going to see my dad, but I have changed my mind." There was another lady hovering behind me, and I was not sure if she was going to get on or not. But I knew for sure that I was not getting on that bus.

My dad had passed away nine years before. So, when I woke up and remembered every part of that dream, including the conversation, I knew for sure that I would live through this. My new life was just beginning, and I knew I had much to do. I looked forward to this second chance with a new beginning and new adventure without even really knowing what that would be. I still had a long way to go before I would feel strong and healthy again, but I knew that I was going to be okay, and it felt good to get that confirmation through my dreams.

While recuperating, I was still very emotional and couldn't really talk about my experiences to anyone because I cried so easily. A friend recommended a local herbalist, Christopher Scipio. It took me a few days to gain enough composure to phone him, as I would start crying if I talked about what I was going through. In the end, it made no difference because I still cried when I phoned him as soon as he asked me my name and why I was phoning him.

He was kind and very patient, which made me feel good about talking to him. As I was crying, Christopher reassured me he was not in any rush and that we had plenty of time, so I should take a deep breath and take as long as I needed. The release of being able to tell my story in my own way and at my own pace made me feel so much better. I then calmed down and made an appointment to see him in person. As I sat with him and we talked, again the emotions came up, but he was very easy to talk to.

Christopher made up an herbal tincture to take on a daily basis, and in just a few days I was noticing a difference! Within a few weeks, the remedy had helped to calm me down, and I became stronger emotionally. I realized that Christopher had come into my life at a time when I needed that remedy for emotional support.

As more time passed, my energy slowly came back. I was eating healthy, organic food and staying away from stress, stressful situations and negative people. During this time I was drawn to start re-reading Louise Hay's *You Can Heal Your Life*. In fact, I had owned this book for many years and had even read it before, but I had not really understood the concepts. Now I was re-reading it, and the second time around it made total sense to me, especially with what I was going through at that time.

My healing was now coming from within, releasing emotions and negative beliefs, and I was doing this on my own. One of Louise Hay's suggestions to assist in your healing is to write affirmations. On the days when I had the energy to drive, I would go down to the beach, taking with me a special journal in which I would write and re-write affirmations on each page.

One of my favorite affirmations is one that was the most important one at that time: "I now go beyond other people's fears and expectations. I create my own healthy life."

As I continued to recuperate, I knew I was still facing 16 radiation treatments which would begin in November, about 12 weeks after my surgery. In the meantime, I developed an infection in my breast at the surgical site and was put on antibiotics. However, even though several different types were tried, they would only be effective for a couple of days and then stop working, allowing the infection to keep coming back.

After a few weeks of different antibiotic treatments, it was decided that I needed to go to Vancouver to see a tropical disease specialist, who decided to put me on one of the strongest intravenous antibiotics. This meant that for the next several weeks I would have to make daily trips to the local hospital for the IV antibiotic treatment. The treatment itself would take several hours for the medicated IV solution to run into my body. These treatments were successful, although it did take a few weeks before the infection was gone.

While I was still on the IV antibiotic treatment, the radiation treatments began. This meant that I would go to the Cancer Hospital for the radiation, then I would have to go to another floor in the hospital for the IV antibiotics. Common sense and my intuition was telling me that it would be better to wait until the infection in my breast had cleared up before beginning the radiation. But because the infection was clearing up nicely, the doctors believed I should go ahead and begin the radiation treatment. At that time I trusted the doctors implicitly and believed everything they said. After all, they were the experts, not me.

But by this time I had started to listen to my body, and if I was tired, I would rest. Rather than having to travel back and forth from the Cancer Hospital in Vancouver each day, I decided it was much more sensible to stay in Vancouver in the local lodge, which was just across the road. Instead of using up my energy spending hours each day commuting, I could conserve my energy by resting, meditating and reading. I discovered I could check out the books from the hospital. There were even shops close by, so it would be easy to just take a walk now and again.

I had my first radiation treatment and that evening experienced such discomfort that I returned to the hospital where luckily, there was a doctor on call. Apparently, hardly anyone has a side effect at such an early stage, but the reaction I experienced was that same as if I been through ten radiation treatments and not just the one. The doctor said that he thought the reaction was a result of the infection in my breast and that it would calm down, which it did to a degree.

I was walking back to the lodge, when a voice/thought that came to my mind: "Is my body letting me know that it had had enough radiation?" But this was all so new to me, I was still not quite sure of these voices. I did not always listen to my body, but I was becoming aware of a pattern that I was being led or directed in a new way. But the Radiation Oncologist told me to continue with the radiation treatment, so I did.

The second and third radiation sessions were uneventful, then I was allowed to go home for the weekend. But on Monday morning after the fourth radiation treatment, I had the same side effect as the first one! This time I was sent for an ultrasound test which confirmed the side effect was from the radiation therapy and not the breast infection, which had been healed.

The Radiation Oncologist agreed to discontinue the radiation therapy temporarily to give me time to think it over. He basically told me I had two options: If I discontinued the radiation, I would need a mastectomy. If I continued with the radiation, then I would have 24 MORE sessions, in addition to the four I already had. I had initially been told I needed 16 total, leaving only 12 more. But now he was saying that I needed 24 more, which would be a total 28 I would receive! In his approach, the four I already had didn't count, and I would have to start over. Since the number of treatments couldn't be reduced, I asked if the radioactive dosage could be made smaller. Again he said, "No. The same dosage."

Although I was in shock, I understood that not only did the doctor know about the side effects I was going through, but he wanted me to have double the amount of radiation therapy sessions than I originally had left! He was so automatic and unfeeling in telling me my "options." All he could "see" was the numbers in front of him. He didn't seem to understand that I was a real person going through horrible side effects on top of still trying to recuperate from surgery. His way of thinking did not make sense to me!

By now, I was learning that my body was sensitive, and I was actually beginning to listen to my body and my intuition! This was a very new but great feeling. Luckily for me the Universe works in wondrous ways, and as I have looked back over this time whilst writing this story, I can see how the synchronistic events have occurred.

For example, after this discussion with the radiation oncologist, I just "happened" to have an appointment the next day with Dr. Klimo, who I trusted implicitly. When I told him what had happened, he said that because the cancer was small, low grade and definitely caught in time, not only did I not need a mastectomy, I didn't need any further radiation treatment either! Basically, I had a third option that the Radiation Oncologist had not suggested: NO FURTHER TREATMENT AT ALL! He said that the only thing I might consider is having my ovary removed (I had had a hysterectomy about 25 years ago), but that wouldn't be necessary for a couple years.

When Dr. Klimo confirmed that I didn't need more radiation or a mastectomy, I was so relieved. Remember, the voice in my head had already told me that my body had had enough radiation. Now Dr. Klimo had confirmed that the radiation therapy sessions I had already received was enough for my body. I was relieved to hear that not only because I wouldn't have to go through any more radiation, but it was also confirmation of the little voice that I heard after the first radiation treatment.

Imagine my surprise when a couple of days later, that same little voice said, "It is time to have the ovary removed." This time I was more inclined to listen and thought to myself, "Yes. That is a good idea. Why go into another year with another surgery hanging over me?"

I received an immediate appointment with the specialist who said I could either wait until the New Year, or have the surgery on December 16th. Well guess what, since I had already decided I did not want to go into a New Year with this hanging over me, I chose to have it done in December. The surgery was again done as an out-patient, and I got to come home the same day.

I knew it was going to take some time to get over the three different surgeries I had now experienced in less than five months. These had all taken a toll on me, and my energy levels were down again. In addition, after this surgery, I felt nauseous, foggy and dizzy, which went on for a few days.

As I previously said, I had achieved Reiki Level Two, but working on yourself when you have no energy seemed impossible to me. To be able to see someone else and just totally relax on a Reiki table seemed so much better, and I knew this would help me heal from within.

I contacted a lovely lady who lived locally. As Martin drove me there, we had to keep stopping because I felt as if I was going to throw up. By going very slowly, we eventually made it to the Reiki appointment. When I came out of my appointment, I felt like a totally different person. I felt so much better - lighter and a bit more energy, no more feeling dizzy or wanting to throw up. I actually felt *normal*, a wonderful feeling that I had not had for a long time.

Now I know this is how my own clients feel after a Reiki treatment. I can see the difference in them from the moment they enter my Healing Room until they leave at the end of a treatment. It is remarkable what Reiki can do for a person no matter what their situation or what health issue they have. Of course, every Reiki session is always different, and the more open and receptive a person is, then the more they can expect from a Reiki treatment.

I was on my healing path and starting to feel much better when I heard that the Canadian Cancer Society was looking for Cancer Connection Volunteers. I had a good feeling about this! I would be trained by the Canadian Cancer Society, then be matched up with women who phoned wanting to talk to someone who had been through a similar cancer experience as they were going through. We were matched by several different things: Age, family, cancer type, medication, treatments etc.

I enjoyed this immensely and, during the three years I volunteered, was able to talk to quite a few women. I believe that what it gave them after being newly diagnosed was HOPE. They learned that women can get through this challenging time and see the light at the end of the tunnel to becoming healthy and whole again.

One day I went to the doctor for just a routine appointment. My own family doctor was on vacation, so I saw the doctor filling in for her. While I was there, I just happened to mention a spot I had on the top of my breast. He inspected it and said that he would make an appointment in a week to remove it. On my subsequent visit after the removal, I was told that the result of the tissue biopsy was that it was a small skin cancer.

I was then referred to a dermatologist who gave me a cream with instructions to use for five days in a row, stop for two then continue this regime for six weeks. Almost immediately, my skin became more itchy with every passing day. By the fifth day it was burning so badly I could not wear any clothing close to that part of the skin. No one had warned me that this might happen, so I consulted with my own family doctor. During that visit, I learned that my skin cancer was the result of sun damage from sunbathing years ago and had nothing to do with the breast cancer.

When my doctor looked up the possible side effects from this cream, we discovered that lo and behold, I had these exact symptoms – further confirmation of how sensitive my body was! After a discussion, we decided to discontinue the cream. Again I was being vigilant with my body, watching and listening to what was going on, and this was ridiculous. My body needed gentleness, not the burning and blistering that the cream was doing. I knew that there was someone or something out there that could answer my questions. It wouldn't take long for the Universe to show me the way.

A few days later, I just "happened" to be watching a local news station with Katolen Yardley, who is an MNIMH – Medical Herbalist, answering questions from the viewers. I had been interested in Herbology for many years, but during that time did not have the energy to pursue learning more. At the end of Katolen's segment, she gave her email address so anyone with questions could contact her to book a consultation for detailed recommendations on their health. Of course, I emailed her right away to ask if there was a gentler way in which to treat the body instead of using the cream that had been prescribed for me. I liked the gentleness, honesty, and integrity that came across in her emails so I made an appointment to see her for a consultation and completed the several page questionnaire she sent before my scheduled visit a couple weeks later in Vancouver.

Upon arriving for my appointment, I immediately felt really comfortable with her and her gentle energy. We talked for almost an hour, or I should say that "I" talked, telling her all about my previous health challenges. And, yes, I did cry when I told her about my breast cancer, it still is a sensitive issue.

She prescribed a tincture to use several times a day, which would last me about four to six weeks. In only a couple weeks after beginning to use the tincture, the difference I felt was incredible. I could actually feel the difference in the energy in my body. My appointments continued with her about every six weeks for awhile. My energy was coming back in leaps and bounds. It was great, I was beginning to feel normal and healthy again!

Prior to the viral infection, I had run a bit previously, and even entered an annual 10K fun run a few times. My energy was so good that by January, 2007, I registered for this same fun run, the Vancouver Sun Run, to be held in April. It felt so good to have the energy to run again, I felt great. For the next three months, I busily trained then completed the distance in 1 hour 30 minutes. My previous "personal best," was around two hours, and I had taken nearly 30 minutes off that! If someone had told me a year before that I would run a 10k race again much less have my best time ever, I would never have believed them.

Because I loved the effect the herbs had on my body, I asked Katolen where I could learn more about herbs to make my own remedies. She referred me to the Dominion College of Herbology in Vancouver, which had a distance learning course. Although the course was really fascinating, it was hard work, and I had to continually motivate myself to keep up the studies and homework. In late 2007, I passed the exam and became a Chartered Herbalist. I began to make my own Herbal Tinctures for myself and friends, and began to sell them as well.

God does not give any diseases that there is not a remedy for.

~ Unknown

I attended a Spiritual Workshop in 2008 and met a lovely lady named Pam. She told me that she had started her own business with Healing Touch. She explained that she had gone on a government-sponsored program to do this, but that you had to be on EI (Unemployment) or Medical EI to qualify.

But I was confident that if Pam could do it, then I could, too. The thought that I could start up my own business venture was exhilarating!

I was a bit concerned whether or not the Medical EI I was on a few years ago would give me eligibility to register, so I spoke to an Employment Coach at the Employment Bureau to check on my status. After confirming my eligibility, the Employment Coach liked my idea of starting a Reiki Energy Healing business and referred me to the Aspire training program.

Now I could do something with my life. I had always wanted to work for myself, but did not know how to go about it. Now it was all at my fingertips. My interview for the Aspire program was scheduled to occur in just a couple of days, which I thought was quick. What I had not realized was that to be accepted into the Aspire training program and actually receive the financial support funds from the Provincial Government, I had to go before an Interview Panel to explain to them what exactly I intended to do and answer questions about my new upcoming business idea.

When you allow your intuition to come through, the Universe will open the doors, but it is up to you to walk through them. Everything started to move a lot faster than I thought it would, but at this time in my life, the change was very positive because I had my energy back.

The only problem was that the date set for the Panel meeting was in the middle of a trip to Australia that Martin and I had previously planned with the Sunshine Dragons Abreast team, a local Dragon Boating team made up solely of Breast Cancer survivors. I had been paddling with them for the past two years, and this was a wonderful opportunity for our team to compete in an international team event.

Getting to explore Australia was an added bonus. Martin's brother, Eddie, lived there with his family, and we had made arrangements to visit them during our trip. So besides Cairns, Sydney, and Caloundra on the Australian Sunshine Coast, where the actual Dragon Boating event was taking place, Adelaide was added to our itinerary. (As an exciting end to the week in Caloundra, we came in first in one of the races!)

When I explained my problem to Niv at Aspire, she suddenly said, "Okay this is what we can do." She handed me forms to fill in, and told me to come back at 4:00 that afternoon since the Panel just "happened" to be there for another meeting. As you can imagine, this was exciting but also intimidating as I did not have the time that most people get to prepare for their meeting. I had less than four hours to prepare everything. Talk about being stressed and put on the spot.

But as I said before, when the Universe puts you on a path, and you listen and follow through, things do happen suddenly. I always use the analogy of putting a jigsaw puzzle together, and if the pieces are sliding in easily and quickly, it is all meant to be. But when you force a piece in, all the other pieces become tight and misplaced.

So I went home and completed the lengthy forms by answering as honestly as I could, returning to the Aspire office just before 4:00. The Panel was still in their meeting, so I had to nervously wait outside. I asked the Angels to guide me with the right words to say, at the right time, and then I was invited into their room and explained the idea that I had for my business, which was treating clients with Reiki and Crystals. I later found out that I had been accepted by the Panel the very same day, and my journey into becoming an Entrepreneur began a few days after I returned from Australia.

Aspire is a wonderful Government program to help you start your own business. I attended workshops for several weeks where we learned about Marketing, Accounting, Networking, and putting a proper business plan together. There was so much great information, and we even brainstormed for business names which was fun. The business name I have now is: Sunshine Reiki Healing Centre. The added bonus to all this was I was actually getting paid by the Provincial Government for the first year to attend these workshops to learn as much as I could about becoming a business owner.

On December 16, 2007, my business, Sunshine Reiki Healing Centre, began. It was slow in the beginning, but I was still learning, so it was all good. Now I am busy treating clients with Reiki, as well as teaching all levels of Reiki Workshops, which I love to do. I know that this was where I was meant to be and is my dream come true.

In 2008, I received an email from the International Reiki Association in the US. The internationally renowned William Rand was teaching Advanced Reiki and Reiki Master/Teacher Workshops in Seattle, about a six-hour drive away. The wonderful butterfly feeling and tingles began as soon as I received the email, and I knew that this was meant for me so I registered straight away. I didn't even have to think about it, the Universe was guiding me, and I knew it was the right thing to do.

Even though I already had my Reiki Master/Teacher level, I had not done the Advanced Reiki and wanted to learn as much as I could about Reiki for myself and my clients. This was such a marvelous and wonderful opportunity. I felt such excitement as I had read all his books, and I still receive their Reiki magazine to this day. I was not disappointed and had an marvelous weekend in Seattle. It was very intense learning new tools for healing and the Reiki attunements. I also met a wonderful lady, Paula. We have stayed in contact, she has even been to visit my home, and we remain very good friends to this day.

In 2009, I felt guided to learn about the Bach Flower Remedies. I had experienced taking these little flower remedies with Katolen, my Herbalist in Vancouver. Bach Flower Remedies have such a powerful but gentle effect emotionally and physically on the body, which is what I like about them for myself and for others. Whether it be Reiki or Bach Flower Remedies, the gentleness of what I do provides powerful healing for our bodies, and is very healing for the Body, Mind and Spirit. I took my Bach Flower Practitioner Level and passed the exam.

As I look back, it seems to me that each year I have done something new to complement working with Reiki. I never really planned this, I just follow my intuition and know that I am always divinely guided to the perfect workshops for me. Every time I see a workshop that is for me, I always have an excited, tingly feeling in my solar plexus along with a knowing feeling that this is the next step to take on my wonderful journey.

In 2010 I heard about Dr. Patricia Crane, who teaches the philosophy and work of Louise Hay in her *Heal Your Life®* Workshops with her husband, Rick Nichols. What I didn't realize until I saw the details about the workshop, was that for a couple of years, I had been practicing Louise's work and including Louise Hay's work in my Reiki treatments with clients by writing out affirmations and telling them about the *You Can Heal Your Life* book.

I had never heard of this kind of workshop before but thought to myself: "Well, the time is right for me now." I was so excited and ready to release and let go of my "emotional baggage" that I had been carrying around with me for years.

I signed up straight away with that tingling feeling again, and the excitement building once more. This was the workshop where I was going to let the past go and heal from within. Of course this would mean being emotional and letting my emotions out, was I ready for this? Not letting my emotions out clearly hadn't worked before – look where I ended up! So this was the time, and I knew it would also show on the outside. And, oh my goodness, it did.

It seemed that time flashed by and suddenly I was off to the *Heal Your Life®* Workshop in San Diego, a place I had never been to before. What a beautiful place to hold a workshop, it was the ideal place. The perfect group always comes together, and the participants in the workshop were great.

My roommate, Sheila, was perfect as well. She was my first roommate ever, and I could not have asked for anyone more ideal. I had arrived a day early so I had time to get settled in before she arrived. As soon as she walked through the door, we were chatting before she could even put her luggage down. We had so much in common, we could not stop talking. Patricia really knew how to match roommates. When we had to say goodbye on the last day of the workshop, we were both very emotional. Sheila and I are still in contact today sharing our stories of how much good has happened in our lives since this wonderful workshop.

The workshop took place over six days, and I loved every minute of it. I could feel the changes happening to me every day, as I felt lighter, more confident. We don't realize how much emotional baggage and feelings of sadness, resentment and anger that we carry around in our bodies. For many reasons we keep the emotions hidden in our body, but now I was open to allowing myself to release anything that I no longer needed or wanted. At the end of the workshop I became a Heal Your Life® Teacher, and I now teach others about the philosophies and work of Louise L Hay.

The transformations I have seen with my students by teaching these classes have been astonishing, and I love to see people heal from the inside by letting go of past hurts and negative beliefs. Once you start healing from within it really does show on the outside as well, you just glow, it is an miraculous feeling.

I truly love what I do and teach, whether it is seeing clients for Reiki, or teaching Reiki, or Heal Your Life® Workshops and Life Coaching. I am continually learning and studying, discovering that "healing" is an ongoing process for each and every one of us.

Before I went to San Diego for training, I had already scheduled a six-week Heal Your Life® Study Group. I knew that I would love the work of Louise L. Hay because I had been using it myself and for my clients. When I arrived back in November, I had ten days in which to put everything together for the study group! Although I was very busy compiling the documentation, I knew that practicing and letting others know about Louise Hay's wonderful work this was the best way for me to do this. I love to pass on and share what I learn with my students and clients.

In February, 2011, I attended the Heal Your Life® advanced workshop for life coaching, which I had signed up for in October before even leaving San Diego. I was just so excited to be sharing these wonderful teachings of Louse L. Hay. The advanced workshop again was a great experience, and it was held in Sedona – another place on my travel list I had not been to before.

So I actually got the best of both worlds: I was able to attend a wonderful workshop in beautiful Sedona, a place of powerful energy and healing where I had always wanted to go.

Included in the workshop were trips to several of the energy vortexes located in the area, which was a huge bonus for me and for everyone else on the workshop. The first one we went to, the Airport Vortex, had very powerful energy. I climbed up the top as if I had the vitality of a child! There was a path to walk up but I wanted to *CLIMB* up, after all, it is not every day I get the opportunity to climb a Vortex! The climb felt really easy until I got almost to the top, and then someone helped me get up the last bit.

I sat at the top in a meditative state, just gently breathing in and out and feeling such peace. All at once I felt an incredible energy coming through my hands and into my body, which lasted for a few minutes. The power of this energy was extraordinary. I felt and knew that a change had occurred in my body. Something similar also happened in the Chapel Vortex a few days later, only this time the energy came down through my head and through my hands, down my body and through my feet. The vortexes were miraculous! What fantastic experiences!

A day or so later I was giving a Reiki treatment to Heather, who was also in the workshop, when I noticed a huge difference in the healing energy. It was still gentle, but more powerful. After I arrived home, my clients immediately noticed and commented on the difference they felt. I love the way the Universe guides me to the perfect workshops, locations and to new healing energies. At the end of the Advanced Heal Your Life® Workshop I became a Life Coach, something I really love doing.

Since my diagnosis, my life has transformed into the life I was meant to be living. I have met some remarkable and wonderful people. I am always reading and learning: I am a student of Life! My life is balanced doing things I truly love: Spending time with family, my work, gardening, reading, and traveling to new and exotic places.

As you can see from my story, breast cancer does not have to be the end of your life, although it could be an end to the old life that you lived. Breast cancer truly gave me a second chance to create a brand new life which went in a totally different direction. I sincerely doubt that if I had not had breast cancer that I would have been brave enough to make the changes necessary to be living this wonderful new life. Yes, breast cancer was a blessing in disguise.

Beautiful Seeds of Change

CONCLUSION

What do you want your life to be? Breast cancer does not define *who you are*, but rather *what you allow yourself to become*. The point of power is always in the present moment, just by changing your thoughts. By changing your thoughts, you can change your life for the better.

What is it you have always wanted to do? Is it to travel for fun, change your career, give up your career, retire early or move to a new home? What is stopping you?

I know I used to be busy working in an office, running around after everyone else, making sure everyone was happy and not taking time for myself. Now I am living my life in balance, taking the time I need for ME. I work several days a week treating clients with Reiki and seeing Life Coaching clients. I still sometimes work on the weekends, but it is doing "work" I love to do, which is teaching either Heal Your Life® or Reiki Workshops. It is a joy to see the transformation of students healing from within.

Do you stop and take time to smell the roses, take walks in nature, meditate? We all seem to be in a hurry and have busy lives, so take time for you because YOU ARE WORTH IT AND YOU DESERVE IT.

Only you can change your life. What are you waiting for? Give yourself permission and allow yourself to be the person you can be. Don't hide behind a disease, or wait for the disease to give you a second chance; see beyond it to what you can achieve. Make a second chance of your own choosing! My second chance gave me a life beyond cancer. I truly believe that anything is possible in life.

About the Author

Elizabeth Candlish is the owner of Intuitive Heart and is a licensed *Heal Your Life*® Workshop Leader and Life Coach. She is also the owner of Sunshine Reiki Healing Center, a Usui/Karuna Reiki Master/Teacher/Practitioner, Chartered Herbalist, Bach Flower Remedy Practitioner, Author and Motivational Speaker.

Elizabeth has been motivated her by own healing journey and is always learning other modalities to empower herself and others on their healing journey.

Elizabeth lives with her husband, Martin, on the beautiful Sunshine Coast, Vancouver, BC, Canada. Elizabeth is passionate about her work, and enjoys gardening, writing, tennis, spending time with friends, and traveling with her husband around the world.

eacandlish@dccnet.com
www.intuitive-heart.ca
www.sunshinereiki.ca

Acknowledgments

Thank you to all my friends and family who have supported my healing journey. I give sincere thanks to all my teachers for your guidance and your wisdom, especially Louise L. Hay, Patricia Crane and Rick Nichols, Canela Michelle Meyers, Hannelore, and Lyn Ayre.

A very special thanks to Norma James, who passed away in June, 2010. Norma was the best friend a woman could ever have and was a huge part of my life for over 30 years.

Thanks to Ann White. We met at a time and supported one another when we each needed a cancer buddy. May we never lose that connection.

Thanks to Ross Beard, my brother in law, Margaret Selvester and Julie Wainwright, who all gave me words of encouragement when I most needed to hear them. May our friendships continue to grow and blossom.

Thank you to Paula Elofson-Gardine whose friendship has been a blessing in disguise. I'm so glad we met in Seattle and connected in such a way.

Thanks to Jean Rice, who was at the right place at the right time during my healing journey. May our friendship grow to the next level.

Jessica Wild

Dedicated to those earth angels who continue to love me enough to stand by me and offer me their strength while I find the depth of my own.

Chapter 13

THE HAND OF GOD

When we least expect it, life sets us a challenge to test our courage and willingness to change; at such a moment, there is no point in pretending that nothing has happened or in saying that we are not ready. The challenge will not wait. Life does not look back.

~ Paulo Coehlo

"I am going to ask you a question," she says to me. "And when I ask you, there will be one answer that pops into your head first. There will be more that want to come in after that, but I only want to hear the first answer. And, I want you to blurt it out as you think of it." "Okay…" I think, "I can do this. Simple." I breathe.

She is my marriage counselor. She is also the woman who trained me to be a hypnotherapist and gave me the gift of Reiki. She taught me how to quiet my mind and listen. I love her. It is near the end of my 12-year marriage. I am newly pregnant with my fifth child. My soon to be ex-husband and I are trying yet again to see if we can or should continue trying to make a marriage work that we both had decided nine years earlier wasn't worth saving. He sees her one week, I see her next, and then we see her together. It is my turn today. She has me close my eyes and reminds me again that I am to blurt my answer with no thought. I assure her I understand.

It is quiet then. She allows me time to clear my mind and find my own inner silent place, then she asks me simply, "Jessica, Why did you marry him?"

The answer from my innermost heart spills from my lips with zero hesitation and such honest flow that it literally stops my heart for a moment. It speaks volumes as to where I was when I married him, and where I still was 12 years later. My voice comes out laced heavily with the sob that immediately follows: "Because I was afraid no one else would ask."

And, as it escapes my lips, I am slammed to the core of my being with sorrow and shame. How did I come to this place? That I not only got married, but stayed married for 12 years, only because "I was afraid no one else would ask." When did I become the woman who lived my life with that much fear of the future? When did I become the woman that believed I had to take the first thing offered to me, even if it was 'stale bread'? When did I decide to devalue myself so much that I married a man I didn't love … because I was afraid no one else would ask?

My counselor sits silently as I wipe tears from my cheeks. I begin to voice all of the questions in my head. They are punctuated with snot and tears and long painful moments during which I can't breathe.

After a few long moments of silence and breathing, I look up at her and say, "What do I do now? I don't know what to do!" She looked at me with the loving eyes of a wise old grandmother and said: "Yes, you do. You are just so scared you can't admit it." She pauses for my mind to process then adds: "Jessica, you have been parked on the side of the road in a mud bog for 12 years. It's time to move now. It's time to get on the road… your life is waiting. You have greatness in you. Stop hiding."

I look down and cover my face with a handful of tissues and say: "I can't do this! I don't know how. I am not that smart. Nothing I have to say means anything to anyone…" I gush all of my fears at her feet – my deepest fears of unworthiness and fear. And, she begins to sing my song. I return to a familiar energy stream that teaches me so much about this cycle of surrender and strength.   She slips into what I call "Doula mode" and softly reminds me how to breathe through the worst of the fear and pain that was encompassing me, and how to believe in my own forgotten strength.

I realize now that I was in Transition again. Some of my greatest teachers on this journey have been the women I am blessed to assist in the births of their children. I remember so many times when I would witness this kind of change in a woman who had asked me to stand with her on her birth journey. I remember singing a woman's 'song' for her, until she could look back and see the miracle of her own transition through this process of surrender.

Transition, in a childbirth setting, is at the end of the labor, the last intense demanding moments where most women turn to those around them and say "I can't do this. I don't want to have a baby today. I need a break." It is a moment that a woman finally purges all of her deepest fears before she begins what she knows will be the most challenging part of her journey with her child.

I am reminded of moments moaning a woman's song of strength and power during the most challenging peaks of her birth journey.   I remember whispering reassurance of my belief in her intuition and her inner knowing about how to make it through transition in labor. I am returned to the moments of raw primal power that some women choose to claim to get through Transition. I recognize this place. I remember what this feels like, and I breathe. I return my mind to the wise counselor in front of me, who is patiently waiting for me to find my way.

I was at a place in my life personally and spiritually that felt like that overwhelming wash of failure. I could no longer deny that I was living a life completely devoid of Authenticity. I was practicing a religion that hadn't resonated with me in 10 years. I was living in a loveless marriage that was on every outward appearance perfect, but in reality was toxic and draining on us both. I was learning lessons at remarkable speeds, and I was realizing that I wanted to share these moments of growth with others. I knew that I had something to say to a larger audience, but I had NO IDEA what.

All of the forces in my life were demanding change. I could not put it off, I couldn't stop the process, and I couldn't delay it with fear. Just like the woman in labor, I could only surrender to this moment of transition and ride the wave of intense growth that comes before the greatest reward. And just like the woman about to give birth and experience miraculous changes within her, I surrounded myself with those would sing my song.

I have lived an amazing, vivid, sad, beautiful, happy, terrifying, incredible, miraculous life. And I don't think the growth part is over, I think it is just beginning. What I hope and want to believe is that something I might say or present an analogy on might help someone learn a lesson or understand a concept or discover a way to find their own authenticity. Because while it SUCKS to grow into that Authentic Self, in the moments you can really feel it... really connect with that Divine part of God within you... that Authentic Self, it is amazing. I have FELT that... that moment that you say: "This is who I am, and I will not apologize. I am strong and powerful and bold. I will speak my truth even if my voice shakes with emotion. I am a grower. I am better today than I was 15 years ago. And maybe, just maybe, I have learned a few lessons. I am me. And that is just fine. You can love me or not. I am okay with either one."

It is a moment of power that usually comes after the darkest nights of the soul, the most intense storm and often examining the depths of our being. It is the feeling that I watch wash over some women after this intense part of labor we call "Transition." I watch it, and I see this transition, this change... from woman to primal divine being. It is a moment of growth that I wait for. To watch her face when she realizes that not only did she come out on the other side, but she did with power and surrender in equal measure.

Flash forward from my session with my Teacher when I faced my deepest fear for the first time to sometime in the last two years. The years following some of the most challenging things I believe I could ever face. Years, when I was gifted to find the strength inside of me through the most intense pain and overwhelming sorrow and shame. Times when I looked at my worthiness and ability and believed I could make a difference in the lives of those around me.

I am reminded often as I continue to grow, how important it is to surround yourself with people who will hold your pain and witness your journey and remind you of the song you sing at your most sacred place of surrender.

I always appreciate synchronicity in all of its beauty. It is as if, at the moment that it will do the most good, we are powerfully reaffirmed in our strength and tenacity. In a blessed, synchronistic moment I found a woman named Elizabeth Potts Weinstein. She wrote a blog some time ago that was the Universe's way of reminding me of a lesson I needed to learn or a hurdle I needed to leap over. I share this blog here, with her permission:

Living Your Truth

This is for those of you who are still holding back.
Who haven't launched the business. Who have not put up that video. Who are not writing the blog posts. Who are not being themselves on twitter. Who are not hosting the event. Who haven't started the book or created the art. Who aren't yet consulting or coaching or teaching or dancing or speaking.

For those of you who are still hiding.
Because you don't think of yourself as amazing as the guru or the girl who graduated from school the same day as you. Because you still have research or practice or courses to take. Because you need to learn the technology or buy a new computer or wait for the kids to start school. Because you're not finished getting ready.

Because you don't find yourself perfect.
Let me confirm your greatest fears.
You are not perfect.
You will make mistakes.
You will fail.
Some of what you launch will not work.
Some people will be mean.
Some people will be disappointed.
Not everyone will like you.

Yes. It sucks.

But.

There are people out there who need you.

Who are waiting for the unique truth you have to speak, for the brilliance you are destined, you are called to bring to this world. People whom only you can help.

And yet you are hiding?

You refuse to share your gifts with the world, just because you are not perfect? Because you are human? Because you don't have every answer to every question ever invented, because you have flaws, because you are still growing and learning yourself?

Stop wasting yourself on all that crap.

Stop thinking. Stop researching. Stop analyzing.

Stop waiting.

Reveal yourself to the world.

Share your truth, your brilliance, your message. Surrender yourself to the perhaps tiny yet unserved segment of people on earth who will passionately resonate with your every word.

Open yourself up.

And let them love you.

That is all

What are you waiting for? What's holding you back from the thing you know you want to do, you are meant to do?

~Elizabeth Potts Weinstein (c) 2010

I will add only this to her straight forward call to arms: In the moments of transition over the last few years, what I have learned about myself is that I will never do anything in my life again "because I am afraid no one else will ask." I am here. The right people will ask. I am not perfect. I will fail. I will be disappointed in myself and others and occasionally in the journey. Some people will be mean, some people will ignore me, not everyone will like me; but I am here. And as Joan of Arc said ... "I am not afraid ... I was born to do this."

And the day came when the risk to remain tight in a bud was more painful than the risk it took to blossom.

~Anais Nin

Peeing Alone – The Art of Intelligent Selfishness

Far more indispensable than food for the physical body is spiritual nourishment for the soul. One can do without food for a considerable time, but a man of the spirit cannot exist for a single second without spiritual nourishment.

~Mohandas Ghandi

"Okay. I think we have done really well today. I am proud of you … let's finish off with some homework." She is my teacher, and we have just had an exhausting emotional session relating to me needing to learn about what makes me feel happy and nourished. The message still isn't settled in; it is obvious to us both as she starts giving me the instructions for my assignment. "Okay. So, I want you to make a list for yourself to refer to. I want you to write down 20 things that make YOU feel good. Things that make you feel nourished." I stare blankly at her. She prompts me, "Tell me a few of them now so we can get your creative juices flowing."

We wait. I scramble in my own mind to throw something out that I think will make her stop staring at me. I blurt something to her. "Nope… that's for your KIDS. What makes YOU happy?" I think for a moment then throw out another thing that I think she wants to hear. "NO. That is for your husband. What nourishes YOU?" I try one last time. "Doesn't count, that is for other people… what makes YOU happy?" We sit in silence and then, she quietly says to me , "Jessica, you really have… NO IDEA… what I am talking about, do you?" I look at her with what must have been an expressionless face. "I guess I don't remember how to do anything JUST for me." I tell her, still wandering in my own thoughts, "I guess I have been putting my own needs on the back burner for SO long now that I have forgotten what makes me feel happy. I guess I have been so busy taking care of the people around me, that I have forgotten how to take care of myself. I don't know that I have really ever taken care of myself." I begin to cry then … we breathe in the realization of this statement. And we are both saddened.

I was once asked what my greatest fear was. I thought about it for a moment, and said, "Watching my children be hungry or cold or in pain." My world revolves around my children. Being a mother is one of the things I do best in life. I am good at it. At this point in my life, I had been pregnant and/or nursing for almost nine years (minus six months between my last two children). I took my children everywhere with me. I very rarely got a babysitter. I had toddlers home with me all of the time, and my world revolved around housework, meals, diapers and mothering. I had made my own needs secondary or tertiary for so many years, I had forgotten who I was. I had become a Martyr Mother. I gave everything to my family and was now finally showing how I was suffering from my constant malnourishment. We both realized that I needed to be reminded of the woman in me because the mother was starving me out.

"Okay... re-start," she patiently says. "Here are the rules: I want 20 things on a list. Whatever you put on the list has to ONLY be FOR YOU. If it makes someone ELSE feel good in any way... it can't go on the list. These things are only for you. This is Intelligent Selfishness. And it is time you learn this principal."

I am reminded in an instant of part of the flight attendant's instructions when you board a plane. We have all heard it: "If you are traveling with others who may need your assistance, please put your own oxygen mask on first." I remember thinking once, when flying with my children, "Oh, I can't do that, if I am going to save anyone, it can't be me. I would put my child's mask on so they would be safe, then take care of my own. I can't be selfish like that." I also remember feeling the slow quiet realization that if I didn't take care of myself, I could not effectively take care of them. And that if I wasn't safe in my OWN right, no one would be safe if there was tragedy. I had to make sure I have enough "oxygen" in me, enough nourishment of body, soul, spirit and mind, to actually care for myself and others. And to do that, I had to learn how to take care of myself first occasionally.

I hug her goodbye and promise to work on my list that night. "Okay. Email me by noon tomorrow with your list. I want to be sure you understand." I promise I will.

I go home that afternoon and do all of the things I had to do as a mother and wife. Dinner, laundry, dishes, laundry, bath times, bed times, laundry, cleaning, more laundry. *laugh* And as I am about to collapse into bed, I remember my homework. "CRAP," I say as I haul myself out of bed and go into my office, where I grab a sheet of paper and a pen.

I sit down and take the lid off of the pen. It is poised over the paper. I wait. I start bouncing it on its point onto the hard desk... waiting... for inspiration ... I am thinking. Still thinking... And... I am ... stuck.

So I repeat my instructions to myself. "Things that make me feel good, that make me feel nourished ... Just for me ... What makes me happy?" I wait some more. Nothing. Hmmm. I quiet my mind and ask myself, when was the last time I felt like I had done something ALL for myself. What do I even WANT to do for myself? What do I like? What makes me feel stronger and more able to cope with life?

OH!! OH!!! I am writing finally! This one works. No one else benefits from it, and it makes me feel good. The first item on my list was: Peeing Alone.

Don't laugh. I was a mother of four children under the age of eight. I quite honestly could count on two hands, the times in the last few years that I had actually peed alone. If I locked the door, someone was going to knock and need me... so why bother, right? I never peed alone. I stopped trying.

Peeing alone. So there it was. Written down. And as I looked at those two pitiful words on my blank page, I realized the depth of my complete and utter depletion. I finally grasped how much I was giving of myself to others at what ultimate cost to myself. Really? Peeing alone would make me feel nourished. Um, yes. Actually having a few minutes to do nothing but breathe.. and pee... yes. That IS nourishing for me. Okay, I am going to be okay with this. There it is, Item #1. Peeing alone.

I was determined to get through this assignment before bed so I made myself start thinking. The creative juices finally started to flow, and I began writing. #2: My down comforter. Sleeping late wrapped in my down comforter. I racked my brain and came up with many more. Oh! Smoked turkey wrapped around a slice of avocado. Good hard purple grapes with Havarti cheese. Music! Quiet, moving music. And, wait..,. I love sitting in the quiet on the porch before dawn and meditating. And... OOOH!!! "MASSAGES!!!" No one else gets to feel good from that so for sure that counts! I am on a roll now.

The list was rounded out with "Time with my friends (sans kids)" and "enough time alone that I can catch my own thoughts." I also added "driving alone in a car," "weekend getaways near the ocean" and "shaving my legs in a huge bubble bath with candles." I was flowing now! I took the time to title it "My Delicious Decadence List." I went to bed dreaming of moments where I could hear my own thoughts and the blissful fantasy that didn't involve anything to do with laundry.

I was so proud of myself when I emailed her my list the next morning. And I was overwhelmed almost to tears when she told me in a reply email: "Good job! Now make the commitment to yourself and to me that you will do at least two of these a day... and that you will add five items a week to your list." Her email continued with something overwhelming like. "Hang the list on your kitchen cabinet. Look at it often. Use it to remember to take care of yourself. Jess, I love you. You are strong and amazing and growing ... but, you are SO depleted. If you are going to be strong enough to do the work you need to do in this life, you must learn how to nourish yourself. No one is going to force you to stay well except yourself. It is a life lesson you have been putting off for too long. Get fierce with yourself. Please put your own oxygen mask on, Jess. Ask for help. You can't do it all alone, sister. I promise you will feel SO much better. I will see you next week. You are worth more than 'Peeing Alone.'"

TWO? A day? I am FAR too busy to create time to do two intelligently selfish things every day. All of my previous worries and statements of judgment about myself flow into my thoughts. I begin writing with them, and as I did, I sat with the energy of that fear, overwhelm and embarrassment of needing this kind or replenishment. "If I take time to do things for myself then things won't get done, and I will only have more work tomorrow to catch up on. I can't do two of these every day. Maybe two a week."

I tell myself the lies over and over. "I am not that selfish. I don't need that much care from others. Other people don't want to help me be selfish. People are going to get upset at me and think I am horrible. I can't go away by myself, how will my life function without me involved in it? No one can do the job that I do as well as I do it. They will all be lost without me. People are counting on me to take care of them. If I nourish myself, then someone ELSE will be depleted. I will have to tell people no. They will think I am weak. I will have to ask for help. They will think I am greedy. I will have to learn to be willing to accept help and be grateful for it. What if they think I am lazy? I will be embarrassed if people know that I am taking care of myself." I hear my own thoughts, and I realized again that I had no idea how to do this ... and the evidence of that bubbled out of my inner voice and tears trickled down my cheeks onto the page upon which I had just scrawled this list of terrifying "What if's."

"What if they realize I can't. Do. It. All. Alone . What if people stop thinking I am a good person because I need time away from my kids, and my life and my partner and my worries to just be selfish. I can't do this; it isn't how I work ... I help people; I don't ask for help ... How am I going to...." My mind races, and I start to slip back into Martyr Mother mode. "STOP!!!!! Stop," I tell myself out loud.

I tell my brain to be quiet so I can think. I have a brief break in mind chatter that allows a quiet moment of reflection... Oxygen masks.. Breathing... Nourishment... Accepting help, receiving graciously, trusting others to help. Listening to my inner voice that tells me how empty I am and how close to collapsing I have become.

I am reminded of Birth once again. I write a lot about women finding beauty within themselves in sacred powerful moments. Moments where we grow into true authentic beauty through surrender to the journey and the reality of Becoming; it is a beautiful, magical miraculous process. Much of my journey is based on layers and reminders of lessons in the same energy stream that helped me remember a feeling of wholeness.

My writing often has to do with lessons I have learned watching women experience the transcendence of birth. The birth of that inner vision that changes who she is forever when she can glimpse it, even for only a moment, to help her remember lessons that were learned in other times and places. It is a magical thing to watch a woman surrender and lean into what can be a shift in her beliefs about herself. Watching others have ah-ha moments is one of the secret joys of my life. And helping them get there feeds my soul and makes me somehow richer.

There really are very few times in a "natural" birth that oxygen is needed barring an emergency. The most common situation is when mom is asked to breathe oxygen while she is at the end of her journey and is doing the hard work of pushing the baby out. Mothers often need extra nourishment during this period. She is carrying and still sustaining the life of a baby in her womb. The baby needs all of the oxygen it can get... and it will take what it needs to survive, often at the cost of the mother. So we nourish the mother with extra oxygen.

I often help mama understand that we aren't offering her oxygen because she is IN jeopardy; but instead, we give oxygen to KEEP her from jeopardy. We give her oxygen for energy, we tell her. So here is mama, tired, achy, depleted and spent. We remind her to breathe deeply. With each breath to take all in that she can, so it will saturate her cells and sustain both of them through the next contraction. That will demand all they both have and more to work through. When she feels weak, we remind her: "Breathe your oxygen, keep your mask on. You are working hard, your baby needs extra right now and so do you. Just breathe, fill your lungs."

I remember now. These two concepts feel the same to me, 'peeing alone' and 'putting on my oxygen mask' ... these are important lessons. I am also reminded of the way I feel after I allow myself to be cared for and, if only a moment, remember that MY needs are important, too.

I remember what it feels like to wake up and think "I have all I need to accomplish my goals for the day." And I am reminded of the days I need to collapse into the arms of someone who is more nourished than I am in that moment... seeking contact, strength, fortitude, and the gift of intelligent selfishness. I am reminded of the times someone has to catch me as I am close to falling and say to me.. "GO. Take care of yourself. We can do this. Get yourself filled."

And I am reminded of the moments in my life where my closest friends stood by me and sang my song of transition and reminded me to breathe. When I forget how to feel nourished, they remind me. When I believe I cannot possibly survive a trial of my faith, they often have to hold the mask over my face for a moment for me to remember how good it feels to breathe. But usually, I remind myself before they need to do that.

"Peeing Alone." They have become reminder words between my closest friends and me. When we call each other in crisis, we often ask: "Are you taking time to Pee Alone?" Those two words have become a stark reminder for me on more than a few planes. One, if peeing alone is nourishing to me in that moment, I am depleted. Two, if I am not remembering to pee alone, I am not being intelligently selfish. We all need nourishing in different ways. How we are nourished isn't nearly as important as that we are actually nourished. *How* we are intelligently selfish isn't nearly as vital as that we are intelligently selfish.

I don't remember what else was on that list now; I have remade it several times. But I will never forget that vision of those two words scrawled at the top of the paper, and how proud I was to have thought of something I do just for me. And, then, the reminder of how little I had been doing to take care of myself. And I am recommitted to the belief that selfishness can be intelligent, and that peeing alone isn't nearly enough to sustain my soul.

I try to remember to get my own mask on before I need it. And, yes. I do still pee alone.

The Hand of God.

> *No one can tell what goes on in between the person you were and the person you become. No one can chart that blue and lonely section of hell. There are no maps of the change. You just... come out the other side. Or you don't.*

> *~Stephen King*

I call her, sobbing: "I need you." I am driving, shaking and I cannot stop crying. "Tell me what's wrong." Her voice, which carries a love for me that I've heard from few others, calms me in an instant. This woman is my sister and my Teacher. She is amazing.

I begin sobbing anew, but take the time to pull over because I was having a full blown panic attack: heart racing, sweating – the works. I couldn't stop the words that began to bubble out of me: "Am I doing the right thing? Should I wait just a little longer to file for divorce? Maybe things will get better. I can't have this baby alone. Can't I just put this off another year? We can pretend that long, we have pretended for nine years. This is SUCH bad timing; I was stupid not to wait. I can't work because I am seven months pregnant and raising five kids on my own now. I can't pay the bills and I have no idea what I am supposed to do next. I am so tired and I can't think….."

I stop to catch my breath, having purged my deepest fears at her feet. "And…" I hiccup a sob and choke out my deepest fear, the one that had plagued my innermost self for weeks now: "Who is going to lie across the bed from me and help me tell her she is beautiful?" A new wave of tears spill down my face. I grab a tissue and try to breathe.

I am due to have our fifth baby in seven weeks. I have just completed my last paid birth assistant work until my baby would be 6 weeks old. Meaning, I was essentially jobless and would have no money for almost five months. At my request, my soon-to-be ex-husband moved out less than a week ago, and I am exhausted. My oldest son is in kindergarten. The other three are home with me. Most of my friends don't know about my pending divorce so I have kind of been in hiding. My mother has just picked up the children for the weekend so I can finish cleaning my husband's things out of the house. I am alone. And I am more scared than I have ever been.

I sit and weep for a moment, not hearing the rest of my phone conversation. I finally hear her voice on the phone: "Where are you?" I take a breath and reply, "I am on my way to your house." I hear her breathe. "How long until you are here?" I get my bearings on the freeway. "Forty minutes," I tell her. "Oh good," she says. "Are you okay until you get here?" Hearing her voice and knowing I will be with her at her home makes me calmer. "I am okay. I will still probably cry the whole time, but I am okay." She replies with a quiet, "See you soon."

I hang up the phone and put my hand on my huge belly bulge and whispered to my unborn daughter the mantra I had been reciting for weeks now, "I am okay. We are okay. This will all be okay. This. Is. Perfect." I say it over and over again as I begin to move forward again. I breathe and attempt to exhale my fears, as I slowly move to finish the drive. And finally, I stop speaking and begin to quietly cry once more because I do not believe myself.

She meets me at the door. Her home is sacred. She is a teacher. Her home is peaceful and powerful all at once. I stumble into her arms, putting my head on her chest, trying to stop the tears long enough to say hello. She holds me. I finally find my voice and say into her breasts. "I don't know what to do. Can I undo this; will I survive if I don't undo it? Should I just say I am sorry and… fake it?" She laughs at me. It makes both of us smile, and we slip into that you-have-to-laugh-because-crying-isn't-doing-it kind of laugh. The laughing is enough to drop some of my overwhelming sorrow. I am safe.

She points into her office. She is a healer. From the moment I met her, I was a better person. I curl up in one of the overstuffed couches and tuck my feet under me. She sits next to me. My eyes had to be that of a deer as it stares down its hunter. I was sure I was about to die. She starts questioning me, in her beautiful therapeutic way. Asking me to walk thru things a step at a time and evaluate each option; reminding me to feel the emotion and energy around my choice. Then she would wait patiently while I chose the right path. She is good for me.

We eventually move into a meditation. I stretch out my legs and relax, centering myself with her as she starts to help me see where I need to go. She takes me through our familiar grounding; I go there quickly with her. We have been many times. And she instructs me to see a light coming from my heart chakra. I am amazed as a twinkle of pink and green light comes out. She asks me what it looks like, so I tell her.

"Okay. Now, make it a road. Make it hard. You are going to walk out on it when you are ready." I work on the image in my mind for a moment then nod that I am ready. She asks me: "What do you see?" "Well… there is a bit of a bridge, but it ends in about 20 feet. I can't quite see, it just looks like it ends." "Good, so start walking those 20 steps." I see, in my mind's eye, where I am walking. I approach the edge and nod.

She asks me, "Where are you?" I tell her I am standing about five feet from the edge of what I can see. She tells me to go look over the edge. I remind her that I am terrified of heights, and we laugh. I stand and wait. Then in my mind, I peek over, wishing for a railing, like at the Grand Canyon. There is no rail. It is only… mist. It wasn't … scary, per se. Just unknown. I visualize in color usually, but this was unfamiliar to me.

So here I am in my mind's eye, peeking over the edge. She asks me how I feel. I tell her I don't like being there, and I have to back up. She waits. I exhale. Then she says in a quiet, near whisper: "Why are you afraid?" "I am not afraid," I reply defensively, knowing I am lying to myself. "I just don't know what's down there." I quickly defend myself, almost opening my eyes. She laughs at me. I smile. "Well, then, what do you need to do to be NOT afraid?" "I want to know what's down there," I tell her in a whine that made us both laugh. "I know I will be safe, and I know I am supposed to go down there. But I don't know if I can fly."

She chuckles again. "Oh, honey, you don't need to know how to fly now, that is something you learn as you go." "But what if I can't fly?" There are fresh tears spilling onto my cheeks. "Well, then you will land somewhere, won't you? Why don't we see where you land today? I am here, you are safe, just go there with me, and we can look at the options together." I exhale and try to get back to the place of peace I am looking for.

She allows me the time to sort thru things in my mind, bringing me quietly back to the problems that are plaguing me about my pending life path, softly coaching me: "What's the worst thing that can really happen?" I would answer. "Okay. How would that feel?" I reply. She takes me into my deepest fears of judgment, unworthiness and failure. And she helps me see that, really, the only thing you can do, is "leave it all on the track." There is a moment of uncertainty that slowly becomes a sense of courage. I am calm. But I am not at all certain I am safe.

I breathe, and I tell her: "Okay, I am going to step over the edge." And, in my mind's eye, I walk cautiously to the edge of my vision. Then I close my eyes and step off. In my mind I am falling. It is pretty amazing. There is mist and pictures and beauty all around me. I recognized that I was falling, but I also felt very safe... almost like that moment when you are flying a paper airplane, and it catches that last bit of air and glides to a stop. I had landed. It wasn't a huge bump, but there was still a deep uncertainty.

I tell her that I am ready to move forward. She begins to speak again and asks me to tell her where I am. I explained to her that when I stepped off the ledge in my mind, I had closed my eyes for the fall. I explained to her that I had been falling with my eyes closed. I am back to looking at my landing, and I kind of try to clear my vision to see where I am.

She then asks me, "Open your eyes, Where are you? Where did you land?" I see myself opening my eyes and inhale the sob that forms in my throat. She gives me a moment to process then asks. "Where are you, Jess?"

I cannot find my voice, and I feel like I can't breathe. I motion that I need a moment. I am awash in... what? Relief? Release? Peace? Gratitude? Probably a swirl of all of them. My voice is unsteady, and I am kissed with hope. The energy surrounding me is that of a peace I had rarely felt in the past months that were the end of my marriage and the beginning of a season in my life, which would, on many occasions, feel suffocating.

My emotions are barely in check as she asks again quietly, "Jess, what do you see?" I take a moment to look around and then all at once as the mist finally clears I am weeping again. I whisper through my hand that has instinctually covered my mouth, "My kids are here. They were patiently waiting. They are here with me, and we are safe. They were already here. They just needed me to launch." I can no longer talk; it is all I can do to breathe. I am awash with emotions that earthly words would diminish, silence is the only option.

"I …." I stop and clear my voice that is thick with tears. "I think I landed in the Hand of God." The words choke out of me in an almost inaudible whisper as fresh, quiet tears come. I breathe. We sit with my message and let it soak in. As I come back to my own awareness, I hear my own voice in my head reminding me of safety and strength, and I take a moment to place my hands on my pregnant belly and whisper aloud: "I am okay. This is okay. We are okay." I breathe to try to soak it in. I think I believe myself now.

She cries with me as I leave to go home; grounded and centered and more sure of my choices. I love her. I have this moment we shared burned on my consciousness. It is a visual I have used many, many times since then. It sustained me through the birth of my child, a divorce and countless hopeless days since.

As a conclusion to this story, we will flash forward about ten weeks. It is the week of New Year's. I am lying in bed nursing my beautiful infant daughter. I am peaceful and confident. It is 3:00 am; our middle of the night feeding. I have the lamp on, and I am curled on one side of the bed with the baby in the middle of the big king sized bed. She finishes nursing and falls asleep. I scoot her to the now empty side of "our" bed and reach for the light just as my "new baby" -enchanted three year old pads in. I hear her pajama-clad feet rustling a sleepy stagger.

She says "Hi mom, I saw your light." She makes me stifle a laugh. "It is still nighttime sis, go back to bed." She gives a small grunt of disgust. "Okay, then I will just climb in for a kiss." My bed is high, and there is a wooden step on the other side of the bed for her. She climbed onto the stool and stopped, gasping in delight. I looked her and said, "What's wrong?" She quickly climbed onto the bed threatening to wake the baby and swooped gently down to place a (rather firm) kiss on her sister's cheek. "Don't wake her. Don't wake her." I whisper, waving her back with a brush of her hair.

And, in that moment, my beautiful three year old angel daughter took me back to the Hand of God. She looked at me with her piercing blue eyes, still swollen from sleep, and her mop of shiny white blonde hair and bubbled quietly: "Oh mom, I am so sorry, but I just HAD to kiss her. Because… because… well… because she is the most beautiful thing I have ever seen in my whole long life!"

And, there were the tears, again. I was awash with the memory, remembering that this journey takes us to the hand of God, and that we were safe. Remembering that I would always be provided with someone to 'lie across the bed from me and tell her she is beautiful'. Once again, my deepest fear vanishes into faith. "Thank you, sister…" I whisper into her still warm sleepy head. "Thank you for bringing me here again." I motion her over and kiss her sweet head. My three year old didn't go back to her own bed that night. She slept on the other side of the baby. And, for a few minutes we lay there holding hands in the lamp light, looking at her and wondering at her beauty and whispering to her; both of us telling her she is beautiful.

As I reached to turn off the lights, I finally knew. We were safe. I was known. And it was all going to be all right. I was being held in the Hand of God. We were safe, and we were known. I remembered. And, finally… I believed it.

Change How You See, Not How You Look or "The Eight Cow Wife"

Confront the dark parts of yourself, and work to banish them with illumination and forgiveness. Your willingness to wrestle with your demons will cause your angels to sing. Use the pain as fuel, as a reminder of your strength.

~August Wilson

My Christmas gift a few years ago from one of my sister-friends is a bumper sticker that says: "Change how you See, not how you Look," and there is a sketch of a beautiful woman with ample curves. We cried together when I opened it. It was so perfect. I believe in synchronicity. I think it is the Universe's way of saying… "Keep going, you are on the right path."

I looked up at her and said, "Where…?" She gushed about stumbling on it on a bizarre shopping trip during a spontaneous trip to Sedona. "I saw it and KNEW it was for you."

This is her goodbye present to me. She was to be moving soon. We learned to talk with our souls, this woman and I. She was sent to me as a gift to help me grow. And my life is richer because she chose to live authentically. I think there is something sacred, about having the kind of friend that you can lay in the sunlight with and talk about life. I think there is something even more sacred, however, in having the kind of friend who makes you look at your dark places. Who sits with you in the quiet and listens to you find your way. Who sits by you and holds space through the dark nights of the soul we all face. And even better; who helps you see that your looks don't define you.

Do you remember the 1980's Pantene shampoo commercial with Kelly LeBrock? The camera pans in to her flawless face and cascading gorgeous brown hair, and she says, "Don't hate me because I am beautiful." Then the commercial goes on to tell us, the viewers, that if we will only buy Pantene shampoo, we will be as beautiful as her.

I always hated that commercial, not because she WAS beautiful, but because she needed us to hate her for it. And because we were expected to mindlessly try whatever magic potion she told us to purchase to attain her level of beauty.

I often sit and think about beauty and how others' perceptions of us can change our perceptions of ourselves and our feelings of self-worth. I am reminded of another defining moment for me as to how I feel about my own "beauty."

One night I was with a friend getting ready for girls' night. I am a pretty casual person, and I thought it was supposed to be a casual evening, so I was in a sun dress and flip flops. She asked me if I would be willing to dress up a bit more to make the evening more fun. I said, of course. And here, is where the next layer of lesson began for me.

I walked into my bedroom and thumbed through my overstuffed closet and pulled out a black dress. It is over four years old and starting to show signs of wear. But it is the perfect little black dress for my body. (Little being a misnomer, I am a size 20.) It shows just the right amount of cleavage, is a sexy length, is cut well and the fabric is amazing. This has long been my "I don't know if I need to be dressy or not" traveling dress. It has been wadded into my suitcase many times. I actually got the dress on the clearance rack. It was one of those synchronous moments where the heavens open and lights from the angels illuminate the dress that happens to be in the right size, the right color and a quarter of its original price. And it was comfortable. I grabbed it. *laugh*

So I slid the dress over my head, fluffed my hair and pulled on a pair of strappy heels like my friend asked and stood up. An instant later, the entire evening was ruined for me. She looked at me, both of us facing the mirrors in my bedroom and said something like, "Well, now you are too pretty. I don't feel pretty enough next to you anymore." I remember looking at her and offering to change back, but we were late and she wouldn't hear of it.

Later in the night she said something to the effect of "I am just so tired of being the Moon to your Sun." I was still so much in shock, I didn't have the clarity of thought then, but it did come later, somehow me being pretty made her, a beautiful, striking woman in her own right, feel "less than pretty."

I told her: "Changing my dress and shoes didn't make me more beautiful. And it MOST certainly didn't make you LESS beautiful." But the energy from that evening stayed with me. I struggled for weeks with the concept of beauty, and how someone else's perceptions can so often shape our own. Whenever I think about it, I am starkly reminded of that Pantene commercial … "Don't hate me because I am beautiful."

Coincidentally, also in the early 1980's, Brigham Young University released a movie called "Johnny Lingo." It was a movie made for youth, to help them look at self-esteem and self-worth differently.

Johnny Lingo is the eligible bachelor on a remote island, and it is time for him to choose a wife. Mahana is one of the girls on the island. Her spoken name is never only her own. It has somehow morphed into "Mahana You Ugly." It was what she was called by all of the villagers. They believed her so ugly that she hid in the trees so they wouldn't taunt her.

The tribe's dowry currency is measured in cows. The day of betrothal comes, and it is made into a village event where Mahana will be insulted in public when her beauty will be judged by how many cows her suitor offers her father.

Mahana's father starts the bargaining. He has teased Mahana that he will start high so it won't be as hard when she only brings one cow. Her father says: "Three cows." And everyone laughs knowing that Mahana-You-Ugly isn't really worth that. Then, in a moment, Mahana's life changed. Johnny Lingo, resident island hunk and respected man says: "Three cows is many, but not enough for Mahana. I will pay eight cows." Everyone is astonished. Johnny tells Mahana's father, "I will bring them in the morning." And then he leaves the villagers and Mahana staring after him to plan for his return the next day.

At the wedding feast, there are boys hiding in the bushes singing in their childlike taunting voices: "Johnny Lingo had a cow, trade it for an ugly wife, Johnny Lingo's married now, he'll be sorry all his life."

Mr. Harris is the local trader helping with the wedding gifts, and he hands Mahana's father the mirror that Johnny has ordered as a gift for Mahana to look into every day. "How do you like that, Tulo." The reply from Mahana's father is: "Ah, it is beautiful, too bad Mahana's face will crack the glass." And the two men laugh.

Johnny Lingo then, in that VERY moment, changes Mahana-You-Ugly's life forever. He begins to explain to the villagers what they missed. He tells them then, in a voice filled with strength and love for his bride: "Always and forever when they speak of marriage settlements, it will be remembered that Johnny Lingo paid eight cows for Mahana." As he leaves with her for his own island, Mr. Harris says: "So that's it. He's neither crazy nor blind. He's just vain. Poor vain fool."

Johnny takes Mahana home to his island and returns some weeks later. The trader looks again at Johnny's new wife, who has been kept away from her own taunting village mates and loved by her new husband, but now, he sees Mahana through Johnny's eyes. "Johnny, I can't get over it, she's beautiful." Johnny replies in a small yet sacred voice to this man who will never understand what he sees. "I have loved her ever since we were children, she was always beautiful. But tell me, do you think eight cows was too high a price for her?" The trader looks at Johnny's beautiful wife, who has now become the envy of all of the women for miles around, tells Johnny, "Oh, no. In fact, eight cows might not have been enough for her."

Trader Harris then looks at Johnny with eyes of realization and says, "I see. In her father's hut, Mahana believed she was worth nothing." And Johnny quietly replies, "Yes, and now she knows she is worth more than any other woman on the island. Think what it must mean to a woman, her future husband meeting with her father to discuss the lowest price for which she can be bought. And later, when the women of the village gather, they boast of what their husbands paid for them - three cows, or five. How does she feel, the woman who was sold for one, or two? This could not happen to my Mahana."

Johnny is met by a respectful glance by the trader as he says, "Johnny, I've misjudged you. I thought you were thinking only of how important you would look to your friends, paying eight cows for a wife. I didn't know you wanted to make Mahana happy."

And, here, is the moment that ties all of this back to the purpose of my writing. Johnny replies by saying "More than happy, Mr. Harris. I wanted her to actually remember and BE an eight-cow woman."

Johnny somehow understood that by allowing Mahana to see her own beauty without the constant taunting voices of the Village, she would allow herself to be reminded of her own worth and beauty.

I think that the obstacle for many of us, me included, is that we are hiding in the trees, waiting for someone to fight off the "villagers" and take us to a place where we can find our own inner (and possibly outer) beauty.   And, I think I have come to believe that no one has to hate anyone for being beautiful.   And, that sometimes, it takes the miracle of another person "reminding us" to declare our value to our own insecure child and those that would mock us.

As I finish editing this writing, my four year old has just left my arms. She came to find me in the quiet of the morning. I looked at her messy hair and sleep laden eyes and said quietly "You are beautiful."

Her response was the perfect ending for this story. It was the quiet manifestation of remembering beauty. I kissed her warm head as I told her she was beautiful, and then she looked at me with her big brown eyes, the same eyes of the baby in my womb when I went to The Hand of God, then she curled into my chest and matter of factly said exactly what I needed to hear to tie all of my thoughts together: "I know, Mom. But thanks for reminding me."   I smiled at her as I felt tears burning my eyes. There is something sacred about the wisdom of a child. I am blessed.

Everything has beauty, but not everyone sees it.

~Confucius

About the Author

JESSICA WILD is a perpetual student of growth and development. She has studied many modalities and sat at the feet of many teachers who have changed her life. Her greatest moments of wisdom are often discovered while sharing a path of growth toward transition and transparency with those she loves. She has been a childbirth professional (Doula) since 2000 and has educated individuals on birth and growth in all aspects of life based on her journey in this profession.

She lives in Mesa, Arizona with her five children who are her greatest source of strength and her loudest cheerleaders.

jessicadwild@yahoo.com
1oilymom@jessicawild.com
www.jessicawild.com

Beautiful Seeds of Change

Acknowledgments

My thanks... to my amazing children for strengthening me in ways I had never imagined. My journey would have meant so much less had I not been blessed to travel it with each of you. To my family for giving me both roots and wings and being willing to watch me fly. To Andrea Fisher, for 'Seeing me' and never for a moment allowing me forget who I am or how strong I am. To my Teachers, both in body and in spirit, thank you for showing up when the student was ready. To Elaine Lemon, Mamie Wheeler, Anne Marie Palzer, for always answering the phone when I called and walking down terrifying paths with me, reminding me that everything is perfect, and that I had come too far and worked too hard to let anyone take my place at the finish line. A sacred thank you to the many, many men and women I can't possibly list who have shared with me your journeys of strength, challenge, despair, love, power and triumph, who stood by me through the darkest nights of my soul and allowed me to witness yours in return. To the many friends who sat with me and listened to the sound of growth in myself and others and celebrated with me. To Paula, for believing in me and launching my last step to claiming the life that was intended for me.

To Lisa and Nancy for helping me share my story and refine my dream. My life became richer the moment each of you entered it. I am humbled.

Jiyun Park

I dedicate this to my mother, who did the best she could to bring me up with the knowledge she had at the time. Also this is dedicated to those experiencing pain and suffering. May God help you to find the path to peace and joy.

Chapter 14

GOD NEVER ABANDONED ME

UNWANTED CHILD

When my father and mother got together in Korea to start their lives of "happily ever after," they knew from the beginning they didn't get along with each other, and they both knew their relationship wasn't going to last long. But by then I was already in my mother's womb getting ready for my new adventure. My mother was worried that she wouldn't be able to take care of me after I was born, so she decided to have an abortion. Unless she could provide me a normal family life and a good education, she didn't want to have me as her child.

She went to several hospitals for the abortion, but the doctors refused to help her because she had progressed too far in her pregnancy. She was devastated and continued to search for a doctor who would help her with an abortion, but to no avail. In the meantime, I was growing bigger, so she had to abandon the idea of getting rid of me. Faced with no other choice, she waited to see me face to face.

When the time came, she didn't have an easy delivery. Her water didn't break from inside, and she endured about 36 painful hours to give birth to me. In the olden days in Korea, mothers didn't go to a hospital for childbirth, so there was no outside aid for an easy delivery. Her abdomen was unusually big, so people expected to see a baby boy. When I finally came out to this world, many people commented that they wished I was a boy.

As soon as I was born, my mother started examining my body. If any part of my body had been severely deformed, she planned to put me into a permanent sleep by pushing my face down to the quilted floor. As she was searching, she found something peculiar about my hands: Both of my hands were tightly clenched into fists. She continued to check to see if anything else was wrong with my body.

When she discovered that everything else was fine except my hands, instead of infanticide, she tried to open my fingers, but they were so tight she couldn't open them up. She carefully made a small opening from my pinkie and put something soft into my folded finger then waited hours so that the muscles could get used to the new position. She continued to open up my fingers one by one and pushed soft objects further inside. She did this very slowly and devoted great attention to it. After a couple of months, my fingers finally opened up completely and stayed open.

One morning when I was six months old, my father brought his girlfriend home to introduce her to my mother. My mother believed that the relationship with my father was over, and she felt by encouraging the relationship with the girlfriend, it could end gracefully with my father still providing support for us. My mother also felt compassion for this other woman, so without hesitation she welcomed his girlfriend, made breakfast for her and began eating with her. When I was laid in between my mother and this woman, I began to kick her. My face turned red with a scolding look, even my voice had a scolding tone. This woman felt so shameful she couldn't eat anymore and dropped the spoon, but my mother encouraged her to continue to eat.

A few days later after this incident, with no warning, my father left us behind with no means of survival. My mother didn't know where he went, and she never heard anything from him after he left. With no more financial support, her struggle began.

The only consolation she had was her younger sister whom she loved very much. After my father left us, my aunt moved in to live with us. Since my mother and my aunt were both struggling financially, they wanted to save money by reducing the rent fee. My aunt loved me dearly and looked upon me as her own baby. Wherever she went, she took me in her arms, showing me off and praising me. She truly gave me unconditional love.

When my mother used to live with all of her sisters in one house, her second sister did not get along with my mother. This sister constantly implied with words and action that my mother wasn't welcome in that house. When my mother decided to leave home, her younger sister wanted to go with her. Before they left, one fortune teller told my mother not to take her younger sister because she would lose her in a tragic way. But her younger sister insisted on going with my mother.

When I was only one year old, I invented my favorite song. If I loosely translate my masterpiece, it is: "It is done. It is complete." I joyously sang this song several times a day, and as I repeated this song, the tempo accelerated. My body moved with the rhythm, and my head bent backward as I sang faster and faster until I was about to fall backwards. My mother used to catch me right before I fell, saying "It's enough my baby. Stop singing now. You are going to fall down." My mother and my aunt both thought it was very auspicious for me to sing this, and they hoped this would bring good luck to them.

Each of them tried to get a job, but it was especially difficult since neither of them had an education or a skill. The only thing they knew how to do at that time was working for a family or a restaurant to clean the house, cook and wash dishes, but even that was extremely hard to find. When they were able to get some food, they fed me first, and whatever remained, they shared together. By then I already learned that it was a rare opportunity to have food, and when they would try to feed me with only a small amount of food, I snatched the spoon away and started eating like an adult.

My aunt was a gentle soul who was very compassionate towards people who were less fortunate than her. One day my mother sent her to their elder sister's house and gave her some money for transportation and food. On the way, she was drawn to a big crowd who had formed a circle around a beggar lady with a baby. It was a winter time, and they only had thin clothing on them, and the baby didn't even have a blanket. Spontaneously my aunt gave all the money she had to this beggar lady thinking to herself, "How could all these many people just watch this poor lady without helping her?"

But as compassionate as she was, she didn't know how to cope with her own difficult life. She left both me and my mother by drowning herself to death in deep water. My mother found out about it from a neighbor and ran to her younger sister only to witness her struggling for her last few breaths. Before the last breath, she told my mother that she was very sorry to leave in such a way and was sorry that she couldn't take care of me. My mother was left feeling very sad and guilty about her younger sister.

After her younger sister committed suicide, my mother lost her mind. Between the fear that she may not be able to take care of me, and having the guilt and painful memory about her younger sister, she faced each moment in guilt, fear and agony.

Since she didn't have any place else to turn, she decided to go back to her parents' home. My grandmother and my first aunt were very happy to meet me. I was the center of attention, and they both loved me so much. But my second aunt was deadly against my mother and me. She was very abusive towards me physically and verbally. This was very hard for me, having such love and such hate towards me in the same house.

One day she took me into another room where my mother wasn't able to see and broke my arm by pulling and twisting it. When my mother heard my painful scream, she realized my aunt had done something horrible to me. She ran into the room, and asked my aunt what she had done. Then my aunt said that she had wanted to dance with me, and gently pulled my arm over towards her, slowly turning me around and my arm got broken.

Another time, during the winter while my mother was away from home, my aunt placed frozen cooked rice on a frozen dish and tried to feed me with a big spoon. I screamed at her saying that I wouldn't eat it. My aunt was getting very angry and yelling at me to eat it. When my mother came back from her chore and saw this drama, she was dumbfounded. I was a fighter even when I was young. I fought with my aunt by screaming and protesting at her whenever she was being abusive toward me. But my mother concluded that it was very dangerous to live there and decided to leave home once again. My first aunt and grandmother were heartbroken when they found out about it.

When I was two years old, I had to experience another separation when my mother was forced to put me in an orphanage. Because she had a child with her, she wasn't able to get a job at a house or a restaurant. After we left my grandparents' house, my first aunt searched for us for months, finally finding me at the orphanage. It was such an emotional reunion for both of us. When I saw her, I cried and ran to her, and as she held me in her bosom, she also cried. Without a hesitation she took me back to her house. When my mother went to the orphanage to look for me, she learned that I was with my aunts. Remembering the abusive behavior of my second aunt towards me, she immediately removed me once again.

As a last solution, she decided to leave me with a foster family to take care of me and promised to visit me once a month. I was despondent and very sad. But as she promised, she came once a month to see me and pay the fee. She didn't earn a lot of money with the work she was doing. Even though the clothing she was wearing was ragged and was mended a few times, she always paid the fee for me.

The foster people were not bad people, but I wasn't treated very well by them. I always was fed with leftover food, and my body and clothing were very dirty. I don't remember having even one egg when I stayed with them. Only when my mother came to pay the money did I see some good and fresh food on a food table, so I told my mother about it. I would have several foster families over the years of separation before my mother settled in one town and brought me back to live with her.

But her life wasn't getting any better, and she was getting more depressed. Often times she would just burst into tears out of the blue, which would scare me and I would cry with her. She tried to commit suicide many times to end her suffering. She didn't want to leave me alone in the world, so she also tried to take me with her. But, if may I borrow her words, she would always wake up from each attempt to find me breathing peacefully. "Alas!" she thought, "I failed again."

By nature she was a very caring person and willing to sacrifice herself for me. But due to her suffering, she became very aggressive and angry. She screamed and yelled at me randomly. She blamed me for her misfortune and everything she had to suffer. She would tell me that I ruined her life by being born as her child. She used to stamp her feet on the floor and yell at me that I was ugly, stupid, was an unwanted child, didn't amount to anything, I should get out and finish my life, etc. She was very resourceful about expressing her anger toward me, and, of course, it was very emotionally painful for me to hear.

While it was very difficult when I was separated from my mother, it was also very difficult living with her. I was already depressed because of the constant separation and change of environments, then I had to bear her regular routine of verbal abuse and her crying outbursts. I became more depressed and scared and didn't feel like I belonged to this world. I felt guilty that I was born to her.

I tried to commit suicide in the fourth grade of elementary school to finish my life. I thought that was the only way to end my miserable and useless life. Ever since then, the thought of suicide haunted me so strongly, I tried unsuccessfully to end my life many times.

SCHOOL TIME

When I became eight years old, my mother took me to register at the elementary school. Even though I was actually eight years old at the time, my birth certificate indicated that I was seven years old. When I was born, my mother didn't register my birth right away, and on the second year she registered me as a one year old child. The school had a rule that if the child is past the age of seven, the child could not be accepted as a student. My mother was afraid that she wouldn't be able to afford to send me to school before I was seven, so she reduced my age.

She was very concerned about my education, and she tried the best she could to educate me in any way she knew how. One way to educate me was by telling me metaphorical stories and wise sayings she had heard from people. She also told me stories about how some people's experiences turned out to be mistakes. She was hoping the stories and wise sayings would help me to become a good person and understand life better.

In the second grade of elementary school, I began going to a Christian church. Deep within me, I loved Jesus Christ very much, and it was a great comfort for me to go to church. It was very natural for me to pray to Him, and the church felt like my own home. I especially loved to go to a patient's house with adults and participate in a prayer for the sick person.

Knowing that I loved God, my mother thought it would be a good idea for me to become a nun. When I was in the fourth grade, she asked me if I wanted to become a nun, and I said yes. So she took me to a Catholic Church and had an interview with a Father. After the meeting she changed her mind and decided not to send me to a church. She was very disappointed at the Father's behavior and said he wasn't a respectable person.

I had a special love for music and dance. I always loved to sing and wanted to learn to play an organ since the piano was unknown to me at that time. I understood that my mother couldn't afford to send me to a teacher for music training, so I used to fold the paper in a zigzag manner to make keyboards and attach them to the floor to play on them.

When I was in my mid-teens, I had a great desire to learn dance. By this time my mother was working in a traditional food market and was making a little bit more money than before. As I expressed my desire to learn dance, she took me to Korean traditional dance school to see if it was affordable. But when I heard how much it would cost me to attend the school, I gave up on the idea of learning dance. I could see on my mother's face that she was disappointed for not being able to send me to dance school. Although my own heart was breaking, I didn't say anything to my mother because I didn't want to cause her more anguish.

Until the end of fifth grade, we lived in the country. When I was in sixth grade, my mother decided to move to Seoul because she wanted to give me a better opportunity for my high school education by moving to the city. She found a school there, but when she tried to register me as one of their students, the school wouldn't accept me as a sixth grade student unless she paid some money. Since she didn't have enough money, she begged them to accept me as a student, so the school finally accepted me as a fifth grade student.

After I graduated from elementary school, I entered high school. There was no scholarship or loan for poor people, so she had to pay the entire fee for my education. After I entered high school, she had to work even harder for my school tuition. At that time there was a house building boom in Korea. People who had money were able to build many houses, then sold them and got richer. She got lucky and found a contractor to hire her.

In the beginning, her work was to clean the construction area by picking up the nails and other debris. Later she asked her boss if she could try painting. When the boss saw her potential, he gave her the painting job which gave her a more money. Even though it was very difficult work for her, she was very happy to get that job.

Knowing how difficult life can be without a school education, my mother was determined to give me as much education as she could. She thought if only I could get a school education, I would live a comfortable life making good money. She never had any kind of education from school or from her parents. My grandmother had been severely abused physically by her stepmother and suffered brain damage before she married my grandfather. My saint-like grandfather strived to live his life with his family of six children.

My mother wanted very much to go to school and get an education, but there was no adult to support it. Both my grandparents were very compassionate towards poor people and generously shared what they had with those in need instead of sending any of their children to school. Sometimes my mother would walk with her friend, carrying her friend's school bag up to the school gate, then gaze at her while she walked the rest of the way to the school building. She envied her friends who could go to school and felt great despair of not being able to go herself.

One day she found a piece of paper in the street with some words on it so she picked it up and brought it to someone who knew how to read. The words were from a famous Korean folk song, which my mother knew. She tried to fit the written words with the song as she sang along. That's how she learned to read and write Korean, which she taught me before I entered the elementary school. Longing for the education she knew she would never have, she sacrificed all her needs and desires, and concentrated on my education.

It was an extremely difficult six years of high school. Tuition payments to the school were often delayed, and one day my mother told me that she didn't have any more money to pay for tuition. I told her that I would quit school and find some work. On my last school day, one very kind teacher provided my tuition so I was able to continue the school. For three years, I went to school in the winter without a coat, gloves or scarf. Due to lack of nutrition and food, we both became very weak.

My mother was getting sick from working hard and not having enough food. She was unable to stop thinking about her younger sister and blamed herself for what happened. She was getting more depressed, and her abusive behavior was also getting worse. My depression was deepening, and my suicidal tendency was continuing. Deep within me, I longed to be healed from the wound, but I didn't know where to go for help. As I talked to a friend about it, she took pity on me and brought me to a teacher from another school thinking that he would help me. But when I went to see him and began to tell him about my depression, he scolded me for coming with such a reason and told me to go home.

TO AMERICA

About a year after I graduated from high school, my youngest aunt invited us to America. My first two aunts had sent their youngest sister to school, and she was able to graduate from university and came to America for further education. Later she met a man and got married. After she settled down, she invited my two aunts to America, and many years later she invited my mother and me as well.

When we came to America, we both started working in stores which were managed by Koreans. But in my heart, I wanted to continue my education and fulfill my dream that I had ever since I was young. From a young age, my heart was always inclined towards sick people. If any of my neighbors had a cut or bruise, I would run home and get a first aid liquid medicine to apply to my neighbor's wound, and console them that they were going to be okay soon. Although it seemed very natural to me, my neighbors thought I was an unusual child.

When I was in the fourth grade of elementary school, I read a book about Florence Nightingale. I was very moved with her story, and I wanted to become a nurse when I grew up. So with great hope, after I came to America, I enrolled in a college to study nursing. It was easy for me to go to school because I was able to get a scholarship. It was my great joy to think that I could help sick people and at the same time I could support my mother after I graduated from school and got a job in a hospital.

But every morning my mother would ask me when I was going to quit school. She was so persistent, it was very difficult to concentrate on my studies under such pressure, so I finally had to stop going to school. Then I wanted to go to bible school since I felt a strong connection with God, and I was continuing to experience the mystic about God. She said the school was located too far from home and would not let me go. So then I asked her if I could go to school to become a designer, and she said it was too expensive.

She was hoping that I would give up on a school education and start working so that she could rest. She was very tired and weak and was getting

Beautiful Seeds of Change

sick. I also wanted to support my mother, but I wanted to get an education first. I didn't want to take any random job just to make money. I was hoping she could wait for me to finish school so that I could get a decent job and be able to support her. But, knowing it wasn't possible to do that, I folded all my dreams and decided to work.

I tried many different jobs, but they didn't last long. It was very difficult to maintain a job when I didn't have the slightest interest or appreciation towards the work I was doing. Then I was introduced to Ballroom and Latin dance and decided to become a dance teacher. My mother didn't like this idea either, but I insisted on becoming a teacher. Since she hadn't allowed me to do anything else I liked to do, I became very stubborn and decided to do things my way. Since I loved dancing so much, I put forth my best effort to become a good teacher and a dancer. But many years later, I quit this work, too.

One day my mother found an empty store to rent out. She thought opening a store would be a good opportunity for both of us, and if I got involved in a small business, I would be very successful. She often used to tell me the story of how good I was at selling things to people when I was only one year old. My aunts had a fabric store, and I spent a lot of time there when we were staying with them for a short period of time.

When the customers came and started to look for fabric to make their own clothing, I tried to get their attention by pulling their long skirts and convincing them how that fabric was beautiful on them. At that time I only knew two words for "sale" – auni (auntie) and boodi (beautiful). I would keep repeating these two words until they paid attention to me and acknowledged my excellent opinion about their choices.

When I was successful, I brought a scissors, paper and string in that order to cut and wrap the fabric and tie it. After that, I received the money from people and put it in the cash register. As I put the money away my job was over. I didn't know how much it cost, or if there was any change to give back to customers. They fell in love with my charm, and this brought a lot of laughter among people.

Remembering this, my mother thought it would be perfect for me to become a business person. She convinced me to sign a lease, borrowed some money from my youngest aunt, and we started a small business selling general merchandise. It was very boring – there was nothing exciting about this work. On the second day of starting this business, I told my mother that I didn't want to work here anymore. When she heard that, her face became pale.

After a year and a half, I sold the business, and I opened up a dance studio. Since I had been a dance teacher for many years, I thought I had enough experience to have a studio. I wanted to be successful with my business so that I could build a center for abused and abandoned children. I was working really hard for my goal, and I thought I finally found my life purpose. But the business wasn't doing well, and I was always behind on the rent.

My stress level went up to the danger zone. I would often cry with no apparent reason and got angry easily. While I was struggling with my second business, my mother and I were injured in a car accident. One day when we were crossing the street, a cab didn't stop and hit both of us. My mother's body was thrown up into the air and dropped into the street, and my hip was dislocated. Then due to the stress, I got very sick and uterine fibroids were developing inside me. I went to doctor and spent a lot of money just to find out that I needed surgery and how much it would cost me.

At that point, I decided to get treatment from a holistic healer thinking that it was more affordable. As I was looking through a health magazine, one particular healer caught my attention, and I felt a strong pull to go to see her. I made an appointment, and began my treatment. I was spending so much money on counseling and holistic medicine, I no longer was able to pay the rent. The intense treatment made me very tired physically, and I was getting out of control with my anger.

I felt like I was totally lost in this world; I was trapped with no way out. I lost all my sense of direction about life. It seemed wherever I turned there was a wall which didn't allow me to move forward. Every dream and mission I had was being shattered. I was very angry at my mother with all her verbal abuse and for not allowing me to be successful with things I was good at. Meanwhile, without knowing how much longer I needed to receive treatment, I continued the healing with this lady

MEETING A SPIRITUAL TEACHER

On one of my visits to the healer, I noticed a picture of an Indian woman on the wall and asked her who she was. As she was explaining about this lady, deep within me I felt a longing to meet her. People call Her Amma, which means Mother. She is also known as the Hugging Saint. She comes to America twice a year for a public program and retreat. When She came to NY for the public program, I went to see Her.

My initial impression on seeing her for the first time was how small She looked. As I spent more time with Her, I felt Her immense Love and Compassion emanating from Her. I began to feel as if unseen hands were guiding me to another direction of my life. She became my goal to achieve. On the second day, when I had my chance to ask questions to Her, I asked Her how I can have Love like Her. I also asked Her if I should remain single to walk the path of spirituality.

A few days later at the retreat, I asked Her if I could be Her disciple, and She accepted me. I decided to go to India to live in Her Ashram, and I didn't know if I would ever come back to New York. I asked my holistic healer to take care of my mother if she ever needed help, which she agreed to do. But when I told my mother, it was very difficult for her to accept my decision. I was all she had, and she was scared to live in America all by herself.

For me at that time this was only choice I felt I had. It was difficult to understand Amma intellectually, but from deep within me, I recognized Her greatness and trusted Her totally. I closed the business and started getting ready to go to India. My mother was having a fit, but I was very firm about my decision.

When I went to India, I spent a lot of time being near Amma and a deep healing began. I experienced an intense clearing and cleansing. I faced all the darkness and sorrow from the past during this healing time. It felt like I was lying on an etheric surgical table, and I was being operated on from head to toe and from the inside out. Meanwhile, my mother received the financial support she needed from the government.

After being in an Ashram for 10 months, I came back to New York and from this point on, I was living in between the Ashram in India and my mother in New York. Every time I came back to New York, I worked in different places when I could. Soon my mother was able to move into a senior apartment.

At first she was skeptical about Amma and worried about me, but when she saw the change in me over time she began to feel relaxed and show her interest about Her. She even blessed me. She said, "Since you took this path, I wish you succeed on it. You may not succeed on it but do the best you can and never give up. If I didn't have you, and if I knew such a path was available to me, I would have walked the same path as you." When I heard those words, I looked at her with awe.

After seven years of intense healing, Amma guided me to different direction. When I was in New York, I had a strong pull to go to a certain yoga center so I enrolled in classes there. As soon as I started to go there, the yoga teacher began proposing to me. But I told him that I was a Hindu nun, and wasn't interested in marriage. After a month and a half of his persistent proposal, Amma told me this was the person I would marry.

It felt like a death sentence. "So was this Her plan? Is She abandoning me? Am I not fit for realization?" was my thought. It was very painful to accept this marriage because I was very happy with my path, and it was only thing I wanted. But at the same time I understood that I needed to go through this experience, because another lesson for my growth was waiting for me through this marriage. I remembered the question I had originally asked Amma about remaining single, and She said She would pray to God for me to find the husband.

After the marriage, I didn't get a chance to go to the Ashram often but my inner journey continued. Now that I was no longer there, I felt I needed to begin looking for full time work, but my inner guide told me not to work. Instead I was guided to go on a pilgrimage to Mount Kailash and Lake Mansarovar in Tibet, and to different Himalayan holy places in India.

DIVINE GUIDANCE

After another seven years, Amma was calling us to India for six months, and I intuitively knew that my life would change and I would start working, but I had no idea what kind of work I would get involved in. Also it was difficult to think about working because I hadn't done any work for seven years. So I asked Amma about this matter, and She told me to first think about what I would like to do, then decide.

It was very difficult for me to figure this all out so I met with a Vedic astrologer to get help, who suggested I work as a counselor and a spiritual guide. He also mentioned many other things that I could do successfully. But where do I begin? I didn't have a counseling degree, and didn't know how to bring people to God. But after I came back to New York, the Universe started guiding me and connected me with people who would help. What came to me intuitively was an energy healing work, Hypnosis and Neuro Linguistic Programming.

Through someone I knew, I found the person who was an energy healer and a teacher, and I got initiated as an energy healer in the healing modality of Rising Star. Then I started taking classes to become a Neuro Linguistic Programming coach. A little later one of my friend mentioned about Louise Hay's book, *Heal Your Body*, and without knowing much about her and her method, my heart was inclined towards it, so I decided to learn her methods as well.

I began thinking that maybe I was trying to learn too many things, so I decided to ask my spirit guide and got in touch with him. After asking him a few questions, his response was to learn all of them. My husband was a yoga teacher before he met me, and he also learned massage. Realizing his talent, he wanted to become a massage therapist and enrolled in school to receive the National and New York certificate. I became very scared about our money situation since I didn't have any income and my husband didn't make enough money. We paid all the tuition and living expenses with credit cards.

MEETING ANOTHER SPIRITUAL TEACHER

As I was continuing my education, I met another extraordinary Being who lives in Ireland. His name is Derek O'Neill. He is a Master Healer and Spiritual Teacher. He has a workshop in Ireland in June every year and also comes to America for His workshop. My energy healing teacher said I must go to see Him in Ireland. Since I was struggling with money, I didn't think it was a good idea.

One day while sitting in a chair, I began thinking about Derek and all of a sudden, my heart began beating so fast I couldn't breathe. My heart was being squeezed and at the same time it was being expanded to the size of Universe. After a few seconds of this amazing experience, I realized that Derek was calling me to Ireland. So I told Him mentally several times that I would go to see Him, and after a minute or so my heart was functioning normally.

When I went to see Him, it didn't take long to recognize Him as a great being. It felt like I knew Him from eons ago. My heart once again started blossoming with such devotion towards God. I knew in my heart I could trust Him. I decided to ask Him about my learning. When I asked Him about it, He looked into my eyes so intently and responded: "Why don't you ask your heart?" Inside I said, "Haven't I done it already? To be absolutely sure that I am doing the right thing I need your guidance." But since He knows my heart, I didn't explain a lot of things. I just told Him, "I want you to tell me."

Then He told me to learn all of them. While I was there, He initiated me as a teacher of the Rising Star healing modality so I could initiate people who would like to become a healer. I also was trained to become a healer and a teacher of Prema Birthing healing modality. These two healing modalities are very powerful and the healing process takes place very effectively.

BEING A HEALER AND A COUNSELOR

After I came back to New York, I was able to finish learning everything I was guided to learn, even though it took quite a period of time. These are tools which helped me to continue my own healing and also help others who would like to be healed. Although I have several titles, they are all designed to help restore people to full health physically, mentally, emotionally and spiritually. These programs help us to learn to love and accept ourselves fully and live a happier and healthier life.

I was very fortunate to meet great Beings like Amma and Derek. They not only healed me personally, they also helped me to become a strong healer. Although I met a lot of life challenges and went through a very difficult childhood and adult life, now I understand I needed to experience them. As difficult as it was for me to go through the pains and sufferings, these helped me to understand the nature of life and develop some degree of compassion towards ailing people. I consider this preparing myself to become a healer who would understand people with their pain.

I am very grateful to two extraordinary Beings who healed me and gave me the tools to continue to heal myself and others. My lifetime desire to become a healer has been granted to me finally. God never abandoned me and my heart's desire. Now I have truly found my life path and am very happy with what I am doing.

About the Author

Jiyun Park is an energy healer and a teacher of Rising Star and Prema Birthing Healing Modalities. She is also a licensed *Heal Your Life*® Coach and Workshop Facilitator, Hypnotist and Neuro Linguistic Programming Coach.

She lives in New Jersey and works in both New Jersey and New York City. Jiyun loves plants and animals and communicates with the many indoor plants she has. She loves to meditate and chant the Divine Names of Goddess.

Jiyun believes that everyone is capable of healing themselves from past wounds and heal the world. Her great wish is that people recognize their Love and Light shine out from their heart.

gentlehealingcenter@gmail.com
www.gentlehealingcenter.org

Acknowledgments

My gratitude to my Gurus, Amma and Derek O'Neill, whose Love and Compassion is the embodiment of Their true nature. Without Them I would not be where I am now. Also thanks to Nancy Newman and Lisa Hardwick for their tireless dedication to make this book beautiful. With their loving and kind encouragement I was able to write a book.

Cris Hitterman

I want to dedicate this to all of those amazing souls out there who are ready to embrace their greatness, and live the amazing life that they are here to live. Simply, because you deserve it!

Chapter 15

WELCOME TO MY GARDEN

I feel honored to share my journey and my amazing garden with you! So thank you for stopping by and being open to exploring my world with me. My intention is to share my stories with you and the many lessons, actual gifts I have received in this journey of my waking up. I wish for you to be able to see with a new set of eyes, and see all of the love that surrounds you and to feel a sense of gratitude for all the many gifts you already possess, and realize just how amazing you are!

There are many metaphors to life; however, I feel a garden and the seeds we plant are a perfect metaphor for life. As, we age with the different cycles of life. It is just like watching our garden grow and mature, from seed to its full potential. Our different moods and emotions are just like weather. Some days are hot and sunny, some windy, some just perfect, and some rainy and cold. All in all weather is constantly changing just like our moods, thoughts and emotions, which in the end has an effect on the seeds that we plant.

One belief is that we are all energy, and in some way, shape or form, we have created our own reality. It is important to be mindful and conscious of the seeds that we plant, furthermore cultivate. We can choose to have a healthy, vibrant garden, full of unlimited opportunities and abundance. Or we can choose to have a garden that may be jeopardized by weeds or the lack of care. You can choose to change the seeds that you plant at any time.

You can focus on different crops, at different times of the year. And some crops you will just have to weed out, as they may no longer serve you for your highest good. Your garden, the seeds that you plant will begin to grow, with the energy and intent you provide for each crop. Each dream, each belief, the choice is up to you to decide which seeds you choose to cultivate and bring to fruition. After all you are a spiritual being having a human experience. You are of divine nature and deserve the absolute very best! This I can say today, and I truly believe it! Two years ago, it would have been a completely different story. I think the best song to sum this up, is from Aladdin, *A Whole New World*.

That is exactly what happened to me, and can happen to anyone at any time. It is up to us to be conscious and be aware of what we are growing in our garden and allowing into our world. Your reality can shift in a blink of an eye. It is up to you to say when, and fully believe that you deserve better.

The next part, is simply to trust and let go, that is where the magic unfolds!

As mentioned, two years ago, I lived in a completely different world. A very dark world. A very depressing and sad world. Ladies and Gentlemen, fasten your seatbelts, as we are about to embark upon a very rocky adventure to the world of Victimhood or better known as "Poor Me."

In the world of Victimhood, it was far from whirly truly gumdrops and having a candy cane forest. I was well over 550 pounds. I was 30 years old, living with my parents, and completely numb to life. I was a zombie. I was fully asleep, and just going through the motions to life, if that.

I had just lost my coffee shop at Skydive Arizona, due to the fear of showing up. I was so embarrassed about my weight that I did not want to be seen out there anymore as it was humiliating. In a sport where there is a deciding factor between a cupcake and more free-fall time, well my decision was always obvious: I always went for the cupcake. And it showed. It became just too humiliating for me to be out there anymore.

But wait, there's more! During this time period, I had also lost my grandpa, who meant the world to me, and always offered huge support and unconditional love for me. My best friend was killed in a car accident. And, my heart had just been broken, by someone I cared about. I felt alone, I felt betrayed, and the list goes on.

My life was a smorgasbord of lower vibrations and depressing energy. I was sleeping through life. I was doing everything to avoid life. Sleeping the day away. Avoiding friends and family, because I was ashamed of my own weight. I even created my work schedule around avoidance. I was too embarrassed to run into anyone. So I took up eBay'ing, as a way to make money.

I would go to the post office at 3:00 a.m. to mail the packages, then off to get a veggie burrito from a local Mexican food restaurant. I was on auto pilot. I tuned out everyone. I watched reruns of *CSI* and *NCIS*, hours on end. I would sleep the day away avoiding the pain I felt from where I was at in life, and the pain, humiliation and disbelief I allowed myself to get to be so heavy! I would numb myself from the pain I felt with food and sleep. Did I mention I was sleeping my life away?

Everywhere I looked, I looked through painful eyes of Victimhood. It hurt watching my parents ignore one another, which brought up the hurt and the confusion of how two people who used to love one another now not even acknowledge one another.

Beautiful Seeds of Change

I can go on and on in Victimhood, and it is quite entertaining. Do you hear the violins in the background? I think you get the picture. Are you familiar with this world? We all have been there. But the question is, is how long do we want to stay there? Pretty much everyone has visited the world of Victimhood before. It is part of human nature. However, it is not a place to make your permanent residence. Some may choose to, but it is not my choice.

SEED: THE HOW IS NONE OF OUR BUSINESS

During this time, I knew there was another world out there besides Victimhood. I knew it existed, but I did not know how, to get there! This was the first seed that made a difference in my journey, was not focusing on the perfect plan. This involved being comfortable and not knowing how – with everything.

As previously mentioned, I was over 550 pounds. I was desperate to release the weight, and just wanted a better life. During my late nights, and my frequent TV watching skills, I came across a popular weight loss program on TV. It just so happened in three weeks, they were doing castings for the show. I was for sure this was the answer. I went to the casting call and got pretty far in the process. At the time, I would have been their biggest female contestant. I am all about accomplishments, but that was not something I would be proud to call an accomplishment.

I was sure this was my answer, and was my HOW. It was the perfect solution in my mind, to get to this whole new world. Well guess what? The Universe had another Master plan in store for me.

Weeks later, I was devastated and crushed of the hope of my dream coming true. Kind of the same feeling like when I was a kid and finding out that Santa Claus is not real. (Well, I still believe in Santa Claus, but to find out, he does not deliver my presents.) With this, the Universe presented me with a wonderful opportunity.

My friend, Doug, was going away for a month and asked me to watch his place. It was like a dream come true. I figured if I was not going to be training, with personal trainers, I would design my own boot camp. I packed everything I could think of that would assist me in my transformational journey. I was focused and ready to go!

SEED: MAKE LEMONADE

As the saying goes, when life hands you lemons, make lemonade.

That is exactly what I did. Although I did not get to be a contestant on the show, I could have stayed in pity mode and put on 50-plus more pounds, or I could do something about it. It was the perfect time to create my own reality and work towards my goal.

During this month, I had a set schedule for Operation Transformation. I had turned my friend, Doug's, place into a Sanctuary. A sanctuary, to help me move forward. I began each day with meditations, I was doing a juice cleanse, I was dry skin brushing, oil pulling, working with angels, positive affirmations. You name it. My focus during this month was to transform myself, while I was away and alone.

Of course, during this time, being over 500 pounds, I was thinking, sure I can release 300 pounds in a month if I do this every day. Not a reality, really. But I seriously thought I could make it one. Then I could catch up on meeting up with all the friends I deeply wanted to connect with, but avoided due to me being ashamed of my weight.

I had gone through my life, delaying meeting with friends and others, thinking I could only meet up with them when I was thin. That was the only time that I would be of value, or worthy of even meeting with them. Until then, I would remain hiding, in my mind. But not really a reality when you are around 550 pounds.

SEED: OUT OF THE BOX

I decided to stretch a little and meet someone I had been putting off meeting for quite some time. I tried everything possible to delay meeting, from finding reasons not to travel, or manifesting chaos or drama to come up, so I did not have to face my fear of rejection. As, I mentioned, I was 550 pounds, I was in a self-pity mode of nobody loves me, and I was shutting everyone out, because deep down inside I did not feel good enough or worthy enough. I did not believe I was worthy of good things, especially love, because I was so huge at this time. All I wanted to do was hide. But I knew if change was going to happen, I needed to take a step in another direction, and just make a small change.

So we after running out of every excuse in the book, we finally met. The whole time, I was hoping and manifesting that he would call and cancel, so I did not have to face my fear.

That plan obviously did not work out, but thank goodness, as we had a great time, and I felt happiness for the first time. I felt love for the first time. I felt like life had been breathed back into me again. Just like in

Sleeping Beauty, when the Prince comes to give her a kiss, and she awakens from a deep sleep. This is how I felt.

My whole world transformed right before me. I was inspired even more to move forward into this new world that was breathed into me and that I had awakened to. I felt for the first time what love felt like and was addicted. I had never allowed anyone to get close to me before, or let someone into my life before. I was always being the martyr trying to do for others. This was different for me. I felt joy. I could not remember the last time, I felt joy, and felt alive.

This new feeling was introduced into my life, all because I was willing to get out of my way, and step towards a fear, instead of running and hiding. It was all about doing something out of the box, that I thought I would never do, or I could not do, until I was thin. With this, I learned we have to take steps in different directions to get different results. It is with this, our vibrations begin to change, and we begin to enter a whole new world.

SEED: GRATITUDE

As the saying goes, all good things must come to an end. But I have learned in this journey this is not true. And I have learned that things just get better and better. During this time at my friend Doug's house, I was grateful for the month there. I had become closer to myself then I ever had before. I had faced fears. And I was feeling strong to move forward.

I admit, I was nervous. Because of all the hard work I had done, I was nervous about backpedaling once I went back to my parent's house. While I was at Doug's house, I had made a vision board.

When I was living in victim mode, it seemed the world was against me, but Doug's place allowed me to see this was not the reality. It was what I had created. I began each day, listing five things I was grateful for, and I would end the day with five things that I was grateful for. With this I also made a gratitude board, to show me all that I have, and all that I am blessed with.

Growing up being obese, sometimes you feel the world is against you, and that you are cursed. By creating a sense of gratitude, you realize that you are surrounded by gifts and abundance. It just depends on how you shape your reality. This also helped me begin to feel safe living. Growing up obese, I always had the excuse of, "when I am thin" I will do this, or I will met so and so, or go somewhere. My weight was an anchor. With gratitude, I began to release the anchors.

As the saying goes. **"When you have gratitude, you are rich."** There is so much to be grateful for! What are some of the things you are grateful for? Trust me, it feels good, spending some time, in the gratitude neighborhood. In fact, I attribute my next journey to stemming from gratitude.

As mentioned before, I made a vision and gratitude board. On my gratitude board, I was grateful for the space and opportunity to spend at Doug's. I was also putting it out there, I was already grateful for the opportunity to continue my journey and release the weight.

SEED: LEARN THROUGH NATURE

With this, the universe began to support me in the process. My Angel Aunt had called and left a message about me coming back east to visit for a bit. I could not believe this. It was a dream come true. So within a month of time, I knew it was time for me to go and continue my journey back east. I had credits left from a flight before, so I was off.

It was the perfect timing. It was almost August, which was exciting for me, as it meant it was almost fall. Living in Arizona my whole life, I had never experienced a true fall before. I am one who learns through nature, and fall was just what I needed to learn the art of letting go. Exactly what my focus was: Letting go. Letting go of it all. The weight, the negative and limiting beliefs and thoughts. The depression. The unhealthy ways of living. I was ready to let go of it all. I wanted to let go of it all, and breathe in and continue filling up with what I felt with my friend, Kyle. I did not know what we had or what I was experiencing. I just know that I was feeling good. And I wanted to continue this journey of feeling good.

I began to continue my walking every day while I was back east. Breathing in fresh crisp air, I began to experience nature and observe the process of letting go, and in trusting that everything will be okay. And, that in order to fill up, you have to let go of the old that no longer serves you. I then was able to realize that this was all a blessing in a disguise. It was all too good to be true. I was in a very happy place; I loved this new life that had been breathed into me. I was focused, and I was focused on moving forward.

I learned to trust the process through watching the trees. How they would bare it all, releasing each and every single last leaf. Fully trusting and believing in themselves to bare all in the winter, and that they would be fully provided for in the spring. The magic begins and voila! Presto, there is an abundance of all new leaves. Sometimes we have to let go of it all, before we can begin to receive.

Beautiful Seeds of Change

SEED: IT'S OKAY TO BE HUMAN

As always, nature has a sense of humor, and once one gets comfortable is when things began to change. This is when I realized, whatever relationship I perceived Kyle and I had, was not the reality of what it was. I was suffocating Kyle, and I was projecting the feeling of love onto another person. I was smothering him; he was a drug for me. He was exactly a love drug for me. I realized I was projecting love onto him, and considered love to be a person, not energy. What I wanted and how I felt was all projected onto him. Love being a possession, and outside of me, instead of within me. I was looking for love in all the wrong places, never realizing it was within me the whole time.

Things began to turn ugly, as I began to become more and more fearful of him leaving me or withdrawing from our connection. I became crazy, a person I did not know – just like a heroin addict not able to get their next fix. I was just the same. I was having withdrawal, from what I perceived to be love.

I had a whole rainbow of emotions going. As I felt rejected, I felt abandoned. I did not feel good enough. I turned into a crazed person, not even recognizing who I was any more. During this time, I thought the only thing that was wrong was I was still too heavy. I was moving forward and had released 55 pounds at this point. I still had a journey forward, and I was dedicated to move forward.

SEED: LEARN TO LOVE YOURSELF

The following morning, after my meditation, I went to get ready to take a shower, and I found an old card, with an angel reading on the back from Sunny Dawn Johnston. I felt guided to look up Sunny's website, as I had not checked this website for years. It just so happened that Sunny was teaching a class based off of the Louise Hay book, You Can Heal Your Life. This was exactly what I needed.

Through this class and awareness, the synchronicities began to unfold. I was a dedicated student. The more and more Kyle withdrew, the more and more I dove into doing my own work. I knew I was being clingy and possessive, and I knew these feelings I felt were causing me to search outside of me when I needed to search within myself. With this, I had to do lots and lots of reprogramming.

I grew up listening to love songs and watching movies of couples living happily ever after, combined with understanding how energy works,

I knew this whole time that the treasure and love I was searching for outside of myself, was actually in there the whole time. I needed to re-shift my focus, and learn new ways of being. New ways of finding love with myself.

And with this, I realized I had to unlearn everything I had learned. This stirred up many emotions, and created great confusion, and anger and frustration. I realized what I perceived as my truths, were actually lies. My reality had been created from a base of many lies from others and from myself.

SEED: GIVE YOURSELF PERMISSION TO BE ANGRY

One of the greatest things, a friend of mine told me was: **"It is okay to be angry, I am glad you are angry."** Just to hear that from a good friend, let alone having permission to be angry and not be judged, but accepted unconditionally meant the world to me. It provided a whole new avenue to release energy.

At this stage in life, I was angry and scared. I felt very confused. Here I was working hard on releasing my weight and committing to myself. I was being good in my eyes. But yet I felt punished, as Kyle was dropping from my universe. We barely spoke anymore, and when we did we were always patching up the past, or addressing my craziness. Out of fear of not being loved, I became clingy and I was constantly apologizing for my actions. I had become Lenny from Mice of Men. I was smothering, and ended up crushing what I loved the most.

I was constantly telling myself things were great, while ignoring my intuition. I did not want to accept the reality of what was really happening. I was living a fantasy. I was fearful of letting love go. What would I have left, if Kyle left my universe?

Definitely a black hole. Emotions I did not even know existed, including ANGER, and lots of it. Emotions that stemmed from my childhood that I had not addressed and had shut off, began to bubble up to the surface. It was a Disneyland of emotions. It was a whole new world to me once Kyle left. But at the same time, was the beginning of my treasure hunt, to find the love within.

I truly believe we are all mirrors for one another. And how we react is a reflection of ourselves. The anger I had was not at Kyle, but anger in general, and it needed to be released. Bottom line, it was pent up anger and frustration that I had felt with myself, that I never allowed to be released, nor even knew existed.

Beautiful Seeds of Change

One morning I was doing a guided meditation to get in touch with my shadow personalities. Personalities that we have that provide opportunities to react in healthier ways.

In this meditation, I connected with my anger, which was called Angry Anthony. I remember calling for him, on a bus full of other sub-personalities, and no one could find him. Angry Anthony was a mouse in my meditation. The whole bus was looking for him. Finally one of the sub-personalities (Ugly Ursula) found him and screamed while trying to kill him, followed by the whole bus being stirred up and all trying to kill Angry Anthony.

I then was able to rescue Angry Anthony and have a talk with him. He mentioned he was scared as everyone disliked him, and every time he was seen, people would try to kill him. It was then that I realized this is exactly what I do with anger. Every time, Angry Anthony would show up, I would try to suffocate him with food. Stuffing my emotions.

Angry Anthony and I then made a pact, that I would put him in this gold cage, so he would be safe. I then took him on the bus and introduced him to everyone. I also told Angry Anthony that he has a front seat on the bus, and I would check in with him every day.

I find it fascinating that anger is the least acknowledged and understood emotion. Yet, contributes to so many diseases and impacts one's life so much. So just remember, it is okay to be angry! Anger does not make you any less of a person. There are many healthy ways to deal with anger. If nothing else, look at the bright side, it is a sign that you are alive. It is just how you express and choose to deal with the anger. Just know you are always loved regardless. There is a thin line between anger and passion.

SEED: EXPLORE YOUR GIFTS

During this time I felt blessed as my mentor for mediumship, Andrea Allen, was living not even 20 minutes away from where I lived. I began to take mediumship classes through her, helping me work on my energetic awareness. Being an empath, clairsentient I was working with energy and not just sorting through my emotions, thoughts and beliefs, but also going through, learning how to discern, what energy or feeling was mine, or which feelings I was picking up from others, or from other realms. Through this process, I was able to really reconnect to myself and find what was mine, and help that energy move forward.

Through this new awareness, I learned the importance of protecting one's energy. It was this protecting my energy with Archangel Michael, that began to change and shift my life. I began to call in Archangel Michael every morning, and imagine surrounding myself with a blue bubble, feeling fully protected and safe. Once I began to do this, my life began to transform at record speed.

I found it easier to move forward with releasing my weight, continuing to walk every day, eating a healthier, raw food lifestyle. With this, my mentor and good friend, Andrea, was able to reintroduce life back into me. I began going out in public again. I was still reserved, but it felt good to go out. I even ventured to a Zumba class, where my heart and soul began to dance.

SEED: MOVEMENT

Growing up, dance was a huge outlet of expression for me. From a young age, dance was in my everyday life. Dance is known to be poetry of the body. Through movement, I began to find myself again. I was connecting with my spirit that had been asleep for so many years. As my body began to move in different motions, I could feel my spirit coming back to life. With the music pumping through my blood, I was alive once again. I was beginning to feel my true emotions.

The act of moving, helped me reshape my body, my mind and emotions. Zumba helped me call back my spirit, and find my true essence. My inner truth. I then began to venture out even more, and felt a strong pull towards Bikram yoga, or better known as hot yoga.

I am going to be honest, in my first class, I was just trying to make it through being in the heat and humidity for 90 minutes and not leave the room. For some strange reason, I have no idea why, but I survived the first class, and found myself wanting to go back. It never made sense to me. I always hated the first hour of class, but something would shift the last 30 minutes. My ego would weaken, and my body would begin rejoicing, shouting out for joy! I would then be so happy and so grateful that I came to class. My body felt so loved, and so appreciative.

I was slowly gaining trust with my body. After years of not being in it, I began to find the gratitude of being in my body. Through hot yoga and Zumba, I was able to see where my thoughts were at. My mind and my body were like a couple in a relationship. Some days, they would get along, and have a great time. Some days, one would try to control one another. And some days, my mind and body were just not in a loving relationship at all. I could always tell where my thoughts were by my body's movement or lack of movement.

Beautiful Seeds of Change

Some days, I could Zumba effortlessly, or hold my poses in yoga. And some days, I was tripping over my own feet, and wanting to just lie down in yoga. I learned to see the relationship my mind and body had with one another, and how just movement alone could help change and transform my thoughts and relationship with my body.

By this time, I had released about 120 pounds within a five-month period. I was feeling good, I was moving forward. Life was good.

I was back east, I was releasing weight. I was experiencing my first fall. I had found Zumba. I had become aware of working with different realms and energies. I had realized I needed to find love within myself. And, I had found a job again, life was good.

SEED: THIS TO SHALL PASS

December 24th, a time to fly home for Christmas. I boarded the plane and received my first Christmas present. For the first time in years I was able to use a seatbelt without an extender. I was able to sit without my legs feeling bruised and indented in. I felt so good, what a way to start things off. And it just got better, as that Christmas would have made the perfect Folgers' coffee commercial. It was a Christmas to remember.

I was ready for a new year, a new me. I was back in Arizona, after an amazing five month opportunity with my Angel Aunt and Incredible Uncle. I was on a roll moving forward, and felt I could continue the process forward at my parents. This next journey just reinforced to me, that the HOW is none of my business as the Universe had a different plan.

I received a phone call from someone I had met while back east, that was looking to hire for their metaphysical book store. I knew I was supposed to go back. I knew this was the Universe telling me to come back. I was fearful of telling my mom and dad that I wanted to go back as I had been gone for so long already. My three weeks of visiting back east had turned into five months. I knew I had more work to do, but I did not want to tell my parents. I was fearful; I did not want to hurt their feelings. I became paralyzed in fear.

But I knew for me to continue forward, I needed to trust in the process and honor what I wanted and what the Universe was providing for me. It was my desire for happiness, good health and just higher vibrations that kept me moving forward. I had two mantras during this time that kept me moving forward. My favorite: **"Just keep swimming, just keep swimming,** "as life is like an ocean to explore, and it is all about moving forward. My second favorite mantra was: **"This too shall pass."** I learned this at a previous ten-day silent meditation retreat I had done earlier in the fall. Nothing is constant, and everything is constantly flowing. We can choose to stay stuck and paralyzed, or can choose to explore, go with the flow, through good and bad, and knowing that it is never permanent. I knew it would be tough to tell my parents. But I knew it had to be done, and the flood gates were open.

I think telling my mom that I wanted to go back was the hardest thing ever for me in my life. I can't recall anything more painful in my life than going through this motion. Leaving the nest so to speak, and me growing up and becoming an adult. I know it was hard for my mom to see my perspective, but I had to do it, and I survived!

SEED: YOUR OPINION OF ME IS NONE OF MY BUSINESS

During this time period I was taking a seashell reading class with Michelle Hansen, an Ocean Oracle. And, it was through the shells that I began to realize my underlying psychology. I realized I was living a life of trying to please others and make others happy, at the expense of sacrificing myself. It was through the shells that I learned I let others opinions have complete control over me, my decisions and lack of decisions. I learned about the fears I had of people disliking me, or me upsetting others, and in the end, if I did so, then I would not be loved.

I was constantly seeking love and approval from others, but yet I was exhausted from wearing all of the masks and trying to making everyone else happy but myself. I needed to make another change: I needed to start to take my power back, and find the love, approval, and happiness within myself, and not seek so much of it in others.

I will be honest, I am still working on this process, but the threshold is wearing thin. But when you take your power back, and don't spend so much time doing things out of outside approval, or fear of upsetting someone, it gives you so much more energy to create, to move forward, and to enjoy life. It is a different type of freedom. I encourage you to try it! After all, we only have our life to live!

SEED: HAPPINESS IS A CHOICE

If the prior lesson was not hard enough to learn, then this next lesson ups the ante. We all want happiness, and we all want to see those we love happy as well. But it is not our job to save them, or make them happy. We all are in one another's life for a reason, and some fall away. I found this is what I had to allow to happen. I was going through life, just wanting to make others happy. Putting tons of energy into it. I surrounded myself with unhappy people, just to find a purpose, a sense of belonging or being needed.

This was hard for me to accept, but I realized that, (huge gulp) I could not make everyone happy, and it is not my responsibility. Just like trying to help someone with an addiction. You cannot save them, or make them change. You can influence a change, but with an addiction, you cannot make the change for them. It has to be something they find on their own and desire to do on their own.

I admit I still do my best every day to spread some cheer and happiness everywhere I go because this is what I truly enjoy. This is part of who I am. However, I have learned to not try so hard. It is up to the other individual to make of it what they chose. They can choose to receive and participate, or they can chose another way. It is all up to them.

Allowing this to flow allowed me to have so much more energy to focus and put forth doing things that made me happy, and that helped me begin to release even more weight. I always say release, as when we say lose, it implies wanting to find it again. I have chosen to give this energy, this weight to Mother Earth, to be used for the highest good. I do not wish to find the weight again. At this point, I had released close to 200 pounds and was still focused on moving forward.

However, I was confused, the weight was not coming off as fast as it used to. I had come to a holding pattern, and did not understand why. I was working out, I was eating RAW, and I was doing my inner work, what was missing?

SEED: BE CAREFUL FOR WHAT YOU WISH FOR

I began to take an "Embrace The Body That Is" class with Sunny Dawn Johnston. It was through this class that I realized what I truly desired was sending mixed messages. My theme for my weight release journey was FREEDOM. I desired to be free from the paralysis of limiting beliefs, from all of the fat I carried, and unhealthy behaviors. I wanted to be free from feeling that I was in a prison with the door wide open, but was too afraid to leave out of the fear of judgment, and out of the fear that I deserved good.

It was through this awareness that I realized this whole time I was manifesting Freedom. But the message I was sending to my body, was I did not want to be in my body. I wanted Freedom from my body, my fat suit. I realized that ultimately, Freedom from the body was death. I realized, the this whole time, my fat had been a message from my body, trying to get me to stay in my body. To be present, to be here on earth. My body, my fat, the whole journey, was about me learning to love myself, and to appreciate my body – flaws and all.

It was through this that I learned to send gratitude to my body for all that it does. I realized without my body, I would not be able to hug, like I love to, to laugh, to walk, to move forward and to live my dreams. My body is truly a gift to be in, regardless of its shape and size. That is what it is about: It is not about the number on the scale or size you wear. It is about the gift of your body that you are loaned for this lifetime. It truly is a vehicle for your soul. I encourage you to take some time, and really see your body for the gifts that it provides. Spend time with your body, sing love songs to it, and tell it you appreciate it. After all, you would not be here without it.

SEED: GET THE LESSON AND GET OUT

At this point in life, I had realized that I had an issue with control, particularly being out of control. I would spiral. I had gotten a strong message from spirit that I needed to go back to Arizona. However, the message was also strong that I needed to live with my two friends at the time, and also not have a vehicle.

It was not the best environment; it was full of negativity, scarcity, and not a very safe part of town. But my fears and limitations had created this reality in my life. I was grateful for them allowing me to stay with them. And I thought things would be like back in the days. But I realized after about a month, that people do change, or they don't change.

I experienced constant criticism, negativity, and control in the environment. It definitely was a final exam from the Universe to test how much I had learned back east, and how much I loved myself. One belief that kept me moving forward is I would imagine I had a child. I do not have one physically, but I would imagine if I had a child, and I would ask myself "what would I do for that child?" I had to learn to begin to nurture myself this way.

As the lesson states, get the lesson and get out. I will not spend time on the negativity. Bottom line, I put myself in an emotionally and energetically abusive situation. It was an opportunity for me to learn to set boundaries and to learn to stand up for myself. To know that I deserve better.

I did not realize the type of environment I was in, until I went to pet sit for my friend, Maria. I was able again to create my sanctuary and do some inner work. It was with this that I was able to see what I was swimming in energetically. There is a quote: **"the fish is the last to see the water."** I had been swimming in this energy field this whole time and did not even realize it. While I was at my friend, Maria's, house, I ended up watching the movie, Aladdin, over and over, and over again. It had to have been more than 10 times. But the theme was a whole new world. and I knew it was time for a whole new world. I knew I would never let my child stay in that type of environment. I knew I had to leave, but had no idea where I was going.

SEED: GET OVER YOURSELF

My friend, Maria, and her family had just come back from holiday. I knew and felt something big was underway. That night we were having our Mind-Body-Spirit class. I had most of my stuff with me, when I went to Maria's, as I was setting up my Sanctuary, again. I was feeling nervous. I am in class, and the class is talking about manifestation. Towards the end of class, Sunny asked me, "What is going on, Cris?" Here I am taking a Mind-Body-Spirit class, I am studying Psychology at another school, and I find myself in an abusive situation. I was too embarrassed to say something, to really tell what was going on. I present like all is great and grand, and here I am in an abusive situation.

It was then that I realized I needed to get over the mold of trying to be perfect and present that all is great. I was then candid with the class, that I was afraid of leaving, but that I was going to leave the house that night. I did not know my plan, but I was going to find a hotel for the night. I was scared. I had never stood up for myself before. But I knew I would never allow my inner child to be in that environment. It was through this I realized the lesson that had been provided to me. I knew I could stay in this critical world, or I could learn to choose to take a step into the unknown, and leave this part of me behind. The choice was there for me to say when and which path I chose.

SEED: LEARN TO ASK FOR HELP

I realized through this process that I had never really learned to ask for help. I was going throughout life, trying to play the DIVINE. Trying to do things alone. I was like an island. I was creating barriers, and secluding myself from others. But yet, I just wanted to join in with others. I was limiting myself. All because I had too much pride to ask for help. I was embarrassed to ask for help, and bottom line,. to learn to say those words, I did not see myself as needing help. I felt this is what I attracted, and I had to do this alone.

It amazed me, all of the support and love I received from my fellow classmates. Numerous offers poured in to help me, for a place to stay, the support to get my belongings, the support to talk, it was an ocean of love, so powerful, that I had to surrender.

SEED: LEARN TO RECEIVE

It was then that an earth angel appeared in my life. My classmate, Paula, came over, gave me a huge hug, and said, **"You are coming home with me."** I barely knew her, as we would miss each other in class.

It was like a Cinderella story. It was about an hour drive home, and she was just incredible. She is opening up and providing unconditional love and support. She is being completely honest and authentic with who she is. I have never met someone so authentic and so full of unconditional love. I mean, she took a complete stranger into her home. I am completely confused at what is going on, my mind and ego are running wild. I am scared about the journey that I am just about to embark upon based off of my choices and by divine intervention.

Just in the hour we talked, I felt like I had known Paula a lifetime. We arrive to a huge home, in a safe neighborhood. This felt so great. I am greeted with a huge hug by another angel, her son, Adam. This felt even greater. At this stage, I felt I was being flooded with love and greatness. It was a complete energetic cleanse that had really resuscitated me. I was scared, but excited at the same time. I cannot even begin to explain what I felt, and what I still feel today.

The next morning, I was greeted by yet another angel, Paula's daughter, Sarah. This was all a dream come true. I felt like I was in a Disney movie. Things were happening so quickly and effortlessly. I had the support and unconditional love from a family that didn't even know me. Support and unconditional love from my classmates.

That day we went over to get my belongings. I was so afraid of my roommate going off on me again. Paula and I called in the angels to help us in this process, as I was so scared.

SEED: FORGIVENESS

The whole time I was there, I had never seen my roommate so calm. I went in and collected my belongings and said my goodbyes. I thanked him for the many lessons and opportunities he provided me with. I told him that I loved him, and that I was not leaving him, I was leaving his behavior. When I was leaving, I was leaving all the negativity, the control, the possessiveness, and the criticism that went on in my head on a daily basis. He was a mirror for this for me. And I chose not to give it any more power and control over my life.

I admit, once I left, I felt bad, as I was not used to upsetting someone. It hurt. But I realized I had a choice. I could be bitter about things and see him as a bad guy, or I could see the gift that he provided me with. It was through this process, that I also learned the art of forgiveness. I learned that there may be people that upset us, or that we may feel hurt by, but ultimately, what it boils down to is that the forgiveness that needs to be done is with one's self.

This is where I first began to discover the art of forgiveness. I encourage you to look at your life and find the blessings in disguise. It makes life a lot more fun, and you see you are surrounded with opportunity, gifts and abundance. Just open your eyes and look around.

SEED: TRUST IN THE PROCESS

I wish I could explain in detail, this whole transition of entering into a whole new world as it has been the most amazing experience ever! Like I said, a fairy tale, so to speak. But it is my reality. I chose to let go of the negativity, control, criticism, fear, and my ego. I chose to open my heart, to live from my heart, and I chose love. I chose to connect with this vibration and only this vibration.

It was through this trust, and letting go of control, that I am connecting with you right now. Deciding to enter a whole new world has connected me with my angel family, and has connected me with the opportunity to be sharing this story with you right now. A dream come true of mine.

I wish I could provide you with a happily ever after. But I truly do not believe that all good things must come to an end. I truly believe things just get better and better! My job is to open my arms wide and receive. To just be me. Each new day and adventure is unfolding, and each day just keeps getting better and better. I truly am living and creating a heaven on earth. You can too, if you just open your heart and let go. Your heart will attract and align you with your true vibration.

SEED: YOU ARE LOVE

This is important to remember. You are love. You are pure love. You are surrounded by love. Just remember your truth. **"Anytime you are experiencing anything other than love, then you have forgotten who you** are." I encourage you to try remembering this. If you are feeling upset, remember, "you are love." It will shift your vibration quickly. If you are feeling jealous, just remember "you are love." If you are feeling happy even, just remember "you are love." That is your nature, through good and bad, the midpoint is love. All you have to be is just you. Let your light shine and be. Love does not require work, it just requires being.

Sometimes, it takes some effort to reconnect, but the choice, just like happiness, is up to you. Each day, I encourage you to create a list, of loving things to do. Simple acts, such as taking out the trash, paying bills, finishing up things one has been procrastinating on, eating loving foods. It will change things completely, if you remember your true nature, and you do things from acts of love and gratitude.

SEED: TLAQUEPAQUE

My final wish for you, is my favorite word: Tlaquepaque. It is an Anasazi saying that means **"the absolute very best of everything from the heart."** And you deserve the absolute very best. There is a garden of yours awaiting, for the many wonderful seeds that you deserve to have to come to fruition. Be mindful of the seeds you chose to plant and cultivate. And always cultivate with gratitude. Cheers to celebrating all of you, and who you really are, LOVE!

About the Author

Cris Hitterman considers herself to be an Instrument of Spirit who has a deep-rooted passion for helping individuals heal and embrace their greatness. She has over 15 years of formal training in a wide variety of modalities from around the world.

The healing arts have been a blessing to Cris, that have helped aid in transforming her own life. She combines the ancient arts of the soul with Transformational Life coaching to help one get to the core root of the matter and release. Cris assists individuals in finding the love, gratitude and forgiveness within themselves.

spiritualstingray@hotmail.com
www.openeyesoflife.com

Acknowledgments

There are so many to thank, and to whom to express my love and appreciation. Mom and Dad, thank you for being the best parents ever, and for being yourself and always believing in me. Shauners, thank you for being you and the tough love. Thank you to all of those mentioned in the story for being some of the best teachers and angels in my life. Thank you angels and guides for always being there through thick and thin. I love you and trust you. Thank you weight, for the amazing journey and being such a wonderful treasure map and adventure to find the journey and buried treasure within. I love you all!

Brad Simkins & Jeri Tourand

Lovingly dedicated to all of humanity, particularly the purpose-driven, heart-centered family that surrounds us and inspires us to be more, bigger, better versions of ourselves.

Chapter 16

THE DAWN OF A NEW DAY

Wake up!!! This is the call that we have been hearing, and it has been becoming increasingly louder leading up to 2012. This is the global awakening. Our children's cries are finally being heard. These powerful beings that have chosen to be here are calling us back home, back into our hearts. Although some have become confused and fearful of all the chaotic energy and huge vibrational contrast that has resulted, and have actually chosen to exit the planet, many are awakening as they hear the cries and are finding they can no longer ignore them. All of our old paradigms, beliefs, systems and infrastructure are being called into question. Our truth is emerging, and we are feeling the sense of urgency to listen to the calling of our hearts and take our place in this new paradigm.

We live in a very dynamic and evolving world of change. We are in the process of releasing what no longer works, and embracing ideas and insights that are new, exciting, and yes, sometimes frightening. Many have been feeling that they have lost sight of who they really are, and fear they have become disconnected with their divine guidance system, with God (Source, the Universe, Love, etc.) and with one another. The truth is, we are all still connected, some have simply blocked that connection because of the walls they put up around their hearts and with the multiple masks that they wear to protect themselves and in the hope of gaining the acceptance and [false] love of others.

Our universal goal is to provide a safety zone for people to be who they are and to remove their masks, unveil their authentic selves and reveal their gifts to themselves as well as sharing them with others. Is that not why we are here?

We need to connect to something greater, bigger than ourselves; we need to connect with our higher purpose, and to take our place in society. One by one, as each of us gets reconnected with our authenticity, we will begin to feel a greater peace, trust and ease than ever before, first within ourselves and eventually within the world.

We can never obtain peace in the outer
world until we make peace with ourselves.

~Dalai Lama

We need to learn to "live from HEART." Even a broken heart can be a good thing. We desperately need more people walking around with their hearts "cracked wide open." Your heart remembers who you really are, and now more than ever, the world needs you to remember, have the courage to release the fear and step into love; to love yourself enough to BE that person.

In our heads there are no answers;
in our hearts there are no questions.

~Buddha

STEP ONE – FINDING YOU

If I ask you to point to yourself, where do you point? Do you point to your head or to your heart? Our HEARTS are our point of connection. When we learn to hear the calling and listen to our hearts, we cannot help but attach to something bigger than ourselves. Living in alignment, we step into our authenticity. As we awaken ourselves to the truth of who we are, we give others permission to do the same, to discover their own authenticity and empowered lives.

Oprah is a good example of one of the few people who has stepped into her authenticity. People care and listen to what Oprah says more than anyone else on TV because of her honesty and transparency. People feel like they know her and can trust her. To be that real and to be that transparent takes courage. We would do well to adopt her courage and be willing to fearlessly be ourselves, instead of who we think everyone wants us to be.

Many people's greatest fear is being discovered, being found out. One of the most common fears is that of intimacy. The biggest reason most people fear emotional intimacy, is the fear that if they allow someone to get emotionally close to them, they will discover that they aren't who they pretend to be. As long as they don't allow people to get too close, they can profess to be anything they choose. But, if they allow someone in, they might be discovered.

Those who have the courage to be real, to be transparent, discover two things: People who don't accept them, don't matter; and those that do matter, embrace them fully. Besides, we cannot change something that remains hidden away. There is no healing in darkness, only light can heal. When we bring our insecurities, flaws, imperfections and greatest fears out of the darkness of denial and into the light of transparency and vulnerability, there is powerful healing available there.

Beautiful Seeds of Change

Here's a beautiful little prayer the authors stumbled across that may help you untie the knots that are holding you back from who you really are and begin the process of freeing yourself.

Dear God:

Please untie the knots
that are in my mind,
my heart and my life.
Remove the have nots,
the can nots and the do nots
that I have in my mind.

Erase the will nots,
may nots, and
might nots that find
a home in my heart.

Release me from the could nots,
would nots and should nots
that obstruct my life.

And most of all, dear God,
I ask that you remove from my mind,
my heart and my life all of the am nots
that I have allowed to hold me back,
especially the thought
that I am not good enough.

Amen.

~ Author known to God

Like many others on the planet, the authors of this chapter have been on, what they like to refer to as an "Accelerated PhD Program of the Soul." It's all been coming to the surface, the garbage we've held on to, the lies that have been passed on to us and that we now tell ourselves, about being unworthy, not enough, unlovable and insignificant. We have been attracting relationships that trigger us, bringing out our wounded parts, our demons from the past, in the form of anger, hurt, and resentment. And what a blessing it's turned out to be! It's these divinely orchestrated relationships that have helped us identify our false programs, what is keeping us stuck and what we need to release to become more... bigger... better.

There has been a massive clearing going on. Did you feel it in 2011? It was clean up time. We can no longer afford to stay small, in our own little lives ... focused on surviving day to day. This is not living and it's not why we are here, especially in such a pivotal time in human history! It is time to let it flow – get triggered, see it, feel it, question it, delve into it, and finally - let it go. Release the negativity, let go of resistance and all the other faces of fear. Let love prevail.

CONNECTING BEHAVIOR TO NEEDS

Our behavior is key in providing us with important information about our needs and how we can best serve others in helping them to recognize and realize their full potential. Conscious parenting instructors will tell you that there is no such thing as "misbehavior" - all behavior is an important form of communication, an expression of a need. Not only our children (although being the sensitive and intuitive beings that our children now are, it seems more blatantly obvious to them) but even as adults, we continue to "act out" or "misbehave." We all have the same underlying needs that are simply not being met.

As human beings, we all have the same basic needs. We need to feel safe. We need to feel loved. And we need to feel valued and important. We need to feel safe enough to express ourselves, our pains, our true feelings, our passions and our gifts. We need to feel loved in order to feel like we are good enough, like we are worthy of accepting all that life has to offer. Finally, we need to feel valued and important; we need to be validated in order to gain the courage to step into our greatness with the faith and trust to know that what we have to offer is important, that we are able to contribute and that our contributions are valuable. We do make a difference.

Isn't that really what all misbehavior boils down to? A trigger is hit (one of those false messages we received from childhood; one of those needs that weren't met) causing us to act out. We act out in a jealous rage because we feel unsafe and insecure in a relationship. We revert back to a crying, pouting and hurt child when we feel unloved or unlovable. We attack with names and blame when we feel unheard and unimportant. And we fall into a deep depression and isolate ourselves when we feel undervalued and unseen. Now the question becomes, "What do we do about it?" How do we meet these rampant unmet needs of so many men, women and children on the planet? Where do we begin to heal the damage we've done?

HEALING THE SELF

Since we cannot give what we do not have, the key in building and maintaining healthy relationships with others must start with a healthy, loving relationship with the self. Here are some powerful techniques to help you begin to heal those deep seated wounds and see yourself in a more loving and supportive way.

1) Daily Self Care:

Spend 30-60 minutes a day, EVERY day doing self care. This can be anything from going for a meditative walk, taking a candlelit bubble bath, to reading from a spiritually uplifting book, etc. There are no absolutes. What would be a self care, energizing activity for one person may not be for another. For example, a ten mile run might energize one person, but cause complete misery for another.

Many people have a hard time even imagining what a self care activity would be for them. Moms have an especially difficult time putting themselves first, or even putting themselves in the picture at all. This is an important part of the process, to take the time and spend the effort to discover what energizes you. And just to clarify, these are NOT energizing activities: Watching TV, taking your child to a soccer game or similar activity (this is child care, not self care), and anything to do with regular hygiene.

The bottom line in choosing a self care activity is this, "do you feel rejuvenated and more energized afterward?"

2) Mirror exercise:

Many people cannot even look themselves in the eye when they look in a mirror. This can be for a variety of reasons, but the core issue is a disconnect between you and you.

For three to five minutes, stand in front of the mirror and look deep into your own eyes. Take a few moments, just looking and connecting. Imagine you are looking into the eyes of the love of your life. What would be your focus? What message would you want to send? What message would you want to receive? Then, gently and lovingly tell the person in the mirror the things you love and appreciate about them.

In other words, you would not tell them you appreciate them, and then add a qualifier, like: "You are a beautiful person, if you could only lose ten pounds." This is a 'No Negativity Zone.' As you are expressing your love and appreciation for yourself, notice what feelings come up. Do you want to argue with the acknowledgements? Do you believe what you are saying? These feelings and reactions can be very useful in helping you see what issues have been holding you in fear, doubt and playing small and thus are the areas that you want to focus your healing intentions upon.

Our deepest fear is not that we are inadequate. Our deepest fear is that we are powerful beyond measure. It is our light, not our darkness that most frightens us. We ask ourselves, Who am I to be brilliant, gorgeous, talented, fabulous? Actually, who are you not to be? You are a child of God. Your playing small does not serve the world. There is nothing enlightened about shrinking so that other people won't feel insecure around you. We are all meant to shine, as children do. We were born to make manifest the glory of God that is within us. It's not just in some of us; it's in everyone. And as we let our own light shine, we unconsciously give other people permission to do the same. As we are liberated from our own fear, our presence automatically liberates others.

~Marianne Williamson

3) Positive Aspects Journal:

The law of attraction states that 'what you focus on grows and expands,' therefore it is essential that we practice mindfulness and tune in to what we are indeed focused on. Keeping a personal journal of positive aspects will help you to shift your focus to the positive, thereby attracting more of the same. In a notebook or journal mark the first section as YOU: "John's Positive Aspects." We suggest you put your family members, friends, and even home, car, etc. in the subsequent sections. Take the time to write in it every day. Record five positive aspects, or things for which you are thankful for each individual, especially yourself. You may not repeat the same thing twice. This will enable you to go deeper and really begin to see your true self and the greatness within.

TAKING CONTROL OF YOUR VIBRATION

Never has there been such a contrast between high and low vibration on the planet. It's like the Universe is saying to us "No more sitting on the fence." The more aware and sensitive people are, the more they are experiencing this huge contrast. Some of us feel like we are losing our minds, in the authors' opinion, not a bad thing ... but never easy. Some have expressed that they sometimes wonder and worry that they may be mentally ill, bipolar or schizophrenic. Many others stay more in the middle. Those who are not as connected and sensitive aren't experiencing the same extreme highs and lows that many of us are feeling.

Please realize there are gifts within this contrast. For one, the lows give us immediate and powerful feedback that our thoughts and focus are not in alignment with what our inner guide knows to be true. The higher we are able to raise our vibrational set point, the more powerful the warning bells sound when we are out of alignment with who we have become. One can raise their set point through meditation, gratitude, music, and even physical activity such as going for a walk or dancing! Ask yourself whenever you feel out of alignment, "What is one thing I can do right now to raise my vibration?"

Have you experienced the incredible rate of manifestation that is taking place today? More and more people are discovering that as they raise their vibration, their ability to manifest what they want becomes more and more profound. The energy on the planet is moving and changing so quickly now that our thoughts and feelings have become extremely powerful and produce rapid results, manifesting exactly what we've been focusing our thoughts and emotions upon. Exciting, isn't it? But also a very good reason that we must be more mindful about what we focus our thoughts on, noticing negative emotions and shifting immediately to a better feeling thought.

A good example of this was when Brad, one of the authors, was running a therapeutic horse ranch for at-risk youth. The staff at the ranch experienced tremendous manifestations, often immediately following an intention.

One evening, Brad was finishing up a staff meeting, when one of the counselors mentioned that they were noticing an increase in the number of clients who had speech challenges. "Would it be possible to hire a part-time speech therapist?" she asked. It was agreed that a grant would be written within the next few weeks to get the funding needed to hire a part time speech therapist.

The very next morning, the phone was ringing when Brad opened the ranch. Upon answering, a young female inquired, "Is this the horse ranch that works with troubled youth?" Brad assured her it was. She then stated, "I saw your story on the news a few months ago, and it moved me to tears. I have wanted to contact you for a few weeks, but have not been able to before now. I am a speech pathologist, and I would like to volunteer some time with your youth. I am sorry I did not contact you earlier. Would it be possible for me to volunteer?"

Brad assured her, that her timing was impeccable. For if she had contacted the ranch any sooner, the need for her therapy would not have yet been identified. She called at the perfect time.

Manifestations like this happened so often at the ranch, that the staff soon did not even blink an eye when the "miracles" continued to occur.

ALIGN YOURSELF WITH SOMETHING BIGGER

We need to get ourselves IN ALIGNMENT with something that is bigger than we are. It is difficult or practically impossible to have a sustained state of bliss and love when one's primary focus is only on oneself. We need to get into that connection with Source, and something bigger than ourselves, in order to increase our vibration for a sustained period of time. Our only purpose, really, is to remember and BE our authentic self and take our place in the grand design. When you get out of your SELF and connect with a higher purpose or design, that is where your bliss lies. You are aligned when you feel purpose, passion, love, and unity.

Sometimes we need to work in reverse. We are so convinced that we are not enough, and not worthy that maybe the only way we can convince ourselves otherwise is to DO something that we deem worthy. Ask yourself, "What do worthy and important people do?" Our beliefs about ourselves are so deeply ingrained in us, that we cannot even see the possibilities, the doors opening before us. Once we uncover some of the limiting beliefs that we have about ourselves - which is much easier than it seems because underneath, we really are all the same - then we can go about proving to ourselves that in fact the exact opposite is true. We can begin to consciously look for and CREATE evidence that we are – worthy – important – and enough.

Ask yourself: What would it take? What HUGE act of kindness and compassion would be BIG ENOUGH to offset all your anger, your pain and your feelings of inadequacy and unworthiness? What beautiful act would be great enough to prove to you, and show others that you matter, you are worthy and that you do make a difference?

COME TOGETHER WITH LOVE

More and more highly conscious, enlightened beings are stepping it up like never before. They are feeling the global unrest; the crazy energy fluctuations, and they are summoning and enlisting other light beings to stand together for peace, for love and for unity. Now, more than ever we must band together in order to shift the energy on the planet from fear to love.

Beautiful Seeds of Change

With a few exceptions (children with mental disease or defect), all babies arrive in this world with a strong connection to the divine. They know only how to love. They are incapable of cruelty, indifference, abuse or any other negative characteristics. All of these negative characteristics are "learned," often times from their parents, their siblings, teachers, classmates, etc.

As a therapist, Brad has often told his clients, if you want to improve a flower bed, you must do more than just pull weeds, you must plant flowers. If we only attempt to remove weeds, we leave a barren flower bed, and it's easy for the weeds to return. Similarly, if we only attempt to remove the negative behaviors, we leave a vacuum, and it's easy for the negative behaviors to return. Positive behaviors (flowers) must be instilled, and implemented into our lives. This requires courage, commitment and action.

We cannot make a change by ignoring it, or pretending it does not exist. That is what has perpetuated it through the generations. Pretending that you are different than your parents, that you are transformed, is as effective as pretending your flower patch isn't full of weeds.

Unconditional love mandates the courage, strength and commitment to take the time to clear out the weeds and plant flowers. In order to do that, we must first accept and love ourselves. Many of the challenges we see in the world can be traced back to a lack of accepting and loving ourselves for who we are.

SETTING OURSELVES FREE

Now is the time to let go. We must let go of all the lies we were told about not being good enough, about being unworthy, and unimportant. EACH of us is an essential piece in the puzzle. If we weren't an important part, we would not be here, now, in this time of transition.

Brad was privileged to be a foster parent for more than 21 years. Over the years, Brad has connected with hundreds of youth, who have become his "kids-of-the-heart." One of Brad's most memorable foster boys was a young man by the name of Jake, who is a perfect example of resilience, courage, unconditional love and forgiveness:

Jake was born a healthy baby; bright, active and full of joy. Unfortunately, the family he was born into was far from joyful, and far from healthy. Jake was the youngest of seven boys. Their father was angry and abusive. Their mother was checked out and consciously absent. Violence and bullying tends to go downhill, and Jake was at the bottom of his family hill. The father beat all the boys, and the boys beat every sibling that was younger and smaller than them, thus Jake got it from all of them.

Despite this, Jake remained a remarkably happy and positive little boy. Even after being beaten by one of his brothers or his dad, he would quickly recover, wipe his eyes and invite the abuser to play with him. Jake was always quick to forgive and anxious to have fun.

When he was approximately five, Jake was out playing in the yard. His brother stormed out of the house, in one of his rages. Ever the caring and loving boy, Jake ran to the car to give his brother a hug (Jake believed that hugs cured everything). His brother, in a storm of rage, started up the car, slammed the gear shift into reverse and floored it. Jake was coming around the back of the car when it exploded out the driveway.

No one could quite understand how Jake lived through the injuries he incurred. Reports say that Jake broke more than half of the bones in his body. He also had a severe concussion, and dramatic closed brain injury. Jake was rushed to the hospital by ambulance and then into emergency surgery. It took nine hours of surgery to mend all the broken bones and stabilize his vital signs. Jake's body quit twice while on the surgery table, but the surgeons worked tirelessly to bring him back each time.

As hard as they worked, the surgeons could only do so much. Even after years of physical therapy, occupational therapy, speech therapy, and every other kind of therapy, Jake's recovery was limited. His busted up body resulted in a pronounced limp on his left side and partial paralysis in his left arm and hand.

Jake vividly recalls being in the recovery room after the surgery. He recalls with great detail waking up in his hospital bed, and hearing the surgeon talking with his parents. The doctor was breaking the news to his mother and father that Jake's recovery would probably be limited, with likely brain damage, resulting in retardation.

Jake remembers laying there, confused and frightened, still in a hazy subconscious condition, but he recalls with great clarity, his father telling the doctor, "You keep him! I don't want a damn vegetable!"

Jake rarely complained, and rarely became discouraged, but from time to time, I would find him lying in his dark bedroom, his muffled cries portraying his pain. Jake did not like to give in to discouragement or depression. His nature was to bounce back every time he was knocked down, with a bigger smile on his face and with renewed determination to succeed.

He was in constant pain, but Jake rarely complained. He pushed his body through the pain, the lack of coordination, and the partial paralysis. When we played basketball, Jake was always there, running around with a big smile on his face, but I do not recall a game that he did not fall down at least three or four times.

Jake has been a constant source of inspiration for me over the years. I will never forget his love, his determination, his beautiful smile, and his undaunting joy.

Jake's story is powerful. It is a beautiful example of choosing to overcome the challenges of our childhood and live our lives with passion and purpose. However, sometimes challenges can be more difficult to identify. Having broken bones and visible scars makes it easier to identify when one has been abused. Yet, often wounds are not as visible, not as easy to identify. Emotional wounds are often just as crippling, perhaps even more, because they are more difficult to find and heal. Because there are no scars, it can be difficult to validate that a wounding has occurred. It can be more difficult to do the healing work necessary, because it's so easy to mask the pain and the abuse. People often dismiss emotional pain, and so the wound remains unhealed and thus, it continues to manifest in our lives with triggers and fears that hold us back from connecting fully with those we love (especially ourselves).

A beautiful example of this is Jeri's story. When Jeri was young, she remembers one time her parents were telling jokes around her at a party:

They used to always tease me about how "dense" I was when I would not laugh at jokes. I told my parents a few times that "I didn't get it" – as it turned out, I often did get the joke, but I just didn't share their sense of humor. I recall one time they were telling raunchy jokes, and one of the adults looked at my Dad, concerned that perhaps they needed to tone it down a touch as I was in the room. I still remember him responding with something similar to "Don't worry about her, she's dense, she won't get it anyway." Message received: I am dense/stupid, and I don't matter.

Another time she remembers was just before she got her ears pierced:

I was really nervous, and I asked my parents how ear piercing was done. They told me that they have an 'ear piercing gun.'

"What if I move and they miss?" I fearfully asked, imagining what would happen if I flinched, and they pierced my cheek instead.

Next thing I knew, I was the brunt of all their jokes. My parents told all their friends and our extended family that I thought ear piercing involved putting me up against some wall and then standing back, taking aim at my earlobe, and shooting!

The telling of this story went on for years! I would get upset, interrupt the story, and insist that 'I never thought that!' They would simply ignore me, or laugh and insist that I did.

When I grew upset, I was told I was 'too sensitive.' They didn't seem to want to let the facts interfere with a good story, even if it clearly caused repeated pain and embarrassment.

Message received: I'm dense, not important, too sensitive and what I say is wrong and doesn't matter.

Boom ... welcome in Jeri, the scared mute. I grew up believing that I was dense, not good enough and not important.

As a result, I never spoke in public. Well, I spoke to my siblings, a very few select friends, and at home when I needed to, but you can ask any one of my teachers from grade school up to University. I'm sure they wondered if I even HAD vocal cords, if they even remembered me at all, that is.

When I did speak as a young child, it ended up coming back and hurting me. Plus, believing I was dense, I was sure it would come out sounding stupid, and that I'd be ridiculed for it. I fought this fear every day and often still find myself slipping back, although it's becoming easier and easier to remove the masks and show people the real me, bits and pieces at a time. I assure you however, it doesn't take much to shut me down. One small criticism or someone misinterpreting what I've said and the walls rise up. Like all of us, I just want to be loved, for who I am.

When the authors were editing this chapter, it was a powerful experience, as Jeri relived this painful time in her life. The embarrassment and shame returned, and she questioned whether it was 'big' enough, or 'important' enough to include it in the chapter: "It seems like such a silly little thing, I'm not sure it's worth including."

But then it became clear that this was a perfect example of how we minimize our own emotional abuse, because it does not seem to compare to physical abuse. This is why this kind of wound can be even worse. Because there are no broken bones or visible scars, it is easy to beat ourselves up, demeaning ourselves for being so bothered by such a 'trivial thing.' Hence, we continue the cycle of emotional abuse within, condemning ourselves for our own feelings and pain.

Beautiful Seeds of Change

We realized that part of Jeri's mission has been to help others who have been through similar experiences, to find their voice, and begin the healing process. We also hope to help parents realize the impact that their seemingly minimal, off hand remarks can have on an impressionable child's life, creating blocks that their children will struggle with the rest of their lives, often preventing them from realizing their potential and pursuing their dreams.

STEPPING INTO LOVE

In life, we get to choose between two forests; the forest of love and the forest of fear. We are always in one of them, and never in both at the same time. When we are in the forest of love, we see the inhabitants of that beautiful forest: joy, peace, security, love, confidence, worthiness, bliss... And when we are in the forest of fear, we experience its habitat: frustration, fear, inner conflict, anxiety, insecurity, feelings of unworthiness...

Looking at life from this perspective, one might wonder; why would anyone choose to spend any time in the forest of fear, when the contrast is so obvious? The problem is, many of us have spent so much of our childhoods and adult lives dwelling in the forest of fear, that it has become what feels familiar, even comfortable in a sense. Spending time in the forest of love can feel good, yet at the same time foreign. We often feel uncomfortable and unworthy.

A powerful analogy is living in a cesspool (yes, I know this is repulsive, it is intended to be). We hate living there, but we have spent so much time there, we have learned to adapt. As disgusting as it is, we have come to feel comfortable with it. Sadly, we have come to feel that the cesspool is what we deserve.

Then, as we evolve and grow, we find presented to us, a beautiful mansion. At first, we are excited. We have been imagining this mansion for a long time, and now it is ours. We plan when and how we are going to move in, but then we start to have second thoughts (forest of fear). We worry that we will not know how to function once we are in the mansion. We won't know the rules. Plus, our friends (who live in their own cesspool) may reject us, accusing us of thinking we are better than they are. What if our neighbors around the mansion do not like us? What if they can tell where we have come from?

We start to feel insecure, unworthy, and anxious (fear). Somehow, we convince ourselves that we are better off in the cesspool, and we dive back in.

It's like kayaking along a river with a strong current. When we "go with the flow," we are able to put the oars of resistance down and easily traverse along the journey of life. So why is it that we so often feel the need to take up those oars, and battle against the current? The more we battle the current, the more frustrated and discouraged we become. And ironically, we are paddling ourselves away from what we really want, our highest good.

Over the years, Brad has worked with a number of clients who seek him out to help them understand why they keep repeating the same mistakes. One single mother (Samantha) had several boyfriends over the years. She came into the office confused and frustrated. She could not figure out why she kept attracting the same kind of man. The men in her life had been white collar, blue collar, tall, short, heavy, skinny, muscular, etc. At first glance, they had nothing in common with each other, except they were all emotionally abusive. They were either verbally abusive, or they were emotionally indifferent. Over the years, she had fluctuated between these apparent polar opposites, going from the verbally abusive to the emotionally indifferent.

She had dated a few emotionally healthy men; men who were loving, supportive and who were emotionally available for her. They listened when she shared her heart, and they reacted with excitement when she succeeded and empathy when she struggled. These relationships never lasted long. She would always sabotage them because of what she came to realize, were her feelings of unworthiness.

Samantha understood the rules of an unhealthy relationship (cesspool). She knew how to deal with the emotionally abusive behavior. In fact, she had even found a way to feel good about it. Whenever a boyfriend would emotionally abuse her, she would tell herself that "the hurtful are hurting," and this brought out the 'rescuer' in her. She could deal with this drama for a short time, but soon it would wear her down. So, she would seek out an emotionally indifferent man, who would give her safety, yet emptiness. Similarly, this emotional vacuum was another form of a cesspool, and eventually the emptiness and lack of passion and interest she felt would return her to the abusive relationship. And the dance continued.

For years she had tried to figure what was wrong with "them," with little if any progress. When she and Brad started working together, he gently, lovingly redirected her focus, from the men in her life to her.

As they explored and evaluated her relationships, she was able to see that while the two extremes might appear to have nothing in common, they actually had a lot in common. First, they left her feeling unimportant

Beautiful Seeds of Change

and second, they mirrored the messages she received from her childhood. The abusive men reminded her of her relationship with her siblings, who had often been emotionally abusive and demeaning. The men who were indifferent mirrored her relationship with her mother, who was rarely, if ever, emotionally available for her or her siblings.

This small but important shift changed her life. She was able to start to examine why she felt she deserved to be treated this way, and that she felt unworthy to be treated like a goddess when she was presented with it; why she felt more comfortable with criticism (cesspool) than she did with acknowledgments (mansion). With this awareness, she has begun to make powerful shifts in her life, and become more accepting of positive feedback as well as acknowledging her own self worth.

Unfortunately, if we keep playing small and refusing to look at and acknowledge who we really are, then we truly are doing a disservice to our children and to the world. Our children are our future. We have the power to change the world, through making the necessary changes in ourselves, which will empower our children, as they watch our example. Our actions are speaking so loudly, our children cannot hear our words.

RECONNECTING WITH OUR INNER GUIDE

So, why do we as humans choose struggle and frustration over ease and bliss? Many of us are trained from our earliest childhood that to struggle is to be valiant, and that nothing worthwhile comes without blood, sweat and tears. We are trained to distrust our Inner Guide (often referred to as our "gut") and to distrust our intuition. We are taught that we must listen to those outside of us, and ignore our own inner wisdom.

So, while our Inner Guide whispers softly to us, to "let go and let God," to allow the bliss and delicious playfulness to be our compass of life; we listen to those around us, who often do not have our best interests at heart. Although they do not deliberately want us to fail, and they often believe they are giving us the best advice, this advice is often filled with jealousy, insecurity and pain. Even if their advice was free of these human tendencies, their recommendations are influenced by their own experiences and inability to connect with their own inner guidance system.

For example, let's say that Barbara, a mother who lives in Miami, Florida decides she wants to drive her family to Disneyland in California. She programs the coordinates into her trusty GPS system, and records the route in her log book. However, feeling insecure, she calls her mom, who lives in New York, and asks her for her suggestions. Mom, never being at a loss for advice, quickly programs Disneyland into her GPS system, and insists that Barbara must follow her route. Confused, Barbara decides that she needs more information, and she contacts her sister who lives in Edmonton, Alberta, Canada. She explains her dilemma, and asks for her advice. Sis instantly programs Disneyland into her own GPS system, and insists that everyone else is wrong and she is right.

Being a people pleaser, Barbara feels stuck. She is afraid to hurt anyone's feelings, and thus feels paralyzed in making any decision. If she chooses mom's advice, she risks offending her sister. If she opts for sister's directions, she is afraid she will hurt mom. And (God forbid) if she listens to her own inner guidance, she is sure she will offend both of them. She either tries to find some kind of compromise, which usually ends up putting her in the middle of the Pacific Ocean, or she cancels the trip all together.

As ridiculous as this sounds, think about some of the compromises you have made, trying to please everyone in your life. Unfortunately, more times than not, it's the people pleaser that suffers the most, and ends up with everyone upset with them. The answer comes, when we gain the courage, faith and confidence to trust our OWN GPS system, AKA, our 'Inner Guidance System.'

MOVING FORWARD

There is hope for a more peaceful and loving world. There are more and more positive and purposeful people awakening to their truth and authenticity, and banning together to lead the change. There is a beautiful awakening spreading throughout the world. Many people are realizing untruths they were "programmed to believe" at a young age, about themselves and others. There is no one to blame here. As parents, teachers and global citizens, we really do the best we can with what we know. Now that we know better, things are happening. We are taking the positive steps to do better, to make the changes in ourselves and therefore to shift the energy of the planet. Everything we do and everything we chose not to do affects the whole.

We are shifting things with this beautiful awakening, with our children at the helm. THEY are the seeds of change. Our children are acting as mirrors for us and for society. We are able to see more clearly than ever before what needs to change. We are more motivated to change as well, as we look ahead to our children's future. Fear can be a good motivator at times, but LOVE is always a better one.

Remember, we are all affecting the world every moment, whether we mean to or not. Our actions and states of mind matter, because we're so deeply interconnected with one another. Working on our own consciousness is the most important thing that we are doing at any moment, and being love is the supreme creative act.

~Ram Dass

In revealing ourselves and our truth in this chapter, our hope is that we have connected with you and ignited a flame or two of passion and purpose. We invite you to join us as we link arms and change the world, from negativity to positivity, from fear to love, and from entrapment to freedom – one person, one family, and one community at a time. As this new day dawns, we have found tremendous freedom, empowerment, and an abundance of other blessings as we have become more and more awakened and have consciously chosen to be more authentic, more loving and passionate, and allowing our light to shine. We are one. We are love. Everything is connected. There is no such thing as an insignificant person, or an insignificant thought, word, or action.

Be the change you wish to see in the world.

~Gandhi

About the Authors

Brad Simkins is a Licensed Counselor, Family Therapist and Coach. He has had more than three decades in the field of healing and growth. Brad has been a counselor, executive director of three nonprofit agencies, professional (foster) parent, advocate, and healer for more than thirty-three years. He has also been blessed to have three awesome grown children, an adopted son, two grandchildren, many wonderful children-of the heart and now grandchildren-of-the-heart.

innerguideempowerment@gmail.com
www.innerguidehealing.com

Jeri N. Tourand, B.Ed.is a heart-centered mother of three extraordinary girls, a teacher, speaker, coach, trainer, workshop leader and facilitator and creator and instructor of her "Parenting from H.E.A.R.T." program for positive parenting.

Jeri resides in Alberta, Canada with her family and is excited about spreading her wings with her amazing business partner, Brad Simkins, and launching their workshops, classes and seminars for healing and growth with their "Inner Guide Empowerment" business, as well as facilitating and expanding "ReSolutions" programs throughout North America.

innerguideempowerment@gmail.com
www.parentingfromheart.com

Acknowledgments

Brad Simkins

I have to first of all acknowledge Nancy Newman & Lisa Hardwick for giving us this wonderful opportunity. Without you, there would be no book. Then I have to acknowledge Jeri Tourand, the Most Amazing Business Partner, Radio Co-Host, ReSolutions Territory Management Partner, Workshop Co-Facilitator, Co-Author, and Absolute Best Friend I could Ever ask for! My awesome children, Rob, Chelsea, Kim and Fernando: You have been patient with me, supported me in my growth and change, and have always been my best teachers. And, my children of the heart. Please know that I love you and appreciate you every day.

Jeri Tourand

Lovingly dedicated to my girls, Mackenzie, Rylee and Morgan, who have inspired me in every way, to be all that I can. To my Dad, Ronald McDougall, who passed over in 2001, but forever resides in my heart and my Mom, Noella Prevost, for her unconditional love. To my husband, Kelly, who truly has stuck with me through thick and thin. And finally to one of the most loving and supportive people I've ever met, my business partner and twin soul, Brad Simkins, without him, I would not living in this beautiful realm of divinely guided possibility.

Resources

The following list of resources are for the national headquarters; search in your yellow pages under "Community Services" for your local resource agencies and support groups.

AIDS

CDC National AIDS Hotline
(800) 342-2437

ALCOHOL ABUSE

Al-Anon Family Group
Headquarters
1600 Corporate Landing Parkway
Virginia Beach, VA 23454-5617
(888) 4AL-ANON
www.al-anon.alateen.org

Alcoholics Anonymous (AA)
General Service Office
475 Riverside Dr., 11th Floor
New York, NY 10115
(212) 870-3400
www.alcoholics-anonymous.org

Children of Alcoholics
Foundation
164 W. 74th Street
New York, NY 10023
(800) 359-COAF
www.coaf.org

Mothers Against Drunk Driving
MADD
P.O. Box 541688
Dallas, TX 75354
(800) GET-MADD
www.madd.org

National Association of Children of
Alcoholics (NACoA)
11426 Rockville Pike, #100
Rockville, MD 20852
(888) 554-2627
www.nacoa.net

Women for Sobriety
P.O. Box 618
Quartertown, PA 18951
(215) 536-8026
www.womenforsobriety.org

CHILDREN'S RESOURCES

Child Molestation
ChildHelp USA/Child Abuse
Hotline
15757 N. 78th St.
Scottsdale, AZ 85260
(800) 422-4453
www.childhelpusa.org

Prevent Child Abuse America
200 South Michigan Avenue,
17th Floor
Chicago, IL 60604
(312) 663-3520
www.preventchildabuse.org

Crisis Intervention
Girls and Boys Town National
Hotline
(800) 448-3000
www.boystown.org

Children's Advocacy Center of
East Central Illinois
*(If your heart feels directed to make a
donation to this center, please include Lisa
Hardwick's name in the memo)*
616 6th Street
Charleston, IL 61920
(217) 345-8250
http://caceci.org

Children of the Night
14530 Sylvan St.
Van Nuys, CA 91411
(800) 551-1300
www.childrenofthenight.org

Covenant House Hotline
(800) 999-9999
www.covenanthouse.org

National Children's Advocacy
Center
210 Pratt Avenue
Huntsville, AL 35801
(256) 533-KIDS (5437)
www.nationalcac.org

CO-DEPENDENCY

Co-Dependents Anonymous
P.O. Box 33577
Phoenix, AZ 85067
(602) 277-7991
www.codependents.org

SUICIDE, DEATH, GRIEF

AARP Grief and Loss Programs
(800) 424-3410
www.aarp.org/griefandloss

Grief Recovery Institute
P.O. Box 6061-382
Sherman Oaks, CA 91413
(818) 907-9600
www.grief-recovery.com

Suicide Awareness Voices of
Education (SAVE)
Minneapolis, MN 55424
(952) 946-7998
Suicide National Hotline
(800) 784-2433

DOMESTIC VIOLENCE

National Coalition Against
Domestic Violence
P.O. Box 18749
Denver, CO 80218
(303) 831-9251
www.ncadv.org

National Domestic Violence
Hotline
P.O. Box 161810
Austin, TX 78716
(800) 799-SAFE
www.ndvh.org

DRUG ABUSE

Cocaine Anonymous National
Referral Line
(800) 347-8998

National Helpline of Phoenix
House
(800) COCAINE
www.drughelp.org

National Institute of Drug Abuse
(NIDA)
6001 Executive Blvd., Room 5213,
Bethesda, MD 20892-9561,
Parklawn Building
Info: (301) 443-6245
Help: (800) 662-4357
www.nida.nih.gov

EATING DISORDERS

Overeaters Anonymous
National Office
P.O. Box 44020
Rio Rancho, NM 87174-4020
(505) 891-2664
www.overeatersanonymous.org

GAMBLING

Gamblers Anonymous
International Service Office
P.O. Box 17173
Los Angeles, CA 90017
(213) 386-8789
www.gamblersanonymous.org

HEALTH ISSUES

American Chronic Pain Association
P.O. Box 850
Rocklin, CA 95677
(916) 632-0922
www.theacpa.org

American Holistic Health
Association
P.O. Box 17400
Anaheim, CA 92817
(714) 779-6152
www.ahha.org

The Chopra Center at
La Costa Resort and Spa
Deepak Chopra, M.D.
2013 Costa Del Mar
Carlsbad, CA 92009
(760) 494-1600
www.chopra.com

The Mind-Body Medical Institute
110 Francis St., Ste. 1A
Boston, MA 02215
(617) 632-9530 Ext. 1
www.mbmi.org

National Health Information Center
P.O. Box 1133
Washington, DC 20013-1133
(800) 336-4797
www.health.gov/NHIC

Preventive Medicine Research
Institute
Dean Ornish, M.D.
900 Brideway, Ste 2
Sausalito, CA 94965
(415) 332-2525
www.pmri.org

MENTAL HEALTH

American Psychiatric Association
of America
1400 K St. NW
Washington, DC 20005
(888) 357-7924
www.psych.org

Anxiety Disorders Association of
America
11900 Parklawn Dr., Ste. 100
Rockville, MD 20852
(310) 231-9350
www.adaa.org

The Help Center of the American
Psychological Association
(800) 964-2000
www.helping.apa.org

National Center for Post Traumatic
Stress Disorder
(802) 296-5132
www.ncptsd.org

National Alliance for the Mentally Ill
2107 Wilson Blvd., Ste. 300
Arlington, VA 22201
(800) 950-6264
www.nami.org

National Depressive and Manic-
Depressive Association
730 N. Franklin St., Ste. 501
Chicago, IL 60610
(800) 826-3632
www.ndmda.org

National Institute of Mental Health
6001 Executive Blvd.
Room 81884, MSC 9663
Bethesda, MD 20892
(301) 443-4513
www.nimh.nih.gov

SEX ISSUES

Rape, Abuse and Incest
National Network
(800) 656-4673
www.rainn.org

National Council on Sexual
Addiction and Compulsivity
P.O. Box 725544
Atlanta, GA 31139
(770) 541-9912
www.ncsac.org

SMOKING

Nicotine Anonymous World
Services
419 Main St., PMB #370
Huntington Beach, CA 92648
(415) 750-0328
www.nicotine-anonymous.org

STRESS ISSUES

The Biofeedback &
Psychophysiology
Clinic
The Menninger Clinic
P.O. Box 829
Topeka, KS 66601-0829
(800) 351-9058
www.menninger.edu

New York Open Center
83 Spring St.
New York, NY 10012
(212) 219-2527
www.opencenter.org

The Stress Reduction Clinic
Center for Mindfulness
University of Massachusetts
Medical Center
55 Lake Ave., North
Worcester, MA 01655
(508) 856-2656

TEEN

Al-Anon/Alateen
1600 Corporate Landing Parkway
Virginia Beach, VA 23454-5617
(888) 425-2666
www.al-anon.alateen.org

Planned Parenthood
810 Seventh Ave.
New York, NY 10019
(800) 230-PLAN
www.plannedparenthood.org

Hotlines for Teenagers
Girls and Boys Town National
Hotline
(800) 448-3000

ChildHelp National Child Abuse
Hotline
(800) 422-4453

Just for Kids Hotline
(888) 594-KIDS

National Child Abuse Hotline
(800) 792-5200

National Runaway Hotline
(800) 621-4000

National Youth Crisis Hotline
(800)-HIT-HOME

Suicide Prevention Hotline
(800) 827-7571

Beautiful Seeds of Change

Bibliography

Beckwith , Michael Bernard.
   "The Life Visioning Process"

Benson, Herbert. (1975).
   The Relaxation Response.
   New York, NY. Harper Torch

Braden, Gregg. (2008.)
   Language of the Divine Matrix and Divine Matrix: Bridging Time, Space Materials and
   Belief
   Canfield, Jack (2005).

The Success Principles: How to Get from Where You Are to Where You Want to Be.
   New York, NY: Collins
   Chopra, Deepak, M.D. (1990.)

Choquette, Sonia.
   The Answer Is Simple... Love yourself, Live your Spirit
   Hay House

Cohen, Alan.
   "Create A Masterpiece; When mistakes turn into miracles."
   healyourlife.com. N.p., 31 Dec. 2010. Web. 13 Mar. 2011.

Crane, Patricia J. (2002.)
   Ordering From the Cosmic Kitchen: The Essential Guide to Powerful,
   Nourishing Affirmations. Bonsall, CA. The Crane's Nest.

Gilbert, Daniel. (2005.)
   Stumbling on Happiness.
   New York, NY. Vintage

Gilligan, Stephen. (1997).
   The Courage to Love: Principles and Practices of Self-Relations Psychotherapy.
   New York, NY. W.W. Norton &Company

Goleman, Daniel. (1995).
   Emotional Intelligence: Why it can matter more than IQ. New York, NY: Bantam Dell
   Hay, Louise L.
   (1982.) Heal Your Body. Carlsbad, CA. Hay House, Inc.
   (1984.) You Can Heal Your Life. Carlsbad, CA. Hay House, Inc.
   (2002.) You Can Heal Your Life Companion Book. Carlsbad, CA. Hay House, Inc.
   (1991.) The Power Is Within You. Carlsbad, CA. Hay House, Inc.

"Inspirational Quotations by Alan Cohen."
   alancohen.com. N.p., n.d. Web. 13 Mar. 2011.

Landrum, Gene. (2005.)
   The Superman Syndrome: You Are What You Believe.
   Lincoln, NE. iUniverse

Lesser, Elizabeth.
    Broken Open.
    N.p.: Random House, 2005. Print

Lipton, Bruce H., Ph.D. (2005.)
    The Biology of Belief: Unleashing the Power of Consciousness,
    Matter & Miracles. Carlsbad, CA.
    Hay House, Inc.194

McErlane, Sharon.
    A Call to Power: The Grandmothers Speak. Bloomington, IN:
    AuthorHouse, 2004. Print.

Millman, Dan.
    The Life You Were Born To Live. Tiburon, CA:
    HJ Kramer Inc, 1993. Print.

Morrissey, Mary. N.p.: n.p., 2009
    Life Solutions That Work, LLC. Print.

Neill, Michael. (2006).
    You Can Have What You Want: Proven Strategies for Inner and Outer Success.
    Hay House

Ruiz , Don Miguel.
    The Four Agreements
    Amber-Allen Publishing
    Time, Space, Miracles, and Belief. Carlsbad, CA.
    Hay House, Inc.

Tobar, Hugo, International College of Neuro Energetic Kinesiology
    Workshops & Certification, www.icnek.com

Tolle, Eckhart. (1999.)
    The Power of Now: A Guide to Spiritual Enlightenment. Novato, CA. New World
    Library.
    A New Earth: awakening to Your Life's Purpose.
    N.p.: Plume, 2008. Print.

Truman, Karol.
    Feelings Buried Alive Never Die. Las Vegas, NV:
    Olympus Distributing, 1991. Print.

Two Wolves Fighting, Native American Proverb

Wolinsky, Stephen. (1991).
    Trances People Live:
    Healing Approaches In Quantum Psychology.
    Falls Village, CT. The Bramble Company

Williamson, Marianne. (2009).
    The Age of Miracles: Embracing the New Midlife.
    Carlsbad, CA. Hay House

Beautiful Seeds of Change

A Call For Authors

Most people have a story that needs to be shared – could *YOU* be one of the contributing authors we are seeking to feature in one of our upcoming books?

Whether you envision yourself participating in an inspiring book with other authors, or whether you have a dream of writing your very own book, we may be the answer *YOU* have been searching for!

Are you interested in experiencing how sharing your message will assist with building your business network, which in turn will result in being able to assist even more people? Or perhaps you are interested in leaving a legacy for your family and friends? Or it may be you simply have an important message your heart is telling you to share with the world. Each person has their own unique reason for desiring to become an author.

Our commitment is to make this planet we call "home" a better place. One of the ways we fulfill this commitment is assisting others in sharing their inspiring messages.

We look forward to hearing from you.

Please visit us at
www.VisionaryInsightPress.com

CPSIA information can be obtained at www.ICGtesting.com
Printed in the USA
BVOW040136220512

290761BV00001B/43/P